INSIDE THE MINDS OF BASEBALL'S BEST MENTAL PERFORMANCE COACHES

CREATED BY

MATT MORSE

Mental Game VIP:

Inside The Minds of Baseball's Best Mental Performance Coaches

Printed in the United States of America

Author/Creator: Matt Morse

ISBN: 1500558303
ISBN-13: 978-1500558307

ENDORSEMENTS

"Mental Game VIP is the greatest mental game program ever made!"

BRIAN CAIN
PEAK PERFORMANCE & MENTAL CONDITIONING COACH
BRIANCAIN.COM

"Mental Game VIP has been a huge success with players and coaches all over the country. When you get the best minds in one product, it will stand the test of time. Mental Game VIP gives you access to all of the best of the best when it comes to mental performance. This a must for all coaches and players. I skim through my copy often pulling great information every time. "

TIM DIXON
ELITE PERFORMANCE COACH
ELITE PERFORMANCE ACADEMY

"Matt Morse set out on a mission to make an impact in the mental training field by compiling research from within the sports psychology and mental training community. The results are beyond impressive! The amount of content and information from so many different teachers in mental training is amazing...and it is truly an honor to be asked to be part of this. Mental Game VIP is for anyone who wants to not only work on their mental game, but have their mental game impacted significantly!"

ALAN JAEGER
JAEGERSPORTS.COM

"Matt Morse has created the premier resource on the mental side of sports performance. It's a one of a kind resource that really transcends sport and teaches how to succeed at the mental game of life. Mental Game VIP provides the intellectual firepower you need to take your game to the next level, whatever game that may be."

JOHN BRUBAKER
AWARD-WINNING AUTHOR, SPEAKER & COACH
COACHBRU.COM

"Mental Game VIP is a one of a kind resource. Combining some of the brightest and most creative minds in the sports industry in one book is genius. Focusing on and coaching the mental aspect of sports performance is vital to achieving excellence in my opinion. I will use the knowledge and experiences in this book for my entire career. "

ZAC WOODFIN
DIRECTOR OF SPORTS PERFORMANCE
SOUTHERN MISS

"Mental Game VIP is a great tool to help your athletes become more well rounded in the mental game because of the variety of perspectives. It has allowed our softball players and coaches to grow and learn from the experts' inexpensive. Matt has evolved into a definite master of the mental game, in sport and in life, throughout his research and production of this tremendous program!"

ERICA SISSON
ASSISTANT SOFTBALL COACH
UNIVERSITY OF ALABAMA AT BIRMINGHAM

"The Mental Game VIP collection of resources is a must for any coach that desires to build champions from within. I personally use a number of the strategies presented with the teams and athletes I am blessed to work with."

"Mental Game VIP is a great book to get you thinking, motivating, and putting together an action plan for the upcoming season. Share pieces with your coaches and team. Everyone is looking to better themselves as a player and a person and this will help them in all phases. Not just for baseball coaches either!"

"Learning from the best helps you get on the right track to become the best. This book does just that! Not only does it help with the game of baseball, but also in your everyday life. Mental Game VIP is a true game-changer."

"I'm not easily impressed & with my background I'm even more skeptical about baseball/sports training information. With that being said, Mental Game VIP is AMAZING! Love the way that so many impressive minds are gathered in one place."

"Mental Game VIP is an absolute game-changer. Whether you're a coach, player, parent or just looking to gain an edge in your profession, Mental Game VIP has it covered. It is a who's who of the sports world in terms of master motivators and sports psychologists. It will most certainly change your life."

"Mental Game VIP is a valuable resource, collecting knowledge from some of the top performance coaches in the country. Extremely applicable on the field and off! As a collegiate athlete, I couldn't more highly recommend Mental Game VIP as a MUST read for any athlete or coach. It is worth your investment of time! It is a pleasure to know and to have played with Matt at the collegiate level because he makes everyone around him better. He possesses an insatiable desire for excellence and is the ultimate competitor!"

"This contains everything you need to know to become a master of the mental game. Mental Game VIP takes you inside the minds of the best mental performance coaches in the country. It's a MUST HAVE for any coach or athlete's library!"

ABOUT THE CREATOR

Matt Morse is a former NCAA Division 1 student-athlete who trained extensively in the mental game during his baseball playing career at UAB. After having the opportunity to learn from and work alongside some of the best mental performance coaches in baseball, Matt had a vision of bringing them all together in an active research type project. As the process evolved, Mental Game VIP was built during Matt's senior season at the University of Alabama at Birmingham.

In addition to hosting, recording, transcribing, editing and sorting the interviews, Matt also designed the logo, built the website, and called the shots within his strategic social media marketing campaigns.

Due to NCAA Compliance restrictions, Matt was unable to promote Mental Game VIP using his name or likeness in any way until his NCAA eligibility was exhausted.

Matt's passion for the game of baseball and helping others become the best they can be on and off the field is strongly evident throughout his coaching and training of highly competitive athletes.

In addition to coaching, Matt also consults with and speaks to teams, organizations, coaches, and athletes around the world. For more information on Matt, to have him come speak to you and your team, or if you want to create your own VIP collection, visit **Matt-Morse.com** and follow @MattMorse_17 on Twitter!

CONTENTS

GAME TIME Q&A

EXTRA INNINGS

ACKNOWLEDGEMENTS

A special thanks to all of those who made this possible, including but not limited to the following excellent individuals:

My parents John and Mary Morse for their never ending love and support in all that I do, my sister Beth and brother-in-law Dusty Behringer for their encouragement to always keep going, my wife Rachel for always keeping me humble and hungry, and Coach Brian Shoop for building a strong foundation of being uncommon, accountable and honoring God in all that I do.

None of this would have been possible without the selfless commitment to furthering the mental game of baseball from all of the Mental Game VIP participants including:

Brian Cain, Ken Ravizza, Dr. Rob Gilbert, Tom Hanson, Alan Jaeger, Steve Springer, Jon Gordon, Tim Dixon, Charlie Maher, Jim Afremow, Jeff Janssen, Rob Bell, John Brubaker, Aaron Weintraub, Christine Rickertsen, Mike Tully, Alan Goldberg, Justin Dehmer, Mike Margolies, Justin Toole, and Justin Dedman.

An additional thanks to my excellent content creation team for their countless hours of executing this mission around the clock:

Jesse Hopkins, Susan Sanford, Talha Haroon and Brandon Barrett.

Finally, thanks to:

YOU for investing into yourself first so that you may have a greater impact and influence on those around you!

MENTAL GAME VIP DEFINED

The Mental Game VIP Program is a compilation of interviews with some of the best mental performance coaches in the game of baseball. These audio interviews have been transcribed and sorted into chapters by topic for you to read, or simply reference while listening to the corresponding audio program.

This program can be read and listened to in any order by selecting specific chapters or audio sections that you wish to learn about.

Meet the Coaches contains a set of specific questions for each featured coach. **GameTime Q&A** is a series of questions asked to all of the coaches and includes their various responses to these frequently asked questions among the baseball community. Each of these also contains a Question Review with a brief summary of the coaches' main points. All of the coaches were then put on the **HotSeat**, where they were asked to provide their initial thoughts on several popular topics. **The Closer** contains recommended reading, insights on the future of the mental game and closing comments from each coach. **Extra Innings** features a bonus interview with a legendary sports psychologist and performance trainer.

The material covered in this program covers a wide variety of topics that are crucial to maximize your potential and experience as a baseball player, coach, parent, fan, mental conditioning coach or sports psychologist! Go deep inside the minds of these experts with the Mental Game VIP program!

*Interviews have been modified and condensed by the Mental Game VIP team.

What is the Mental Game?
by Ken Ravizza & Justin Toole

Ravizza: The mental game is part of it. It's not the whole thing. You've got to have a certain amount of talent and you definitely have to do the work and the preparation. There's nothing magical about it, but you have to pay your dues and work hard to get yourself where you need to be. The mental game is like frosting on the cake. The mental game may be just 2% of it, but that 2% can make a difference.

Toole: The mental game to me is huge. Baseball is a game of failure. If you go out there and fail seven out of ten times, you're considered to be a good hitter. A lot of people spend hours in the cage working on their swing, on the field taking ground balls, or in the bullpen working on their different pitches, but people hardly ever spend time working on the mental game.

The six inches between your ears is the most important part when it comes to sports, being a professional athlete, and playing baseball with guys that are extremely talented. The difference between the people who make it to the big leagues and the people who don't is usually the mental game. The talent level doesn't change too much. A lot of it is mental, going out there believing that you can do it, going out there with a plan and believing in yourself.

The *Mental Game VIP* program is huge. I definitely would advise anyone to get into the mental game. It's taken my career from a decent high school player, to a good college player, to a good professional player. I've seen it work personally in my life and I know it can work in yours as well.

MEET THE COACHES

Introductions + Exclusive Q&A

Brian Cain

Mental Conditioning Coach and Best-Selling Author

For more from Cain, visit MentalGameVIP.com/BrianCain

You played college baseball at Vermont and then received your Masters Degree in Sports Psychology from Cal State Fullerton with Ken Ravizza. What led you from Vermont to Cal State Fullerton?

Cain: I went to the University of Vermont like many players who go into Division 1 college baseball and have high expectations and not a very clear sense of reality. I went in there on a scholarship thinking I was going to be the Friday guy, a number one starter out of the gate, and I don't think I ever cracked the pitching rotation.

I went in there as a young baseball player from a small town in Massachusetts, which makes you like the best ice hockey player in the country of Mexico. It's a jaded sense of how good you are compared to other people around the globe. When I went to Vermont, I failed!

That was the first time in my life I'd ever failed, the first time I ever got hit hard, first time I ever didn't have success by just rearing back and trying to throw harder, which can get guys out in high school. If you're a college pitcher, that doesn't work when you get to a level where the talent is even. You have to learn to pitch. You have to learn to work smarter, not harder.

My whole mentality was, 'I'm not good enough and I'm not getting the success, so I have to work harder.' It was 2 or 3 hours a day in the weight room without a plan. We didn't have a strength coach and didn't have a full-time pitching coach. So I was on my own trying to figure out a lot of that stuff. Lo and behold, I was hurt all the time. I spent more time in the training room than I did in my dorm room, in the clubhouse or at the baseball field.

In my junior year, I had shoulder surgery and came across the book *Heads Up Baseball* in Boston on July 4 at Barnes & Noble. At that time, I wasn't a big book guy. I didn't read but I was searching. I went to the baseball section and came across *Heads-Up Baseball*. I opened it up and the coolest thing about that book are the little boxes you can read in less than 10 minutes to get a snapshot of the key points. I read through those boxes and thought, 'Oh man, this is really good, but do I really want to buy a book? I'm a 21-year-old college student. Am I really going to buy a book? It's the 4th of July, I should be at the bar.'

I end up buying the book, read it cover to cover two or three times and then emailed Dr. Ravizza, the author. I said, 'Hey, I wanted to be a pro baseball player, but I've realized that's not going to happen. The next best thing for me is that I would like to be a coach in high school or college. Do you have a Master's degree in this?' I got a phone call from him 3 or 4 weeks later and he said, 'Hey, I got your email. I don't do email, but yeah, we have a program. You need to fly up here and check it out.'

I went out there and met Ravizza, Coach Horton and the baseball staff at Cal State Fullerton. My real motivator for going out there wasn't necessarily to get into the mental game of baseball. It was to be a baseball coach. I thought, 'If I can be a baseball coach and learn the mental game of baseball, then that's going to be a great win for me.' Coach Horton was very honest and said to me, 'Look, a lot of people come out here, a lot of people want to volunteer and help out with the program. We would love to have you, but realize it's not a glamorous job. You're going to be here long hours, you're going to do things you probably don't want to do, and you're not going to have a lot of responsibilities. Is that something you are interested in?' I said, 'Sign me up. Let's roll!'

I went out there, across the country from Vermont, not knowing anybody, and had the best 2 years of my life.

What is the first thing you do when you go in to work with a collegiate baseball program?

Cain: The first thing is to figure out where the staff and the players are at. Everybody is in one of four stages of acceptance for the mental game, because there's still a stigma out there that people who need sports psychology are weak and that sports psychology is a crutch.

My first objective and first mission is to change the perspective. I say I'm a mental conditioning coach, not a sports psychologist, because of the stigma that psychology has in the athletic world that if you're seeing a psychologist there's something wrong with you. If you want to get better, you go to a coach. If you want to get stronger, you go to a strength coach. If you want to be a better hitter, you go to the hitting coach. If you want to be a better pitcher, you go to the pitching coach. If you want to become more mentally tough, come to the mental conditioning coach. We'll figure out where you're at and how we can close the gap between where you are and where you want to be.

The first thing you have to try to do is knock down those barriers of people being apprehensive and saying 'this ain't for me.' That's the first of the four stages that people go through in acceptance. This ain't for me. I was there as an athlete and everyone has been there before.

The second step is, 'Ok, this might be ok for others.' I get people to this stage by using the 3 R's: Research, Report, and Results. I tell them about the research and what everyone is doing. Here's how Cal State Fullerton won a national championship in '04. Here's what guys in the big leagues are doing. Here's how George St. Pierre went from getting knocked out in the first round by Matt Serra in 2006, to going undefeated and not losing a round for the next seven years.

9

I show videos and video testimonials and get the people in the room to say, 'Ok, this is ok for others.' Then I get them out of their seats and get them to interact and to participate in different activities, whether it's eating fire, breaking boards, bending rebar, doing mental imagery or falling off a ladder and having their teammates catch them. All of these different things, called experiential learning, are to get people to engage and actually experience the skills that we're trying to teach.

That's when they get to level 3: 'Ok, I'll try it.' Once we get them to 'Ok, I'll try it,' they do it for a year. The key part of that whole mix is the head coach of the program. If the head coach of the program isn't going to emphasize every day the mental conditioning program, we're all wasting our time. I make sure I spend a lot of my time with the head coach. This is different than it was years ago. I learned in the last few years that the head coach is probably the most important factor in the whole thing.

Ultimately they get to stage four, which is 'I can't believe I did it any other way.' Many people who have gone through the program know that it is a life-changing program because you're changing people's perspective. When you change perspective from winners and losers to winners and learners, from the outcome to the process, from I either play good or bad to I always play good and bad, you change people's lives because you change their perspective.

4 Levels of Acceptance

1. This is not for me.

2. This might be OK for others.

3. I'll try it.

4. I can't believe I did it any other way!

The goal is to get them along that continuum as quickly as possible. Again, the most important player in the whole thing is the head coach.

There are signs posted in dugouts of some of the top programs in the country that you work with. What are these for?

Cain: Those are what we call *Signs of Success,* reminders to the team, the coaches and the players of the mindset they want to have. Some examples are: So What? Turn 'Have To' into 'Want To.' Trust Your Routine. Get Big.

When the players see them, they remind them, 'Oh yes, this is what I'm supposed to be doing. I'm supposed to walk like I'm ten feet tall and bulletproof. I'm supposed to trust that my routine and my breath will bring me into this moment. When adversity strikes, which it always will, I'm supposed to say 'so what' and get to the next pitch.' Those signs are great reminders for the players and the staff of the mindset that they want to have.

If you could see inside of my office right now, I've got two windows in front of me. I took a dry-erase marker and I've got my goals, thoughts, and mindset written there. For example it says, 'Be abnormal. Be uncommon. Avoid the loser's limp.' Those are things that I've talked about in the past, but that I need to bring back out. I've got my goals there, on my window, so that when I sit in my room I see them every single day. It's a technique that I've taught for a number of years.

I recently had the opportunity to hear Marcus Luttrell from 'The Lone Survivor' speak to the Arizona State football team. One of the things that Marcus shared with the athletes was that when he was retiring from the Navy SEALs, it was like being an athlete. You do your whole life committed to this one thing, and you have to get ready for this at some point because it's coming for you, as it does for every baseball player. Your whole life has been hitting balls, fielding balls, working out, and being a baseball player. There's going to come a day, and it may be you are playing for a national championship. You're at the absolute height of your baseball career, and then you lose. Your season is over and you didn't get drafted, and now your career's over.

All of a sudden, it's not like a dimmer switch that comes to a slow halt and it's going to be over. It's like jumping off a cliff. One of the things Luttrell said was, 'I had to take a dry-erase marker and write on my mirror my goals and who I wanted to become, because when I looked into the mirror I didn't want to see who I was. I wanted to see who I was working to become.' The signs of success advertise that mindset that you're working to become, and that's what the dry-erase on the mirror does also. It reminds you of who it is you're trying to become.

George St. Pierre used a dry-erase marker to write on the mirror in his hotel prior to a competition. Could a baseball player on the road, staying in a hotel, write down some of the main points they're trying to focus on that weekend in the hotel on the mirror?

Cain: If George St. Pierre was here right now, he would say, 'Absolutely, you want to take that dry-erase marker and you want to write down the mindset that you want to have on your mirror.' If you are a baseball player, you want to write down your key thoughts for that weekend and what it is you are going to try to do, not what it is they are going to try to do to you. George would write those things down, and he'd encourage you to do the same thing as a baseball player. Write down your final thoughts. Write down your ABCs for performance. That pertains to any athlete going into any competition. What are the three aspects you're working on?

Saul Miller wrote the book *Hockey Tough* when I was working with the University of Vermont men's ice hockey team. I wanted to learn more about ice hockey, having never been a player myself. So I read *Hockey Tough.* One of the best strategies for success I got out of that was creating ABCs.

Going into a game, what are the three things you're going to focus on? For a hitter, ABCs might be: get my foot down, see the ball up, line drive. As a pitcher it might be: one pitch at a time, out front, pound the zone. Your ABCs are going to be physical reminders or mental reminders, or it can be a combination of both.

I was down at the IMG Academy in Florida a number of years ago. I got the chance to hear a track athlete who competed in the Olympics, talking to some guys getting ready for the NFL combine. 'Look fellas, the NFL combine is a track meet, it's not football. You go in, you're going to bench press, sprint, jump, and all these things. It's a track meet. How do I prepare for a track meet?' He says, 'I set ABCs.' My ABCs for the 200: explode out of the block, pump your arms, I'm a human bullet.'

When you hear explode out of the block, is that mental, physical, or both for you? I could say I see explosion out of the block like I'm getting shot out of a cannon. So I could argue, it could be both. The second one is 'pump your arms'. Is that mental or physical? That's going to be a physical reminder. The last one was, 'I'm a human bullet,' a mental reminder that I'm sleek, straight and I'm getting shot out of this cannon a hundred miles per hour and running.

What inspired you to write *The Daily Dominator*?

Cain: Developing mental toughness is like bathing. What happens to you if you work out every day and don't bathe on a consistent basis? You start to stink. Developing mental toughness is the same way. You have to do a little a lot, not a lot a little. It comes back to doing the total immersion program. You have to follow that up with doing a little, a lot. I'm a proponent of one or two days of boot camp. Shut the phones off and let's absolutely engage and attack this thing! Leave yourself with something to do a little, a lot. *The Daily Dominator* is the entire mental conditioning system, broken down into one page a day. Most of the athletes I work with will have that book on their iPhone and read the page of the day when they wake up. In there, you can interact with the text and answer some questions. I picked up this fantastic learning strategy in *Heads-Up Baseball*, where you actually answer questions in the book. That helps the athletes and coaches to develop a consistent system. Every day, everyone in the program has read *The Daily Dominator* and they can talk about it when they get to the field.

You are widely regarded as one of the top mental conditioning coaches in the world. How do you maintain such a high level of energy as you travel around the world, working with the top coaches, athletes and teams?

Cain: There are peaks and valleys. When you have to be on and you're with people, you've got to flip the switch and bring up the energy level. There are other times where I get drained and beat up and need a little vacation to decompress like anybody. But the most important thing is being passionate about what you do and having it be your mission.

There are four stages of commitment to what you do. First people go to a job. Second they do work. Third, where a lot of people may be, they have a career. When I went to Cal State Fullerton, coaching baseball was what I wanted my career to be. When I got into the mental game, I realized that coaching the mental game, coaching people how to have more character, how to have more mental toughness, how to succeed in life through sports—that is my mission. It's the first thing I think about when I wake up, it's the last thing I think about before I go to bed. I've dedicated my entire life to it. I'm 35 years old, never been married and don't have any children. This has been my entire life. That's what really drives me to try to be the best that I can be. Let everyone else judge where you fit against anyone else. That doesn't concern me.

So the first thing is finding that mission, why you do what you do, which is to make a difference in the life of other people, to give them skills that I never had as an athlete. If I did, I might have had more success. There is my mission.

The other important thing is working out every day. The first thing I do when I wake up in the morning is get up, take my vitamins, get a little breakfast, and I am right to the weight room or going on a run. If I am on the road, I break out the suspension trainer in the room or I am just doing body weight stuff. You've got to take care of your physical self. Once your physical self breaks down, everything else will break down. You've got to take care of the machine that you live in, which is your physical body. Doing a 'little bit a lot' of exercise is critical, then also making sure that you know why you are doing what you are doing because your WHY is the fuel that will build the fire that is your mission.

How can the readers get access to your Monday Messages?

Cain: If they want the Monday Message and the excellence that comes out every Monday, the stories, the videos, the strategies for success, the interviews with top college coaches and athletes, they can simply go to *BrianCain.com* and sign up for the Monday Message. If they want to view some previous Monday Messages, they can go to *BrianCain.com/Monday*. It's an email that I send out every week that shows up in your inbox.

For the readers of this exclusive content here, I'll give you a little secret. If you reply to the Monday Message, I will get that and reply to you. If you're looking to have a question answered, for a way I could get involved and help you take your performance to where you want to be, close that gap with the right map, just reply to that email and I'll get right back with you.

How does a coach or player get into contact with you to set up a mental conditioning program?

Cain: It really is dependent on what the head coach is willing to commit to. The best thing for them to do is email me at *Brian@BrianCain.com*.

I'll give you the overview of programs. Some programs I go in for one day and it's a boot camp. We're going 8am until 9-10pm with a combination of staff meetings, team meetings, individual player meetings, on-field work, team-building, establishing core values and a championship culture, leadership training with *The Leadership Clock*, going through the PRIDE program or the *Mental Conditioning Manual* program in that day. That's beneficial because it is total immersion for the whole day and that is one of the best ways to learn.

But, how much can you digest in a day? There are two schools of thought on that. Some prefer bite-size chunks so that they can maintain and have something consistently. Other coaches want to get the entire thing in one day.

The most common program is where I go in for two days at a time, up to four or five times a year. Generally, for a college baseball program, I come in early August or September. That's when we're going to talk about the routines, the championship culture where you build rapport with the players, and give the staff a once-per-week lesson plan that they're going to execute every week until the next visit.

I come back in the first or second week of October, which is when they're on the field, so I am giving observation, shooting video, breaking it down with the coaching staff so that they can have a better understanding. I meet with players individually, take the team through mental imagery and through different aspects of pitching and hitting performance, baserunning and defensive play, always leaving them with audios.

Every time we meet, we always record the player and me directly on their cell phone so they can listen to it on a consistent basis. I'll then come back in January or February with a heavy team-building emphasis, getting ready to go into the season. Also, I will visit during the season, usually around March, and then come back in May, video taping every pitch of the game, breaking it down with the coaching staff afterward, saying, 'Here is what I see, what do you see?' It is then that I get them able to better communicate aspects of the mental game.

We continue with individual meetings with players and an entire system that we put together, a very comprehensive system. It is a system that any coach, in any program, in any sport, would find tremendous benefit from. I back it up with a guarantee. If they bring me in for a year and don't feel like it was a life-changing and season-changing program, I refund them the money. If they don't find the value in it, then I don't want to have them make the financial investment.

For more great content from Brian Cain, visit MentalGameVIP.com/BrianCain

Tom Hanson

Owner of Play Big Academy and Co-Author of *Heads-Up Baseball*

**For more from Hanson, visit
MentalGameVIP.com/TomHanson**

How early do you think a proper mindset can be developed with kids, especially with the low attention span kids have today? Can it be taught, or should we just let them go?

Hanson: The goal would be to minimize the erosion of the mindset that they start with. Typically, a kid will come and love to play. My son would hit Wiffle balls and play in the pool. In baseball it's hit this and throw that. The bigger issue is the 'adultification' of youth sports, pressing this adult model onto kids. I've brought him to the park just to drop him off so he could play pickup baseball with other kids who would be there during someone else's game, because I grew up doing that and that's what we want to do. Working with a player, I'll say, 'Hey, it's like playing Wiffle ball as a kid.' Now it's less and less often that they even did that. They start off with this great mindset and I want to help protect it, rather than feeling like it needs to be taught.

You often speak on the 'performance gap' between where you are and where your potential lies. Could you expand on that briefly?

Hanson: One of the drivers for my work is Performance = Potential - Interference. I got it from Tim Gallwey in *The Inner Game of Tennis.* Performance equals your potential (how well you can play) minus the interference (what gets in the way). That interference makes the gap between how well you can play and how well you actually do play. No one plays over their head, of course. That's just a misnomer. No one can play better than they can play, so when someone is playing 'over their head', they're actually playing very close to what they're really capable of playing. Most people obviously don't do that very often, so it becomes about how to consistently play at or near your best, regardless of circumstances. I first heard this definition of mental toughness from Jim Loehr: 'Mental toughness is the ability to play consistently at or near your best, regardless of circumstances.' I'm looking to help people minimize that gap. You're never going to close the gap between how well you can play and how well you actually do play. Typically it shows up in practice, where somebody is much better in practice than they are in a game. That's the gap, the territory I work in.

Many have said that their careers were crushed by the 'yips' before you cured them of this destructive pattern. What is the process that you take a player through to combat the yips?

Hanson: Well, if we keep with this Performance = Potential - Interference, someone with the yips has got extreme interference. There's something in the way. I don't see the yips as a standalone issue—it's a continuum. On the right end would be freedom, joy and full self-expression. That's someone playing at their best. At the extreme left would be the yips, choking and average performance. All kinds of other things would fall on that continuum. The yips is just extreme choking.

We look at the fundamentals of how a human operates, to reverse-engineer how this works. If I have problems with my computer, I call a computer guy. Why? Because he's got the knowledge of how my computer works, so he can identify what isn't working. A lot of coaches and other mental game guys fall short in terms of asking how this whole thing is working. How does this whole machine work, and how can we fix it when we've got a lot of interference, when it is breaking down? The number one problem faced by humans today is that we're not well-designed for the world that we've created. We're not designed for our current cortexes. We're designed more for our current reptilian brain, the lower part of our brain. If there's a perception of stress or threat, there's a contraction. Apparently this fight-or-flight response has enabled us to survive, so if we're confronted with a threat, our body goes into this fight-or-flight response. It would contract, stop breathing and tense up. You lose the feel in your fingers because the blood goes to your bigger muscles so you can run. Apparently that's great, because we're here. That worked, but then, as our cortex developed, we developed this world, including baseball. If you perceive a threat, the last thing you want is to lose the blood from your fingers and tighten up your muscles, yet those were the very things that have apparently helped us survive.

What my work entails, in terms of the mental game, is to help upgrade the operating system of the person so they don't have that blockage, that same response to a perception of threat. With the yips, the person has had an experience akin to a trauma experience. They've had some experience with a simple task, throwing the ball, putting or whatever it might be, so that now it is perceived as a threat. This kicks in this ancient response, causing the tightness, which then causes the atrocious performance. It is true with choking in general, in a performance. It is the same mechanism. It just might not be as severe.

If that's the model, where is that belief coming from? Whenever you have an experience, whatever you're doing, if you perceive a threat, you're going to contract. Our midbrain has what we call an inner umpire, and the inner umpire is constantly saying, 'Am I safe? Am I safe? Am I safe?' If yes, then you have full access to your talent. The cortex runs, the body can stay loose and free. If no, you get this fight-or-flight contraction. The reptilian brain takes over and is now running the show. You may think, 'I should just relax. Mom said to go out and have fun,' but you can't do it. Why? Because the lower brain has grabbed the wheel of your ship and is steering it based on its belief.

Where is it getting this belief? Why is it perceiving this threat? That is the lynchpin of the whole thing. Why is the perception of threat here? That has to do with the belief system. I believe I'm not safe. Why? What happened? Something happened that has now created the belief that I'm not safe, so it kicks in the fight-or-flight. What is the key to fixing the yips, to gaining more freedom, moving to the right on the continuum, moving towards freedom? How do you upgrade the belief system by upgrading your operating system, so you see yourself as safe when you're out there playing baseball?

When I interviewed Derek Jeter, I was working for the Yankees in 2001. I said, 'How do you handle the pressure of being in Yankee Stadium?' He said, 'It's just like Little League. It's not pressure, it's fun. With more people, it's more fun.' That's his belief system, and anyone could say that, but does it actually show up? That has to be your lizard brain's belief system. It can't be your cortex's belief system. Yes, I'm just going have fun. We'll see. I saw the College World Series—we should have fun, right? It depends on the belief system.

You ask, 'How do you get your belief system?' You have experiences. I had an experience that caused me to believe that throwing the ball back to the pitcher, if you're a catcher, is a dangerous thing. Something bad could happen, so I'm going to contract. Lizard takes over, contraction, another bad throw. 'See, I told you, something bad could happen, and look how embarrassing!'

How do you break that cycle? You can't talk someone out of it. You can't say, 'Hey man, just relax and have fun,' because you're talking to the cortex when the problem is in the lizard brain. You have to change the memory, change how the guy's brain holds the memory of these past events. That's where I use this thing called tapping, where you literally tap different spots on your body. It's like an emotional laxative that helps process an emotion or an experience, so it is not informing or dominating the creation of a belief system that says throwing is dangerous.

If a coach or player wanted your help in fighting the yips and removing that interference, how would they go about contacting you?

Hanson: That is at *YipsBeGone.com*. I was learning how to make websites a few years ago, and I started working with some players and had some success. I put that website up, and now it's become a mainstay for what I do. It's certainly not what I set out to do, to work with that problem, but I happen to have found a way to help people. There's very little help for them out there, because none of the traditional stuff really gets at this underlying mechanism that I just went through.

Is there anything you teach in the world of sports and baseball that has a direct correlation to the world of business and the entrepreneurs you work with?

Hanson: Everything revolves around safety. In all human relationships, the most important issue is safety. Do you feel safe in that relationship? Are you safe to speak up and say this? In the business world, is someone safe to say, 'Boss, if we buy this part instead of that part, this is going to break down, then we'll have this problem, and it will cost so much, and someone might get killed.' Do you feel safe to say that, or do you not say it because you've got to cover your butt, because you've got to keep your job, and you've got your wife and kids? It's all about safety. In a relationship, do you say something to your spouse? Do you say something to your coach? Do you say something to your teammate? The communication all hinges around safety.

With performance, if you're going up to bat, do you feel safe? I don't think I'm going to get hit. I'm not talking about physical safety. It's emotional safety.

The midbrain is the mammalian brain, it's all about groups. Mammals like to be in groups.

Why do we get so nervous and afraid of what's going to happen? If we get hit by a ball, that ends up being minor for most hitters. It's because we don't want to get kicked out of the tribe. If we're hunter-gatherers and you get kicked out of the tribe, you're dead. You're not going to be able to eat very well, and you're certainly not going to be able to mate. You've got to stay in the group, so you don't want to be ostracized or criticized by the group. If you think you might be ostracized, it kicks in the fight-or-flight and you choke. That actually makes it more likely that you're going to get kicked out of the group, but the lower functioning brain is dominant. It's all safety. Whether you're a pizza delivery guy, a Fortune 500 CEO, or a baseball player, the number one thing is safety. It all hinges on the brain's question to that ongoing question, 'Am I safe?' because it's all about survival.

How can a listener sign up to receive the latest tips and blog updates from you?

Hanson: Go to *PlayBigBaseball.com*, where you can check out what I'm up to and sign up. I've got a free program there. Once you sign up, you start to get emails every once in a while. They come when I feel moved, I don't have a set schedule that I use. Sometimes I do a little bit more or a little bit less. If I feel like something is worthy of being shared, then I'll share it. I'll just sit down and crank it out.

I played through college myself. I was a hitting coach at Virginia for three years while getting my Ph.D. I was head coach and tenured professor at Skidmore College in upstate New York, before being hired by the Rangers and then the Yankees. Now I've got a ten-year-old son who's into the whole travel ball thing. I'm still just getting acclimated to what the world of youth baseball has become. I coached his Little League team this year, watched them play travel ball and got a sense of that. When I see things that get me motivated to sit down and write, I crank one out.

For more great content from Tom Hanson, visit MentalGameVIP.com/TomHanson

Alan Jaeger

Master of Feeding the Arm & Mind and Owner of Jaeger Sports

For more from Jaeger, visit
MentalGameVIP.com/AlanJaeger

Where did the philosophy of your J-Bands and throwing program originate?

Jaeger: Surgical tubing has been around for maybe forty years. It was found in a medical place, a rehab facility, a physical therapy kind of environment. Band work in general has always been used more as a rehab deal. When I was introduced to the exercises in 1994, it was interesting how good it made my arm feel. With a background in yoga, I was really sensitive to my body, so the concept of prehab versus rehab must have hit me between the eyes. To stretch your hamstrings out before you go on a run, or if you're going to do anything with your body, to get it prepared, made so much sense to me. We know that the rotator cuff is made of very small muscles, and the idea of actually doing something right before you throw, made so much sense to me.

The bands and tubing have been around a long time, but we took the concept and brought it out to the baseball field. We made it something that you do right before you throw again, as pre-hab, an unbelievable warm up, as opposed to just physical therapy.

Jaeger Sports was founded on the principle that athletes need to develop both their physical and mental skills in order to be successful. How important is the mental side of the game to a player who is looking to play at the highest level?

Jaeger: It's 99.9% mental at the highest level. If you look at the major league player, it's almost 100%. It doesn't change much down to rookie ball. I would even go out and say, if you're in a D1 program, it's 95-98%. It doesn't change much. It's pretty much 90+% for just about anybody except for maybe Little

League kids or kids approaching high school, because they can out-physical their opponent.

The mind is the engine to the car. We can make the rims look nice and the upholstery look nice, we can have a great paint job, but at the end of the day, the engine has to run well. We can argue whether it's 99% or 93%, or maybe below the high school level it's 72%. For anybody who's serious about baseball and wants to have a chance to play college, and hopefully have a chance to play professionally one day, it's like a pyramid. As you get to the top of the pyramid, that top point gets sharper and sharper, and the mental game becomes more and more crucial. I usually say it's at least 95%, but to make it very clear, it's 99.9% at the highest level, and that's at the highest level of any sport.

As a meditation enthusiast with your training in Yoga and Zen, how can a player best implement these in their daily routines or pre-game preparation?

Jaeger: I started meditating almost 30 years ago. I dabbled a little bit in other areas, but my core is in meditation and yoga. We can use the term 'mental practice', because it is practice. If you want to get better at bunting, going in the hole to your left and right as an infielder, it's always about practice. If it's easier to substitute the words 'mental practice' for meditation, it's the same. The idea is spending time in a place where you're devoting your attention and your awareness to how to clear your mind. 'How much can I relax my mind? How much can I get my mind to be more focused and more disciplined?'

One of the biggest things that people don't know about, that isn't talked about much, is the benefit of getting good at sitting somewhere for 15 or 20 minutes.

When thoughts come into my mind that are distracting, or something about the future or the past, I get better at not engaging these thoughts and not getting into a conversation with these thoughts. This is skill training. I get really good at being neutral to these thoughts. I can let them be like a scout in the stands, or someone calling me names from the other dugout. I can get really good at being neutral to those thoughts, and practice bringing my attention back to the present moment. That describes a peak state of mind. When you're in a peak state of mind, there is no future and no past. If stuff comes up in your mind, you don't even hear it any more. You're consumed by the flow of the game or the action.

Mental practice and meditation helps you to acclimate your mind and your body to that ideal state of mind. You're practicing not allowing thoughts to distract you. You're learning how to deal with thoughts to where you're not getting into this big conversation with them.

For example, you're in the on-deck circle and you're 0-for-3. The bases are loaded. The winning run is on third and you're not having a good game. You're thinking about how you are struggling, causing you to stress. You need to come through, and you start worrying about a lot of inconsequential stuff.

If you had a meditation practice in place, with practice and time, you start hearing those thoughts and right away you start addressing them. You say, 'Wait a minute! It doesn't matter if I'm 0-for-3. It doesn't matter what the situation is. What really matters is, what's my process? I need to take a deep breath. I need to see the ball well, I need to hit it hard. That's the process I wrote down three months ago that I'm working on every day in practice at the field.' Whether it's meditation or mental practice, at the end of the day, it's the single most important and influential part of developing your mental game and mental health.

You are very well known for merging the mechanics of the Western athlete with the insight of the Far Eastern mind to help baseball players realize and maximize their potential on and off the field. What are the mechanics of a Western athlete?

Jaeger: I received my bachelor's in Psychology and there was great value to that, but I didn't go on to get my master's or Ph.D. so I can only go based on my instinct.

When I got into meditation and the Far Eastern approach, Zen helped me the most. Zen is about trusting your instincts and discounting your thoughts, not allowing your thoughts to be right or wrong, good or bad, but just leaping into action and trusting your instincts. I relate to that as an athlete because we all know that we are at our best when we are not thinking and we just trust our instincts.

For people who don't really know what Zen is, you don't have to go heavy into anything religious. You can just take the simple part of it, which is very innocent. It's more of a life thing, not a religious thing. More about a way, a philosophy. The philosophy is to trust your instinct and know that thoughts are going to slow you down or distract you.

When I studied psychology, it felt to me like, if you had a problem, you were going to use words to figure it out. In talk therapy, you're going to talk through it. That's fine, there's a great place for that and it can be very helpful. But the Far Eastern approach that I studied was interesting. You can still use exchange and discussion, which is important, but the idea was to stop trusting or worrying about the thoughts, and start trusting your instinct. It was more of a cut to the chase, feel-instinct-rhythm kind of thing, so that's where I came up with that plan.

In the West, there is a lot of left-brain thinking. There are a lot of things going on about the future and the past, a lot of worrying about how I look, what kind of car do I own, what kind of house do I own. There are peer pressure, the draft, recruiting, showcases, a lot of stuff that our left-brain can get caught up into. I call it drama. The left-brain is more analytical, linear, and mechanical. The East represents more of the right brain: the feel, the instinct, the action and the spontaneity.

The mechanics are a pitching or hitting coach saying to you, 'Hey, we've got to put the mechanics in place.' I get that, but every day becomes an hour or two hammering your mechanics over and over. At some point I have got to trust my mechanics. I just need to see the ball and go into action mode. When I say the Eastern mind, it's about what I studied—Zen and eventually Yoga.

What if a coach or player wanted to work with you and your team more?

Jaeger: We have a guy named Tim Dixon who pitched for Augie Garrido at Fullerton in the College World Series. He's a powerful guy. Talk about high-energy and passion! If they want information on someone from Jaeger Sports to come out, *JaegerSports.com* is the easiest thing to do. There's a ton of free information and we have a lot of articles on our website about the mental game.

For more great content from Alan Jaeger, visit MentalGameVIP.com/AlanJaeger

Steve Springer

Quality At Bat Guru & Toronto Blue Jays Mental Coach

**For more from Springer, visit
MentalGameVIP.com/SteveSpringer**

You've worked with a ton of big leaguers. What is one thing they all have in common that helped them get to the highest level of the game?

Springer: I teach the same thing whether I'm talking to a big leaguer or the parent of a twelve-year-old. What I figured out by going 1-for-20 thirty times is that I'm good when I'm confident. How to create confidence is the question.

We bypass that by thinking we have to get hits. I played in 1591 minor league games and ended up getting 1592 hits. I was really glad to see that. People ask me if I have a psychology degree. I tell them, 'I can't spell psychology. I have a school of hard knocks degree. I'm not a doctor, I'm a baseball player.' Fortunately, God put me in AAA for 11 years so I can do what I'm doing now—teaching kids how to compete, how to not underachieve.

We get so caught up in what we think of as success by getting a hit. What is my batting average? Batting average is the biggest trap in the game. It destroys more young kids than anything else in the game, hands down. When big leaguers such as Trumbo, A.J. Pollock, or Paul Goldschmidt call me, I talk to them the same way I talk to a dad who ordered my CD—how to get little Johnny to be a great competitor.

When you buy into hit the ball hard, you win, and help your team win. It's not about you, it's about helping your team. You want your 'good player' to show up, but your good player doesn't show up all the time. I'll tell Trumbo, 'Confident Mark Trumbo' is a star and 'non-confident Mark Trumbo' sucks. How do we get confident Mark Trumbo to show up? It's a daily goal that is attainable.

My job is to be the best competitor on the field. Everybody says that we're playing a sport where you fail all the time. I call it the biggest self-esteem-destroying sport in the world. You had better change how you think about success now. That is why the batting average is the devil. You do everything right and you go 0-for-4. You hit four rockets right on the screws right at somebody. You beat the pitcher, and the pitcher knows you beat him. The pitcher's mom knows you beat him! Now you're going to lose confidence because your batting average went down? It makes no sense.

How or why did you evolve from player to coach, agent, scout and now mental coach?

Springer: It's crazy. When you break it down, I feel like a baseball version of Rudy, the 4'11" 90-pound high school freshman. I got three at-bats. I barely made the team because my brother was a star. My sophomore year, I played fresh-soph again, but I got to play. My junior year, all my buddies were on varsity and I was on JV, but I got to play. My senior year was my year. There was nobody in my way. I was going to show them that I could play. Well, a sophomore took my job.

So, I'm sitting on the bench, coaching first base as a senior in high school. It didn't get me a lot of girls, but I grew from tiny to small. I went from 4' 11" to 5' 8", 140 pounds. I didn't know what I was going to do and I didn't get recruited by anybody.

I went to Golden West Junior College. My brother was a star. I was thinking that my coach knew I was coming. He didn't even need to call me. I went out for the team and I got cut. That wasn't the plan. Three days later, I was home watching Oprah with my mom. Fortunately, three guys quit and my brother came with a uniform for me. I was nineteen years old. I got three at-bats the whole year.

I was coaching first base and I ended up playing in the big leagues. To inspire kids: 'Don't quit.' You have to have talent. Sometimes I may mislead people, but I guess my story was so crazy that they feel they can do it. I felt I had talent, but I was a little too small and not strong enough. I'm not saying you need to be a six footer—you need to be strong, you need to be a baseball player, and you need to be a great competitor. I was always like that. It was fortunate that I grew 4 inches when I was 20 years old. I ended up getting drafted by the New York Mets and played for 14 years, 11 spent in AAA.

In my eleventh year in AAA, I had a buddy named Louis Medina, who got a job with the Diamondbacks as the area scout. He said, 'Steve, your playing career is killing your scouting career.' Three days later I was a scout. So I went into scouting for 5 years. I had Southern California for two and then I was a cross-checker for three. I never made enough money to buy a house or take care of my family. Those fourteen years in the minor leagues didn't set me up for life.

I got approached to be an agent. I did that for seven years and we got Kirk Sarloos, who is now the pitching coach at TCU. He was my first client. I got these guys, and holding onto them was a little bit different. I did that for seven years, then I got into scouting and cross-checking with the Diamondbacks.

I met Tony Lacava of the Blue Jays. At that time, I was an agent. He loved my CD, loved it, and he planned on bringing me to Toronto. I went there to scout for the first year. For the last five years, I've been on both scouting and player development, doing a little bit of both. Until this year, they called me up and said, 'Steve, I just want you to be around my players and I want you scouting.' Now I'm a roving mental and hitting coach. It's awesome.

What inspired the QAB CD?

Springer: When I was playing, I had a coach named Tommy McGraw, a great hitting coach. Every time he was around, I was a stud, but he was a roving guy. He would come in for three days, get my mind right. He taught me how to watch the game, when to start, pick up the paper in the morning and see who's pitching, and then start visualizing.

As dumb as I was, I was smart enough to realize that when this guy was around, I was good. I brought a tape recorder to his room and he was nice enough to talk to me for twenty minutes about me. It changed my life. I listened to that thing every single day for seven years. If I was in my car, I put it on. We give ourselves too much credit to remember what we're taught. I can give you guys my whole spiel. And if you don't have it recorded, in two weeks, what I said has been forgotten.

When I became an agent, I wanted to help my kids get a mental game. I just started talking into a microphone. I didn't know if they listened to it or not, but I found out that they did.

It took on life of its own. It's as hot now as it's ever been. I don't mean to boast, but I believe it's hot because it's right. We give ourselves too much credit to remember what we're taught. Too often, players let the mind get in the way of their ability. I make an individual CD for every one of my players. Every player has his own personal talk, just as Tommy did with me about what he thought I needed to do with my staples to play in the big leagues.

For more great content from Steve Springer, visit MentalGameVIP.com/SteveSpringer

Jon Gordon

Best-Selling Author, Coach, Speaker and Consultant

**For more from Gordon, visit
MentalGameVIP.com/JonGordon**

The Carpenter was an immediate Wall Street Journal bestseller. What are the main principles in that book?

Gordon: The main principles are the greatest success strategies of all: love, serve and care.

We love what we do. We love it so much that we are willing to overcome all the adversities and challenges in order to be great at it.

We serve others. With our knowledge, our ability, and our skill, we put ourselves out for our teammates. Your team doesn't care if you're a superstar. They care if you're a super teammate. It's about serving, putting the team first, and making sure that you give everything to the team and not just yourself. That's what service is all about.

We care. You stand out when you care because a lot of people don't care. When you care, people can tell that you put your heart and soul into your work, your practice, your craft and your job. We know when someone cares and when someone doesn't. When you care, people want to work with you, people are drawn to you and you stand out.

Is it really that simple?

Gordon: It is simple, but simple doesn't mean easy, right? The greatest strategies of all are always simple. It's about putting them into action, making them part of our lives, making them a habit. Again, it doesn't mean it is easy, but it is simple.

It is not easy to love when you're fearful. It is not easy to serve when the world says to focus on yourself. When you have so much stress and pressure on yourself, it's hard not to think about yourself, so it's hard to serve. It's hard to care when you're busy and stressed, and that busyness and stress prevent you from caring about the things and the people that you're supposed to care about. Instead of caring, you're just trying to get through the day, trying to make it and trying to survive. You're not thinking about helping others and caring. In this world, it's not easy, but these principles put the joy into our lives. We take this simple and powerful strategy and we act upon it. That's when we see results.

Can you talk more about the benefits of positivity and the cost of negativity?

Gordon: That comes from my books *The Energy Bus* and *The Positive Dog*. We know being positive is not just a nice way to live, it is *the* way to live. Research shows it enhances your health, performance, ability, and leadership, and your ability to be a teammate.

Positivity makes you a better person, a better leader, a better teammate, or a better performer. Research shows that when you're positive, you're more creative. Optimistic salespeople out perform pessimistic salespeople. Positive leaders are more likely to support their team and move them in the right direction. We know that nine out of ten people work better in a positive environment.

We also know that negativity affects your performance. It leads to heart attacks, causes stress and more illness. All of these are costs of negativity. It sabotages the team, and sabotages customer service. Negativity brings us down, whereas positive energy is life-giving and sustaining.

You work with numerous high-performing teams around the world. What is one of the first

things you might do when you speak to or consult with a baseball team?

Gordon: I approach any sports team the same. I find out what they are about, what their culture is like, what their challenges are. I always want to speak to their challenges. What's their vision? What are their goals? Where do they want to go? What message does the coach want to reinforce? Once you know their challenges, you know what their vision is and what their goals are, then you can really speak to them and their challenges and ambitions. You can help them get where they need to go.

Many of your fans rave about creating One Word with you for their year or season. What does the process of coming to that One Word consist of?

Gordon: That's a great thing to do with a team. Every person on the team comes up with a word for the year. Each player will have a word and it will be his driving force. What's the word that is meant for you? What's missing? What do you need most? What do you need to focus on? What word would drive you to be your best?

It might be discipline, habit, passion, fearless or relentless, whatever word is meant for you. When you focus on it, it becomes a driving force in your life. You never forget your word and you can't forget your teammate's word either. When a team is together and everyone lives their words for the season, and everyone focuses on their word, it becomes a powerful momentum builder, team builder and a great focuser.

Remember your word, remember your focus! When you're going out to bat, your word might be 'focus' or 'aware.' Whatever that word is, that could help you be your best. Imagine the whole team doing it together! A group of people sharing and living their words becomes very powerful.

For more great content from Jon Gordon, visit MentalGameVIP.com/JonGordon

Tim Dixon

Speaker, Coach, Motivator, and Creator of the Mental Locker

For more from Dixon, visit
MentalGameVIP.com/TimDixon

Can you tell us about how you got to where you are today?

Dixon: My journey begins a long time ago. I was haunted by this dream of playing professional baseball. I didn't really have the answers. I just knew that I had to work. My journey was not a straight path. I went to a bunch of different schools. I actually went to four schools in four years. Back then you didn't have the rule that if you transfer in, you have to sit out for a year. I ended up landing on my feet at Cal State Fullerton, and that's where I was introduced to sports psychology and Ken Ravizza, who is the best. It really changed everything. I was an average guy, and when I learned how to use my mind, I went 13-0 as part of a national championship team. As soon as I got done playing professional baseball, I immediately got my Master's in sports psychology, and began coaching. I began sharing how important what you think is, your perception, the breath, and all that great stuff that we talk about as psychologists. It changed the outcome of my life, learning how to use my mind as an ally and not as an enemy.

What inspired you to create *The Mental Locker*?

Dixon: *The Mental Locker* is around 25 years of my experience as a player and a coach, seeing some of the things that I've done. It has six modules: goal setting, controlling the controllables, the power of perception, breath and relaxation, visualization, and routine. It's a very intimate and detailed program where you get three emails a week, including three videos and downloadable PDFs. It's very interactive. It dissects what it takes to be the best at whatever you want to do. We set goals, we get a plan, and then we start attacking that plan one day at a time, step by step. Many people, when they have a dream, want to jump right to the end. They want it now. We live in a 'microwave lifestyle'. Many people want instant results, and if they don't get them, they quit.

The Mental Locker is all about being the best and maximizing who you are. It's a process and it takes a long time. We don't want to worry about the end result, because when you're trying to be the best, there is no end. You constantly strive to get better. I'm really, really proud of the product. I have a free download of a pitcher's evaluation, because *The Mental Locker* is geared just for pitchers. We're in the process of creating *The Mental Locker* for position players, hitters, golf, tennis, soccer, and gymnastics as well. We've already been asked to do one for coaches, parents, and even in Spanish. It's just the beginning. I'm really proud, and there's nothing else out there like this. A lot of people write great books, and there are a lot of really great YouTube videos, but this is an intimate, detailed description of what I've done as a player and coach and seen very, very good results.

You are very well known as a pitching coach and mental consultant around the country. How important is the mental game for pitchers in particular?

Dixon: It's the missing ingredient for a lot of people. Baseball is one of the most difficult sports to reach the top. It's less than 1%. You could throw 96, have the dirtiest slider, be 6'4", lean, long, loose, everything that scouts and coaches look for in a pitcher, but if you don't know how to handle failure and deal with adversity, if you can't make the pitches when it counts, you're going to get lost.

During my six years of playing professional baseball, I saw some of the most talented athletes I've ever been around never get out of AA. The mental part, the grind of what it takes to be a professional baseball player, gets to them and weeds them out. The mental game is the number one ingredient for success at an elite level, and probably the number one misunderstood piece of the puzzle. We have the best gloves, we have the best cleats, we spend thousands of dollars on travel ball, we buy the best of everything, but we're missing a big part of it. That's why so many people fizzle out and you never hear of them. It's important! The mental game is important and people know it's important. But they're uneducated on how important it is. Listen to Derek Jeter or some of the best that ever played, it's what they talk about, being in the moment, staying in the present. Look at those guys who are the best. When the game is on the line there are millions of people watching them. They're calm, been there, done that, and it is the difference. It separates good from great.

For more great content from Tim Dixon, visit MentalGameVIP.com/TimDixon

Charlie Maher

Cleveland Indians Baseball Psychologist

For more from Maher, visit
MentalGameVIP.com/CharlieMaher

As a psychologist for major league baseball players, what do you see as the basic necessity to making the transition to professional baseball?

Maher: One of the biggest and most basic things is for the individual to let go of 'himself'. He needs to stop identifying with his results, with his talent and things that essentially are in the past. He must learn to focus on how to play the game of professional baseball, which is a lot different than high school and college baseball. As long as he can let go of things having to do with himself, with what he identifies with, and focus on his effort and development, the individual will make that transition more efficiently.

You developed a program that helps a player learn about his mental game as soon as he enters professional baseball. What does that program consist of?

Maher: We have an orientation, a mini-organization, training and indoctrination period. When we orient players into the organization, we start by emphasizing to them that baseball is what they do, but it's not who they are. The program focuses on helping them learn more about themselves, their values, over and above baseball. It leads into making a commitment to balance baseball with the rest of their life as they move forward, not just their first year of baseball, but throughout their career. We call it a personal development program that emphasizes values, clarification and perspective.

How many MLB organizations have full-time psychologists or mental skills consultants working with their players?

Maher: It depends on how you define it. I would say there are probably about six or seven who are employed full-time by the organization. Most organizations have some form of consultation, but it is widely variable across the major and minor league level. I am president of the Professional Baseball Performance Psychology Group, which consists of mental skills consultants and psychologists who work with various teams. So I'm pretty accurate on the number. If you were to ask every major league organization whether they have a psychologist working in the mental skills area, all of them would say yes. But what they are doing would be widely variable.

How much do off-the-field circumstances and experiences affect players' performances on the field?

Maher: That will depend on the particular player, whether a player has developed good routines to separate baseball from the rest of their lives. When things happen off the field, those can leak into the game. Has he learned how to cope with what we call the 'PPTs'—people, places and things that can drag him down? It depends on the player. But it can affect them if they don't have a plan to separate those things out. Of course, there are also people, places and things that can build them up.

For more great content from Charlie Maher, visit MentalGameVIP.com/CharlieMaher

Dr. Jim Afremow

Mental Performance Consultant and Author of *The Champion's Mind*

For more from Afremow, visit MentalGameVIP.com/JimAfremow

The Champion's Mind is one of the greatest sports psychology books ever written. What inspired you to write this book?

Afremow: I've always been interested in human psychology, what makes people tick and how they can tick better. I've also always been a big fan of sports and peak performance, so sports psychology is a perfect marriage of my two interests.

In terms of writing the book, on a professional level, I wanted to share a bit of my sports psychology approach with a wider audience, which a book allows me to do. On a personal level, I thought it would be a lot of fun and a great challenge to write such a book, and it definitely was. I can tell you that I had to practice what I preach in order to accomplish the task. I had to set goals, stay confident, focus and refocus. I used visualization and a lot of positive self talk to get through the project.

As a former sports psychologist at Arizona State, one of the nation's top collegiate baseball powerhouses, what do you think is the most important thing for a college baseball player to be aware of?

Afremow: The main difference between a player's best and worst performances always hinges on their mental performance. Understanding the importance of the mental game is key. In addition to working on the mental game, college players must also get really good in terms of energy and time management. For time management, the key is to compete in the classroom and study with a purpose. In terms of energy management, baseball players need to protect their rest and recovery time and stick to a good sleep schedule.

I would say that most college baseball players work hard, but if you really want to get an edge over the competition, you also need to rest well to get your regeneration. It's important for baseball players to realize that no one has ever graduated from college wishing they had drunk more alcohol, used more drugs, or partied more often. Keep the big picture in mind, your goal of what you want to accomplish in baseball.

If somebody wants to get your coaching services, how would they go about beginning that process?

Afremow: My website is *GoldMedalMind.net* and that's synonymous with *The Champion's Mind*. When we're at our gold self, we're championing ourselves and being the best we can be. My book, *The Champion's Mind*, is available wherever books are sold. I'm also happy to answer any questions coaches, players, or parents might have about mental performance coaching services, to determine if we would be a good fit together. My phone and email address are available on my website.

For more great content from Jim Afremow, visit MentalGameVIP.com/JimAfremow

Jeff Janssen

Leadership and Championship Culture Guru

**For more from Janssen, visit
MentalGameVIP.com/JeffJanssen**

The results and success that you have produced among teams and organizations at the highest level are astonishing. Can you begin by explaining a little bit about how you got to where you are today?

Janssen: When I was a junior in high school, I read *The Psychology of Coaching* by Tom Tutko. That book showed me all the intangible things that go into the sporting world. I was always an athlete, and was always intrigued that the most talented team or the most talented individual didn't always win. I went to Marquette University, got my degree in psychology and minored in coaching. While I was there, I started volunteering for the men's basketball program, an opportunity to see college athletics at the Division 1 level.

I went on to the University of Arizona and got my Master's degree in Sports Psychology under Jean Williams. I volunteered for Mike Candrea, the softball coach, who gave me a great opportunity, as did their basketball coach. That blossomed into a full-time job working with all the teams at Arizona, which I did for eight years or so. I had a lot of requests from other schools to come in and do programs and workshops. So I decided to go out on my own and be a consultant and facilitator for other teams.

I started the Leadership Academy ten years ago with the University of North Carolina. That's gone remarkably well, and since then we've had about twenty different schools create Leadership Academies with us. It has been a dream career for me, doing exactly what I love to do, with people whom I love to do it with, each and every day. I'm really a fortunate guy.

What are a few ways that you get teams connected with each other and create the synergy that so many championship teams have?

Janssen: It's critical to have that common goal of what we're trying to do together as a group. Once you have like-minded people going after a similar vision and a common goal, they make decisions that are in the best interest of the entire group. Clarifying that is a huge part of it, coming up with a clear and compelling vision of where it is that we want to go.

Second, you're looking at commitment levels. I've developed a tool called the *Commitment Continuum*. It looks at seven different levels of commitment that athletes, coaches and managers, can display towards that common goal. Obviously, if you're going to be a successful team, or even a successful individual, you've got to put in that time and commitment. If you're going to have the respect of your teammates and coaches, you've got to do that not only for yourself, but for them too.

The third part is the leaders. Leaders have such a big impact on team chemistry and everything else that's going on. If you can get the team leaders to continually model what it is that you're looking for, and then manage the culture with everybody else, you've got a chance to have that chemistry and synergy that you're talking about.

Do you encourage coaches you work with to appoint team captains?

Janssen: There are different ways that coaches use their leaders. Some name them themselves. Some do the vote. Some do leadership councils. Some make their seniors automatically captains. I always tell coaches that you don't have to have captains, but you do have to have leaders. What you need to do is take a look at the makeup of your team, where your program is right now, and decide which of these different methods might be best for this particular group this year. If you give the players a say in who their captains are, they're going to be much more involved and committed to those people. Certainly, having a person the coach trusts and respects is going to be important. So a lot of times there's a hybrid version that works best for a particular team.

It's a good idea to step in front of the team and say, 'These are guys who really understand our philosophy, who live it each and every day. I want you to look to them for leadership.' Whether you officially give them the title of captain or make a leadership council is up to each particular coach and season. You don't have to have captains, but you do have to have leaders who are going to set the tone for everyone else and enforce the rules and standards of your program.

How important do you think it is for a team or athletic program to establish core values? Is there a process that you use to identify these?

Janssen: It's really important, whether you're a sports team or a business, to be clear about your purpose, your passion and your principles, to create a vision, a mission and core values, your unshakable bedrock principles. No matter what our record, no matter what's going on in our program, we are going to uphold these with ourselves and others. You take a long-term view of your program and understand that, if we do these things, we're going to be successful. I want to make sure teams know what they stand for, because once you have those things in place, it's going to help you recruit, help you make tough decisions, help you reward your best people, and help you coach and correct those people who really aren't on board as well.

When I sit down with teams, we take a look at core values. Sometimes they have them in place a little bit already, or they kind of assume that they have core values but maybe they're not written down. You get them to elaborate and point out what they were. I've just written *How To Build and Sustain a Championship Culture*. I studied the core values of both sports teams and business teams. They revolve around the five following areas:

Character: how we want people to conduct themselves. Core values often revolve around character, honesty and integrity.

Commitment: you need a great investment of people in the program if you're going to be successful.

Relationships: how do we treat each other as teammates and what it means to be good teammates.

Results: How important are results, and how much are we going to base our group around getting those successful, winning results and championships.

Positivity: the vibe, the enthusiasm, the passion, the excitement levels, the engagement levels are all important.

When I work with a team, those five areas are something we highlight to make sure those core values create the kind of culture that's fun to be around, and hopefully give you a chance at being successful.

How would a coach begin the process of establishing a leadership development system with the Janssen Sports Leadership Center?

Janssen: I created the *Team Captain's Leadership Manual*, a ten-module program in bite-sized chunks that a lot of coaches use, especially in the off season, with their emerging or existing leaders. They usually assign a chapter a week with lots of evaluations, assessments, fill in the blanks and simple homework projects. Then the coach and players meet for 20 to 40 minutes and talk about how that chapter impacts them, what that looks like in their program, how that really impacts them as leaders. It is a catalyst to get at some of those key intangible parts of a program that are often assumed or not talked about. They get into the same room and talk about how this really impacts our team.

A lot of coaches have used that captain's manual as a catalyst and springboard with their leaders, resulting in some great discussions. Sometimes after people use that, I'll get a call saying they want to go a lot deeper into this, and what are the next steps? That's usually how coaches and their existing or emerging leaders get on board with leadership training.

How can the readers start receiving your blog updates and content available via e-mail?

Janssen: The easiest thing is to go to our website *JanssenSportsLeadership.com*. I've got a simple sign-up box that people can join on. We usually do our monthly blog there and have a lot of other stuff as well, evaluations and material for both coaches and athletes.

I also have a daily motivational tweet during the week, *@JanssenLeader* on Twitter. So those are easy ways people can use if they're looking for some information that would be very practical for their athletes and team.

For more great content from Jeff Janssen, visit MentalGameVIP.com/JeffJanssen

Dr. Rob Bell

Sport Psychologist and Mental Toughness Trainer

**For more from Dr. Rob Bell, visit
MentalGameVIP.com/RobBell**

Can you share a bit of your background and how you got started in this field?

Bell: I knew what I wanted to do early on, back in 1996. When it hit me about the mental side of sports and the importance of mental toughness, I was drawn in. I did anything I could to speak with elite athletes, learn the research, and exactly how people play their best when it matters the most. When things were great, I would never think, I would just act. When things got a little bit off, I thought too much, and I would get off at the wrong exit. I could never play consistently. It was all or nothing. I knew about the mental side of the game towards the end of my career, but to help athletes play their best when it matters the most is what I love doing. It's my passion.

If there's one thing you would teach the young high school or college athlete and baseball players today, what would it be?

Bell: Mental skill is the most important and the most important mental skill is confidence. It's trust, belief in yourself and in what you're trying to accomplish. I don't think we even understand how important that is. When we're playing well, I always ask great athletes, Hey what are you thinking about when you're playing well, when you're throwing well or you're hitting? What are you thinking about? The answer is always the same. The answer is nothing. I just see the ball, hit the ball.

When we're not playing our best, when things aren't going well, what are we thinking about? We're thinking about techniques, about results, we're not focused on the process, we're focused on the product. When we're confident, we're like a fountain. But when we lose confidence, we're like a drain and we start searching. The one thing I want to share is to be confident. We work on our confidence through our other mental skills, through our focus and our motivation, then through our refocus, how to let go of mistakes. That's how we get confidence. Confidence a lot of times is trust. It's just a feeling, that's all it is.

Why do you refer to it as the 'hinge moment'? What is the definition or an example of what makes a hinge moment?

Bell: Every door has a hinge. A door without a hinge is a wall. It just doesn't work. The hinge is that one moment, that one person or that one event that's going to make all the difference in our lives. It's going to connect who we are with who we become. The thing is that we don't know when that moment is, or when that person is coming. It's our ability to be ready, to keep giving ourselves opportunity, because we don't know when that hinge moment is going to happen, but it's going to happen in our lives. What we need to do is trust our guts and know that it's going to happen.

Sometimes our mess becomes our message. Sometimes tragedies, the really bad things that happen in our lives, become immediate hinges. From that moment on, everything is different. For athletes, that one time when they come through with men on second and third, or that one time they go out there and it's lights out, everything from that moment on is changed. If they have a little more belief in themselves, that they can get it done, it just happens. The hinges are out of our control, but what I always try to coach is, it's how we respond to things, not how things happen to us. That's all the hinge is about. I just believe that every one of us is getting ready for that moment and opportunity, but we don't know when it's coming. That's the real importance of mental toughness, to know that we can't ever take any play off, we can't take any day off, because we have no idea when it's coming. We might not even know when that hinge connected until months or years later, what the impact was of that one play, one game or one season. We look at a great season or a great game where there was that hinge moment that made all the difference. That one play. That's what it boils down to.

For more great content from Dr. Rob Bell, visit MentalGameVIP.com/RobBell

John Brubaker

Performance Consultant, Speaker and Award-Winning Author

**For more from Brubaker, visit
MentalGameVIP.com/JohnBrubaker**

Can you expand on what you call GR2GR Syndrome?

Brubaker: GR2GR syndrome is Getting Ready To Get Ready. I believe it's an epidemic that everybody has been afflicted with it at some point—paralysis by analysis. We say, 'I'm going to change someday,' but someday never arrives. Today is never the right day. We think we're not ready, so we continue to get ready to get ready. In reality, if you're waiting for a perfect time, it's never going to happen. There is never a perfect time for anything.

Players who go from the bench to starting lineup may not be ready, but they're thrust into that role, so they'd better act ready. When the assistant coach has the opportunity to become head coach, maybe a little ahead of schedule, he may not be ready, he may be getting ready to be ready, but he's got to do it anyway. That's the great thing about athletes, comparing the locker room to the boardroom: athletes take action. They tend not to be plagued by getting ready to get ready syndrome quite as much, because they're only one play away from starting, one hiring decision away from becoming head coach. It doesn't always work out that way for entrepreneurs who have that paralysis by analysis. What I do as a performance consultant is help people get out of their own way and just get started.

As a former coach yourself, what are a few ways that you can get your team connected with each other and create the synergy that so many championship teams have?

Brubaker: I really want to focus on the one way that is the foundation of everything. If you can't get this right, those other ways will never get right, so they just don't matter. If you cannot build trust, you're never going to have synergy. It's the foundation for everything.

Many athletes, coaches and teams focus on building the team on the field, on the court, and they forget that the most important part of team dynamics often takes place outside of practice or the game situation. It is having people connect with each other as opposed to being off on their own, being on their own islands.

I really like to cut through the boundaries right away. Coach Don Meyer, who recently passed away, the winningest NCAA basketball coach, calls it the foxhole test. Who would you want in your foxhole if you're at war, and why? So I'll ask you that, who you want in your foxhole? You choose him because you trust him, that when times get tough, he's not going to turn and run.

There are people who may not be quitting physically on the field, but they've quit on that team mentally, in spirit. Using the foxhole test, you draw a circle on a piece of paper, and put yourself in the middle of the foxhole. Put a line to the left, a line to the right, and a line to the back. The teammate who has your back is the most important person in the foxhole, because you don't know what's behind you. You don't have a rearview mirror. You have each player on the team fill in the names of the three teammates they would want in the foxhole with them.

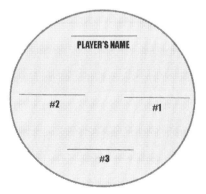

The person who gets put in the back position gets three points. The left side, like a quarterback being protected, is the blind side. We tend to be right hand, right eye dominant, so we don't look to our left. We don't look to our left in the foxhole, either. So the left gets two points and the position to your right gets one point. Then the coach compiles all of that and looks for trends, to see who the go-to guys are when times get tough.

That one exercise cuts through all the politics. Sometimes, things can become popularity contests on teams, and this exercise cuts to the heart of the matter. Who do you trust? Who is not going to turn and run when things get tough? That will expose weaker players who need to ratchet up their commitment a bit, and lets everybody know exactly where they stand in the team dynamics.

If you think about it, without building that foundation of trust, somebody might be that go-to guy and not even know their teammates think that highly of them.

The knock on guys in particular is that we are not great communicators, we don't share our feelings well. When we're lost, we don't even ask for directions in the car—that would be a sign of weakness. Just to be able to communicate more, let people know exactly who you are, what you're about, and where they stand with you, is hugely important on a team. Get the little things right, and all the big things take care of themselves.

This is one of the tools that would help determine the leaders of a team. I never use the word captain. I always use the word leader because 'captain' is a title. Leader implies an actual role that is action-oriented, and I approach it like a job. Everybody has to apply, and they are going to be interviewed. They have to list references. I really had a screening process for how our leaders were chosen. If you're a student athlete, that is a realistic preview of what life is going to be like when you graduate.

You consult and speak to numerous top-level businesses around the country. Do you see that success on the field translates to success in business and in life as well?

Brubaker: There are 101 reasons why you should hire an athlete. As I look at organizations that perform at a high level, the people within those companies who enjoy what they do are action-oriented people. Athletes are, by their very nature, action-oriented. They're not afraid of failure. They understand that failure is a part of the process and that they need to dust themselves off and get back in the batter's box.

Team building is also crucial. In the corporate environment, companies are hiring people to come on to an existing team. They may not have been an athlete at any stage in their life, but all of a sudden, they are expected to be a team player, and they don't know how. The number one reason to hire an athlete is because they know it is service above self. They are participating in something that's bigger than just them.

Many of the most successful players, coaches, and businesses are fully engaged in what they are doing, and excited to get after it each day. How does one connect with their true passion?

Brubaker: There is a connection between your passion and your need to be able to monetize it. We all have to make a living after we are done playing or coaching.

If you can find an environment where your passion and your purpose intersect, you will find where your unique talent or your unique ability lies. Entrepreneurs naturally get what their unique talent or ability is. They have a certain passion, but then they need to make that the distribution channel to the market place, where they're going to be compensated for doing just that.

I don't really think it is something that someone from the outside could come in and identify for you, or force. It's a big self-discovery process, and you need to start taking that journey and explore. Just like an athlete, when you're fully engaged, present and excited to get after it, you're willing to put in that extra effort because you care. You know what you care about and how it is an outlet you can monetize later in life. That knowledge is hugely important, because there are a lot of disengaged people in the workplace.

For more great content from John Brubaker, visit MentalGameVIP.com/JohnBrubaker

Aaron Weintraub

Mental Skills Coach, Consultant and Author

**For more from Weintraub, visit
MentalGameVIP.com/AaronWeintraub**

One of your mentors, Harvey Dorfman, was one of the greatest mental game coaches ever. What did he mean to you and how did you get started with him?

Weintraub: Harvey was probably the greatest coach I ever met. He was working for the Florida Marlins, as was I, in 1995 when I got to meet him. I had read *The Mental Game of Baseball*, and picked his brain every chance I got.

I was the clubbie for the Portland Sea Dogs at the time, an affiliate of the Marlins. The next year I got a coaching job at Brevard College and was very fortunate to find out that Harvey lived in Brevard, North Carolina. He came and spoke to our team and spent hours with us. One afternoon, he had me over to his house for dinner, and basically, I took advantage of his graciousness and learned so much.

I was very young and getting started in the college baseball world at that time. I was smart enough to know that I had found a good man, someone I could learn a lot from. The cool thing about Harvey was that I had heard him speak to teams on many occasions and I'd read all of his books, but it was the kind of thing where sometimes I would think about calling him, but would find it not necessary because I knew what he was going to say. The cool thing about Harvey is in spite of all that, every time I was around the man, I left smarter. Wow! I thought I had understood what he'd been teaching all along, but he just made it clearer and showed me something new.

You authored The Coach's Guide to Winning the Mental Game. What is that book about? What

inspired you to write it? How can the readers get access to that book?

Weintraub: I tried to take all the information that I had found. First on the list of sources would be Harvey's work, along with much of the work of John Wooden and Tony Robbins. I took the best information I could find about how to coach the mental game and put it together in *The Coach's Guide to Winning the Mental Game*.

Coaching the mental game or winning the mental game is all about leading by example—how to give your best effort one pitch at a time, accept whatever happens, and do it again. The leadership book is really built around how to lead by example, but then also discusses in some detail how to make your teammates better, how to connect with them, how to have a vision of where you're going. Both of the books are available on my website which is CoachTraub.com. They're also available on Amazon, but certainly I appreciate when people visit my website.

If a coach wants to bring you in to speak to the team, what is the best way to go about contacting you to begin that process?

Weintraub: Go on my website CoachTraub.com. I'm one of the few mental skills coaches that put my cell phone number and my prices on the website. It is an investment of both time and money, but there is power in an outside voice. I certainly am passionate about delivering value and so I am appreciative if anyone does that.

For more great content from Aaron Weintraub, visit MentalGameVIP.com/AaronWeintraub

Christine Rickertsen

Training Consultant and Contributor to STACK Magazine

**For more from Rickertsen, visit
MentalGameVIP.com/ChristineRickertsen**

Your articles on *SelfMadeAthlete* and in *STACK* are outstanding. What inspires your writing and where else is your work published?

Rickertsen: I got my Master's degree in California at John F. Kennedy University, and it was actually an internship I did at the time with a baseball team. I was working with a collegiate-level summer baseball team, and I got to be an intern working with them. I really got into working with baseball and loved the game. Of course, I loved the game before that, but didn't know exactly how my career could fit into that. I ended up having a lot of great connections out of that. I got really excited and started working with some athletes after I graduated. It kind of blossomed after that. I definitely have a passion for the sport, and I feel very grateful that I get to work in baseball and work with the athletes.

I started writing a couple of years ago. What inspires me to write comes from the athletes. I'll meet with a client about what they're going through that week, something that they're struggling with, or a sort of an 'aha moment' they've had. I'll take those tidbits and work them into my blog or into the articles I write for *STACK*. To be honest, they inspire me, not always the other way around. It's my way of giving back to them for inspiring me. There are some weekly tidbits about ideas that have been brought to me from clients I have worked with and other baseball players. That way, others who may be struggling with or feeling the same about certain topics have a chance to read it and learn something from the blog. I'm very lucky in the way they bring it to me and that, in a big way, is why it's so inspiring.

The average athlete performs in the zone only 10-20 percent of the time. What is the plan for the other 80-90 percent?

Rickertsen: That's the piece that gets me really excited about mental training. You have about 10 or 20% of the time where it doesn't matter what you do, it just kind of naturally happens. It's that feeling that gets athletes excited, because you have the potential to get there and perform there consistently. But 80 or 90% of the time, it's going to be something that you have to get yourself into, because it's just not happening for whatever reason.

In research, the zone is called 'flow', and so getting in this state of flow is what athletes are always trying to reach for. When athletes describe that feeling, it usually has something to do with total concentration on whatever they're doing. They have a very clear goal, or a loss of self-consciousness, or maybe a really heightened state of awareness. Those pieces that they pull out of this zone, or flow, are all skills that can be developed.

The really exciting part for me is the other 80 or 90% of the time, where it's not happening naturally. You can develop skills to help you get there. That's what I'm able to do a lot of times with the clients that I work with. 'Ok, explain to me what that zone feels like, and let's enhance those pieces for the time when you're just not getting there naturally. Let's be more deliberate about that process, so we can make it happen more than 10 to 20% of the time. Let's try to make it happen as much as possible.' That's what's exciting to me.

Have you experienced any resistance or objections as a female in the baseball mental training industry?

Rickertsen: I have to be honest with you that I've actually experienced quite the opposite as far as working with athletes and working with teams. Initially there may be some apprehension, because obviously I haven't played the sport before. There's a tendency to think, 'How much could you possibly know about it? You've never really been in my shoes.' Once I get to know them and really try and understand their situation, I've actually experienced the opposite. The athletes who are genuinely interested in improving their skills and improving their ability to perform when it really counts are the ones who are coming to me. At that point, my being a male or a female doesn't really matter to them.

Another thing that has ended up working in my favor is that I haven't played baseball. I know that sounds strange. It makes me a better listener because I'm not trying to put my experience into what they're telling me. It's easier for me to separate. 'Let me just listen very carefully to what you're telling me, and we'll figure it out from there,' as opposed to, 'This is my experience when I played, so I wonder if you're feeling the same way.' It's actually made me a much better consultant. I've learned so much, not just from being around them, but also from really listening to the players I work with. Listening to their experiences, they're able to teach me some things, and I'm able to teach them some things. In that way, we create a great working relationship. In a lot of cases, they feel more comfortable talking to me than to someone who has played baseball, because I'm not projecting my experience onto them.

In addition to your work with baseball players, what else do you do?

Rickertsen: I did personal training when I was in college. I got my certification, and it was always something that I really liked doing. I liked exercising and I was a four-sport athlete in high school. I had scholarships to run track in college, so sports and exercise has always been a big part of my life. That was a job that I had when I went through school, and I just really liked it. Whenever I have spare time, I like to do some training. I'm also TRX certified so I like to do that as well. It's a great way for me to get a workout while helping other people, so that's exciting. I've been doing that for fun to fill in any extra time, and I like to have time to do that, so that's been a fun piece to keep. Unfortunately, it died down just a little bit since I got quite a bit busier, but I do enjoy doing it.

I was hired as a contractor for the United States Army to do Master Resilience Training. That comes out of positive psychology. We're teaching that to the Army and the active duty forces. The side I'm really excited about is doing performance enhancement with soldiers in the army. This is either pre-deployment or post-deployment, or maybe they're going for a second deployment, a third or a fourth, whatever it is. If they have any sort of quantifiable performance coming up, then we're able to work with them and teach them performance enhancement techniques, much like we would do with baseball players or athletes. The performances may look a little bit different, but teaching the skills looks very similar. You just have to make it apply to whatever performance they're working on. That has been taking up most of my time, but it's a job that I'm really enjoying. I'm definitely humbled with the soldier population that I'm working with, and I'm learning a lot from them as well. Balancing my work with the Army, and also keeping baseball in my life, has been a fun challenge. I am very much enjoying the variety in my day. It's also challenging me to stay current on research and new ways of teaching material to help different populations understand. It's making me a much better consultant, and helping all the different types of people I get to work with.

If a coach wanted to bring you in to speak with or consult with his players, how would they go about contacting you and what would that process consist of?

Rickertsen: My phone number is 308-325-3357, and that's probably the best way because I always have that around me. The other way is email: *christine.rickertsen@gmail.com.*

The way that process usually works is that either a coach, or an athletic director, or a player would contact me. We'd have a little chat about what it is that they're looking for, why the interest in mental performance, and learn a little bit about their team or them as an individual. We can see if we can't work out a program designed specifically for them because so much of this is individualized and unique. There definitely needs to be some time taken to figure out how that fits into your season, how that fits into your practice, and things like that. A lot of discussion goes on back and forth. It's usually a lengthy process, but it gives me some good background information so I can help design a program that would fit each specific team the best.

For more great content from Christine Rickertsen, visit MentalGameVIP.com/ChristineRickertsen

Mike Tully

Author and Founder of Total Game Plan

**For more from Tully, visit
MentalGameVIP.com/MikeTully**

How did you get to where you are today?

Tully: Let me pick out two influences. One, I had the opportunity to be an international sports writer. That means I spent 12 years around the world's greatest athletes. At one time, I saw more than 100 consecutive World Series games, several Stanley Cup playoffs, and was at four Olympics, including the Miracle on Ice. You'd have to be a dummy not to pick up something when you're around the world's greatest coaches and athletes.

The other influence was that I began coaching in a really tiny all-girls private school, with a gym that was an all-purpose facility. One day I showed up to practice, and the gym had been set for a banquet. That got through my thick skull that I was going to have to make the most of whatever precious time I did have in that gym, because I could be thrown out at any time for any reason. I became fascinated by getting the most out of practice time. Those were two primary influences—the opportunity to be around the greatest coaches and athletes in the world, and fascination with how the greatest athletes and performers in the world practice.

What inspired you to create the *Total Game Plan*?

Tully: Economics had something to do with it. I was in the newspaper industry for several years. I knew that industry was not doing well, and I was going to have to do something. I had this fascination. I felt that I had some information to share. I guess I'm a ham at heart. I like to get up in front of groups and speak, I like to write, so it all kind of fit.

We have this 'holistic' approach to practice. It's more than just a series of activities in the gym or on the field. There has to be unity of physical involvement, mental involvement, and emotional involvement. When you get those three things running on high, you pull off miracles like the Miracle on Ice.

What would be the first thing you do when working with a baseball team or program?

Tully: I'm so glad you asked that question because I have the answer. It's a good answer and a really important answer for anyone who's coaching! If I was going to take over a new team, I would first decide what needed to be done. Number two, do what needs to be done.

How important is it to practice the mental and emotional aspects in baseball?

Tully: Yogi said that half this game is 90% mental, yet how often do we practice? Rob Gilbert was my co-author on *Think Better, Win More: How Sports Psychology Can Make You a Champion*. He asked every coach and general manager in the country, how many reps did your players get in the batting cage? Probably a lot. How many fielding reps did your players get today? Probably a lot. How many weight room reps did they get? Depending on what time of year, they probably got a lot. Now here's the jackpot question: How many mental reps did they get? Oops. That's where it breaks down.

This part of the game has to be practiced just as much as the other half, if what Yogi said is true, that 90% of this game is half mental, and I do believe he's right.

How would a player or coach go about contacting you and beginning the process of working with you?

Tully: CoachTully@TotalGamePlan.com. You're welcome to reach out to me on LinkedIn and I'm also available on Facebook.

For more great content from Coach Mike Tully, visit MentalGameVIP.com/MikeTully

Alan Goldberg

International Expert in Applied Sport Psychology

**For more from Goldberg, visit
MentalGameVIP.com/AlanGoldberg**

You've authored 35 mental toughness training programs. What inspires you to keep creating new content and reaching more athletes?

Goldberg: I started off as an athlete and I still am. I was a tennis player as a junior, played in high school and college, and was very interested in the mental side of the sport as a competitor. I started teaching tennis professionally, summers in college, then full time after that. That made me even more interested in the mental side of learning, and what happens to athletes when they're too anxious or focus on the wrong things. That got me pursuing my interest in sports psychology. I started training in traditional psychology and got a degree in counseling psych, but my love of sport and my interest in the mental side of it never went away. Both interests, the psychology and the sports, blended, so this is all I do full time and I've been doing it for almost 30 years.

How important is mental toughness training in baseball?

Goldberg: I would give you the same statistics for any sport. Baseball has a lot of mental demands, but I would say it's in every sport. So if you want to get good in practice, we could say it's 95% physical and 5% mental, which means you have to pay your physical dues to get good at anything. You have to develop a training base. You have to learn the skills. You have to practice the skills. You have to develop strength. But when you step into a game situation, you're a pitcher and now you step onto the mound. Or you're a hitter and get into the batter's box. Your success percentages kind of flip-flop. Your success is now 95% mental and 5% physical. I say that because the muscle memory is there for good technique and mechanics. You've got the skills, you've got the endurance, and you've got the strength. Whether you perform to your potential or not rests entirely on what's going on between your ears. Specifically, are you able to stay calm under pressure? Are you able to focus on the right things? Are you able to manage last minute negative thinking and doubts? Can you bounce back from a bad at-bat or an error? Your success in a game situation is almost all mental.

For more great content from Alan Goldberg, visit MentalGameVIP.com/AlanGoldberg

Mike Margolies

Certified Mental Trainer, Author, Consultant and Public Speaker

**For more from Margolies, visit
MentalGameVIP.com/MikeMargolies**

What inspired you to write *The Athlete Within You*?

Margolies: I had a contract three decades ago to write a book on sports psychology and the mental game, and I couldn't get it done. Even though I was working with the athletes, I didn't have the confidence to write it at that point in time, so it only took me 32 years to get done. I wanted a book that talked about the journey an athlete goes through, using the mental game to find that athlete within them. I wanted something that any athlete could feel comfortable reading and get something from, not just a 'do this, do that' kind of thing that was very dry and hard to get through.

When and where did you begin to learn about the importance of the mental game?

Margolies: I was a failed athlete. I failed in four sports in high school, so what did that mean? That meant I played college athletics. I didn't play football in high school because my parents wouldn't let me, so I walked onto a Division 1 football team and made it. Then I quit because I didn't have the confidence to continue. I didn't believe I was good enough. The coach was always yelling at me, so I quit. When I quit, he just about fell out of his chair, because I was slated to be the number one wide receiver the next year. I didn't understand that I had to pay my dues. The guy who was ahead of me went into the NFL.

I transferred to a Division 3 school where the coach wouldn't let me play football. It had something to do with having hair down to my shoulders and a beard. I was a physical education major and I had to take a class in how to coach soccer. After about six weeks, the coach said, 'You know, you're good enough that you might be able to do this if you work hard at it.' My senior year I played soccer. Then I played a year professionally. But I always kept walking away. I thought it was all the coaches' fault, because who wants to blame themselves?

I had gone to the University of Denver to work on my Master's degree and become a better coach. The first person I met was a guy named Bruce. Bruce was the best friend of the department chair. I was assigned to sit down and talk to Bruce while my boss was on the phone. He asked me questions about myself and my athletic background, and I told him where I had failed. I was still playing professional soccer at the time, and he just laughed at me. He said, 'You know, you're just missing a few skills.' That guy's name is Bruce Ogilvie, and Bruce is probably credited as being the father of modern sports psychology. He happened to be the best friend of the guy at the University of Denver whom I was going to study from. Between Bruce and Marv Klein, I got sucked into the dark side. I got away from coaching to working with athletes primarily on the mental side of things.

How would a coach or player listening to this get into contact with you to begin the process of getting coached by you?

Margolies: The easiest thing to do is to just give me a phone call at 425-241-6539, or they can email me at *Margolies@TheMental-Game.com* or *TheMental-Game.com* or *MikeMargolies.com*.

For more great content from Mike Margolies, visit MentalGameVIP.com/MikeMargolies

Justin Toole

Professional Baseball Player and Author of 9 in 9

**For more from Toole, visit
MentalGameVIP.com/JustinToole**

How did you get to where you are today?

Toole: I grew up in Iowa. I was lucky enough to attend the University of Iowa for four years. I broke my arm my senior year, so I didn't get drafted. I played independent ball for a week and got signed by the Cleveland Indians. I'm just finishing my sixth season with them. I bounced around within the minor league organization, playing as high as AAA.

I spent a lot of time bouncing around back and forth, from team to team, based on the needs of the team. I'm the utility infield guy, so wherever they need a guy, they'll send me. I've hung my hat on being the grinder, the guy who does the dirty work behind the scenes that you don't get a lot of credit for. As a result, I've had to use the mental game to try to make sure that I'm ready when my number's called. I've been with the Indians for six years and I've had a blast.

When and where did you begin to learn about the importance of the mental game?

Toole: In high school I took a couple of psychology classes. In college I decided to major in psychology. My sophomore year at the University of Iowa, we worked with Brian Cain, and that's when the mental game took off for me. My dad was a coach, so growing up I would do mental imagery and use positive self-talk but I didn't necessarily have a term or know what I was doing. I was just taught that this is what you do. After working with Cain, I could put a term to what I was doing and have an understanding of why I do it. I did not have a very good year my freshman year. I came back my sophomore year, after working with him, and hit .360+, not necessarily because my physical abilities had changed, but because my mental assets changed. I had a better approach at the plate, better routines, and I worked on visualization. I got myself to a point where I believed that I could get the job done. I went up to the plate and I wasn't worried about my mechanics, I wasn't worried about anything other than seeing the ball. My sophomore year in college was the big step for me to take my game to the next level because of the mental game.

How do you implement some of these mental techniques on a daily basis throughout the grind of professional baseball?

Toole: It's hard. We play about 140 games during the season, but a lot of it comes down to your routines. You go out and take batting practice and ground balls every day. As a guy who doesn't necessarily play every day, I take batting practice and ground balls very seriously. I've got a good routine, at home or on the road, I'm always doing the same thing in the cage, always taking the same ground balls. Then when you get into the game you don't have to worry, because you've spent the time and effort putting things together before you get into the game. You can just relax, go into the game, have fun, and play. I don't have to worry about if my hands are in the right spot or if I've taken enough swings. All of that has been taken care of. When the game comes, you can go out there and play it.

Throughout a long season, it sometimes gets tough. You can get into a roller coaster ride. I was taught growing up that you never want to be too high and you never want to be too low. Your good games are never as good as you think, and your bad games are never as bad as you think. Trying to stay on an even keel through a 140-game season is huge. The biggest way to do that is putting in the work during practice. So when the game comes, that training can take over and you can just go out there, have fun, and play the game.

How did you get to play 9 positions in one game? Where can the readers pick up your book?

Toole: Actually as kind of a joke, my manager said the coaching staff told him that I could play all nine positions, and he didn't really believe that I could play everywhere. After playing with him for a couple of weeks, he came up to me and said, 'Hey, you really can play everywhere. If you're still here at the end of the year, would you like to play everywhere?' I said, 'Sure!' At the end of the year I was still there, so we picked a day, went ahead and did it, and it was a blast.

My book is available online at Amazon.com, Barnes&Noble.com, BooksAMillion.com, and also available through the publisher's website, BookLocker.com.

For more great content from Justin Toole, visit MentalGameVIP.com/JustinToole

Dr. Rob Gilbert

Sport Psychology Professor and Founder of the Success Hotline

For more from Dr. Gilbert, visit MentalGameVIP.com/RobGilbert

What inspired you to begin the Success Hotline?

Gilbert: I'm teaching at Montclair State and in graduate school I coached baseball and wrestling. When I started teaching, I realized that, especially with my graduate students, there's something wrong. How can I be with my students every single day even though I have class only once a week? I had this idea that I'd leave messages on the phone, and that's how it started. I started it for my students. I never had any bigger vision than that. I was going to leave a message every day of the semester, about 100 days. I liked doing it, and other people started calling, so I've been doing it since 1992.

What is the most important attribute for success?

Gilbert: It's like a recipe. If they ask what is the most important ingredient in cake, you say it's probably flour and then it might be sugar and so on.

The most important ingredient is, what's your biggest weakness? In baseball, if you have a great swing but you don't have confidence, then it's confidence.

Let's look at another thing, desire. You've got to want to do it. There are so many kids doing it because their parents want it, or they're doing it because they want to fit in. Do you want to hear a great quote? There's a movie called *Adaptation*. It's about a guy writing a screenplay. This is such a heavy quote. He said, 'You are what you love, not what loves you.' Are you playing sports because you love the sport, or do you only want the status, to fit in, for people to admire you? It has to do with you. In the end, whether baseball players or writers, you have to have passion.

It might all start with desire. Many years ago, I had a guest speaker in my class, one of the strongest men in the world. His name is Bud Jeffries. His website is *StrongerMan.com*. He's in Lakeland, Florida. He came to my class and started doing some strength feats. He's about 5'10" and at that time, he weighed about 350 lbs. He started ripping phone books, bending steel and breaking chisels. He put his pinky finger in the loop of a kid's jeans and pressed him up into the air effortlessly. He did 10-15 minutes of strength feats, and then he said, 'Are there any questions?' People asked, 'Were your parents strong? Do you take supplements? Do you lift with machines or free weights?' They were asking all these questions, and every time he answered the question. He then said, 'You know, I'd be very happy to answer all your questions, or I can answer any question you ever had in just two words.' Somebody said, 'What are the two words?' He said, 'Desire wins. Desire beats genetics. Desire beats nutrition. Desire beats machines. Desire beats everything.' You know, as they say, it's not the size of the dog in the fight. It's the size of the fight in the dog. So, if you have the desire, who is going to stop you? Who's going to stop you from going to the gym? Who's going to stop you from getting extra practice? Who's going to stop you from hitting a ball off the tee? Nobody is going to stop you if you have the desire.

Growing up in Boston, my boyhood hero was Ted Williams. Everybody said Ted Williams had this unbelievable eyesight. If you read his book, the first chapter was when Ted Williams was a kid growing up. He was a poor kid, but he took his lunch money and paid kids to pitch batting practice to him. After he graduated high school, he was playing with the San Diego minor league team. He was probably 18 years old. Every once in a while he'd go up to the manager and ask for any old baseballs they were going to throw out. The manager said, 'Sure, but what do you need them for, Ted?' He said he had to go back home and have kids pitch batting practice to him. The manager didn't quite believe him, because Ted was at the ballpark all day. He did his practicing at the game. One day the manager, unbeknownst to Williams, drove by Williams' house and found the local field. There Ted Williams was, using those balls, having people pitch to him. Ted Williams used to take batting practice until his hands bled.

If you don't have that desire, how are you going to compete against somebody who does? Find something else to do. If you're playing baseball recreationally, that's fine. However, if you want to be a pro, and you're not working like Ted Williams—well, that's why Ted Williams is Ted Williams. Anybody could work like Ted Williams. You might not develop Ted Williams' skill, but you could develop Ted Williams' work ethic.

There are certain things that aren't a choice. Our height isn't our choice. Our eye color isn't our choice. However, we could choose our level of intensity. We could choose our effort. We could choose our attitude. That is the exciting thing in sport psychology, the things we can choose. If there's anything underlined, bold, and italics in sports psychology, it's a book on sales written in 1947 by Frank Bettger, *How I Raised Myself from a Failure to Success in Selling*. The first chapter told about Frank Bettger being a minor league baseball player in 1907. He wanted to make it to the major leagues. One day the manager called him into his office and said, 'Frank, I hate to do this to you, but I'm cutting you from the team.' And Frank said, 'Cutting me from the team?' He said, 'Frank, how old are you?' He said, '20 years old.' The manager said, 'Frank, you carry yourself around the field like you're an old guy. I don't know if you're going to play ball after you leave here, but whatever you do, put some energy into your game.'

Finally, Bettger was playing in New Haven, and he made this pact with himself. He said, 'I'm not going to be able throw better or hit better or run better, but nobody is ever going to accuse me of being lazy again.' Basically, he put all these batteries inside himself and he became like a Pete Rose. He ran off the field. He ran onto the field. He was the most energized guy on the field. When they asked him how come he was so nonchalant before, he said he thought acting relaxed would cure him of his nervousness and his fears. He found that when he started acting more energized, he cured himself of his nervousness and fears. They started calling him Pep Bettger. Not only did he energize himself, he started energizing the whole team. In a few years, he made it to the St. Louis Cardinals. He was their third baseman.

I'm not going to give away the rest of the story, but I have the people I work with and coach read this chapter at least 28 days in a row, until it becomes part of their DNA, until they become Frank Bettger, because this will be their competitive advantage. The old term is 'Fake it til you make it.' I'm not saying that's not right, but the real term is 'Fake it til you feel it.' You have to fake it until you feel that desire, that enthusiasm. Spell enthusiasm. The last four letters, I-A-S-M, say I Am Sold Myself. You have to sell yourself on yourself. That's the biggest sales job in the world. You have to fake it 'til you make it, fake it 'til you feel it. All the answers are right in that Frank Bettger first chapter. Read it over and over again until you have every word memorized. This is like the bible in sports psychology. There's nothing more important in applied sports psychology. If you want to know the technique that will separate you from other people, this is it.

I give my students this assignment during the NCAA championships or the NBA playoffs. I say, 'Turn on the game in the last couple of minutes with the sound off. Have somebody cover up the score on the screen, so you're just watching the game, not hearing anything, just watching the players. I'll bet, 100 times out of 100, you'll be able to tell who's winning just by their body posture. Winners act like winners and losers act like losers.'

Rarely do you see a losing team act like winners. They're deflated. Winners act like winners and losers act like losers, but here's the key: champions act like winners whether winning or losing. You want to be a champion, not just a winner. Anybody can win. You do it over and over again. Anybody can practice hard today, and do it over and over. This is what they call mastery.

Imagine if you were passionate about 50 things. You'd never be good at any one. However, we're not passionate about 50 things. Find out what you really want, and then get rid of all the other stuff.

Suppose you had a problem with your feet and you found a doctor and you thought this doctor was really great with feet. He's also a dentist, a psychiatrist, a cardiologist and an oncologist, and he delivers babies. You think, 'No, no, no. He can't be that great. He's probably not devoting enough time to feet.' When I'm having problems with my right knee, and I'm going to have to have a knee replacement, who do you think I want? I would want the guy who does nothing but knees. I don't want a general practitioner and I don't want a guy who does knees, hips, and shoulders. I want a guy who has done 18,000 knee operations.

It all begins with desire. I'm currently writing a book, *The One Most Important Question*. What do you think the one most important decision any athlete will ever make is? What's the most important decision you'll ever make in your life? In sports and out of sports, when people wonder where to go to school, what to major in, who are you going to marry, whether to be religious or not? Those are all important decisions, but the most important decision you'll ever make is this: are you going to go all out or are you going to hold back? Are you going to be 'in' a relationship or 'into' a relationship? In America, so many marriages end in divorce because people are 'in' relationships, but not 'into' relationships.

When I speak in high school assemblies, I ask how many are in school? They look at me like, well, what do you mean? I'm in school. They all raise their hands, and it's not such a dumb question. Now I ask, 'How many are 'into' school?' They look at me like I don't know prepositions, but that's what I wanted to say—into it. I tell my students, 'What's your attendance policy? I don't want you 'in' this class. I want you 'into' this class.' Your parents don't want you in their family. They want you into their family. Your preacher doesn't want you in church. He wants you into the church. The one most important decision any of us will ever make is this: are you going to be in it or into it? If you're going to be in it, how are you going to compete with the people who are into it? If you think it's going to be hard to be into it, imagine how hard it's going to be to compete against somebody who is if you're not. If you think it's going to be hard to work out like Pete Rose, Ted Williams or Jerry Rice, imagine how hard it will be to compete against people like that if you don't.

It's not height, weight, speed or how many times you can lift 225 pounds in the bench press. Anybody can be into it. That's the exciting thing. Anybody could decide right now, 'I might not be the best. I might not be the most skilled. I might not be the most genetically gifted. But nobody is going to outwork me. Nobody is ever going to outwork me!'

People talk about most valuable player. Who cares about most valuable? I wanted to work with the hardest-working player, because if you're the hardest-working player, day after day, month after month, season after season, eventually you're going to be the best player. Desire wins.

Nobody in the world has given more motivational talks than me, because every morning I give my *Success Hotline* motivational talk. I'm always practicing. Not only am I always practicing, I want to practice. It's not an effort.

As a sports psychology professor, do you have any tips for college students?

Gilbert: I wrote a whole book on this because I wasn't a good student. I flunked out of school. I probably have the worst grades of anybody who has ever gotten a Ph.D. in the history of the world. I failed ten three-credit courses in undergraduate school, and they threw me out. This is UMass

Amherst. When I got back in school, I had to get a 3.7 grade point average for three semesters in a row. After I passed my requirements, I became a psychology major, but I was taking every easy course I could: Introduction Recreation, Introduction Art, Introduction Film, Introduction Television. I take Introduction Physical Education!

At that time, UMass hired Walter Crow from the University of Texas, who is one of the founders of the whole field of sports psychology. He became my mentor over the next ten years. I wrote *How to Have Fun Without Failing Out: 430 Tips from a College Professor*. Most people will write books on college success because they have been successful. I wasn't. I know all the mistakes you could make. If I was speaking to a student, I'd ask them to tell me a difficult course they had last semester. They could tell me any course. I'd say there were no difficult courses in college. There are just time-consuming courses. They just take time. Are they really difficult? No.

I have this whole list of the secrets of college success. You show up, you pay attention. If you show up but you don't pay attention, it really doesn't matter that you showed up. So, show up. Pay attention. Ask questions. Ask for help. Help others. A very, very important one is do not cheat and do more than expected.

I interview experts, people who are really good at what they do, and there is a common denominator among all these people. In my 34 years at Montclair State, I've only known one student ever to graduate with a perfect 4.0 average. Her name is Melissa Sapio. She graduated in the year 2001. She took 44 courses and she got 44 A's. She never even got an A minus! She got a perfect 4.0 average. I interviewed her and I wrote some articles about her. Over the years, she came with me to a lot of talks I gave. Even when I'm speaking to sales people, I have her come, because she has to give out the secret. She said she never pulled an all-nighter, but she studied from one to three hours every day. She would never miss a day of study. After she goes through all that, I say, 'Melissa, there must be something more.' And she said there is. In the second week of her first semester in college, a little voice came to her that made all the difference in the world. The little voice said, 'Do more than what is expected.' So, for each and every assignment, she started doing more than expected. If the math professor said the assignment for tomorrow is problems 1, 3 and 5, Melissa would do 1-5. If the history professor said the assignment for next time is to read chapter one, she'd read one and part of chapter two.

What do you think Jerry Rice or Pete Rose did? What do you think all these people we're talking about did? They all did more than expected. If you have the desire to do more than expected, you're going to beat everybody.

I love what I'm teaching, and sports psychology is the most interesting subject in the world. In 34 years of teaching, I've only had 8 students ever come up to me and say, 'Dr. Gilbert, that stuff about concentration and motivation, that's really interesting. How can I learn more about it?' I've only had eight people ever ask how they can learn more about it. I've had 8,000 people ask how they can get extra credit. Very few people are in love with learning. Most just want the result.

Which is more important, to win or to go all out? If I speak to 100 athletes, 99 will say, to win. No, it's going all out. It's much better to go all out and lose, than to hold back and win, because if you hold back and win, you're training yourself to hold back.

For more great content from Dr. Rob Gilbert, visit MentalGameVIP.com/RobGilbert

Justin Dehmer

Founder of 1 Pitch Warrior

**For more from Dehmer, visit
MentalGameVIP.com/JustinDehmer**

What inspired the *1 Pitch Warrior* mentality?

Dehmer: I had been coaching as an assistant for a couple of years and I finally stepped into a head coaching position at the same school. We made improvements and we made strides, but it always felt like we were missing something. Once I became the head coach, I started implementing the *Quality At Bat System* with our offense, and they really latched onto it. I thought, 'If I'm doing this with the offense, I need to do something with our pitchers as well.' I felt like I needed to come up with something that could measure the process instead of the outcomes—like wins, losses, strikeouts, ERA, the typical stuff that so many people get infatuated by and fascinated with. I came up with *Quality Innings*, and it kind of blossomed from there. I took the job at Martinsdale St. Mary's, where we won three state titles and had an 88-game win streak. We kept adding new stuff in. B.A.S.E. 2 is one of those things we put in, and other things like A3P, Strike, TPI, any way we could think about measuring the process instead of the outcome that would give our guys a little bit more insight into what we were doing well, and maybe what we weren't doing so well. It was an ongoing evolution of adding stuff each year as the guys felt more comfortable with it. As we felt more comfortable with it, we continued to add pieces.

How important do you think the mental side of the game is to a player who is looking to play this game at the highest level?

Dehmer: It's something that can be worked on, that can be trained and learned. I don't think it's something you're necessarily born with. I always say at coaching clinics that there is no such thing as a 'mental toughness gene' that I am aware of. It's one of those things that kids have to learn and practice and be taught. It boils down to, do you really have a philosophy that you can implement and actually teach kids? That's where coaches fall a bit short. They know it's so important, but they fail to teach it to kids, to give it a terminology and a foundation for their program.

How can our listeners get access to your newsletter?

Dehmer: The website is *1PitchWarrior.com/free*. They can fill in their email address and that'll start delivering them content. Those nine innings that you spoke of, some of them are audio, some of them are videos that I've done at clinics. If they'd like more, they can contact me through my website or via Twitter. There's a lot of other content that isn't part of the *9 Innings* or the *1PitchWarrior* system that helps coaches implement everything once they get that foundation and understanding of what it's all about from a coaching and player perspective. They can see the value in it for their players and their programs.

For more great content from Justin Dehmer, visit MentalGameVIP.com/JustinDehmer

Justin Dedman

Collegiate Baseball Coach and Mental Game Guru

For more from Dedman, visit
MentalGameVIP.com/JustinDedman

How did you get to where you are today?

Dedman: I went to college at Denison University in Granville, Ohio. It's a private liberal arts university just east of Columbus with a Division 3 athletics program. I originally wanted to play baseball at a place as great as the University of North Carolina, but realized after going to play at their camp that it was above my talent level at that point. I ended up at Denison as a student athlete and played baseball there for four years. I was an English writing major. My father and stepmother were both journalists, and I always had a passion for writing and thought that I might be a sports journalist myself. That was the route I was looking at initially. I knew that I'd want to coach at some point, but I really didn't have any idea, when I was in college, how soon or at what level. Right out of college, I had an internship in Asheville, North Carolina and one of my roles there was to follow the Asheville Tourists, a minor league affiliate of the Rockies.

I found myself, being a baseball nut and former player, going to the yard two or three hours before the games to watch the other coaches working with the players and getting the extra work in. I very quickly realized that I was not going to be very happy working essentially a desk job. I wanted to be hands-on. The coach I played for, Barry Craddock, offered me an opportunity, so that's where I began my coaching career.

What is the mental game? How important is the mental game in college baseball?

Dedman: First of all, the mental game is whatever a player needs to do for himself to put himself in the most confident place. Tom House, Brian Cain, Ken Ravizza and certainly Dorfman as well, talk about 'the zone', what that is and what that means. Everyone wants to be 'in the zone' and it's tough to get into. So a lot of them have created systems or given hitters or athletes nuggets on how to get closer to that zone more frequently. To me, in hitting or in any sport, the mental game is how to get to be consistent enough that you can be in a committed and confident place even when your most recent opportunities have had more failure than success. That's first of all what we seek to teach in the mental game, to get people to believe in themselves even when their most recent opportunity was not successful. That necessitates practice and a lot of trials and tribulations for different people, because it's difficult to put your hands on something that is not so tangible when we're talking about the mind.

It's as important as they want it to be. The easy answer would be that it's extraordinarily important, but every player is going to buy in at their own level. If we're trying to sell everybody at the 10 out of 10 level, we turn some kids off. Some kids just aren't ready for that. I don't think we're doing them a service by making everybody get to a certain level, dismissing their intentions or their attitudes if they're not wanting to get there. Kids are at different places in their lives. They've had different experiences. They've had different opportunities to trust individuals. The way we teach and communicate about the mental game is what you're trying to build to become a confident athlete. You're trying to trust yourself and your preparation.

Wooden said, "When opportunity comes, it's too late to prepare." Certainly, we have to work hard before we get those opportunities, but everybody's got a different mind and a different path and learns in a different way. We try to reach them with different energy levels. Some guys may only be ready for a little nugget here and there. Some guys may be ready to dive all in. You give them what they desire. Because if you're trying to give everybody everything, you may only catch the elite group that's ready for that, and you may turn some of the others off.

As a college coach, how do you implement this training on a daily basis with your guys?

Dedman: Certainly I use the experiences of the coaches of the mental game that I've been able to learn from, because those are the ones that we believe in. It starts with Dorfman, Ravizza, Cain, certainly there's some Tom House in there, but those first three are probably the core three that we are teaching— their books, photos, images, verbiage, the way they model things. The system that we actually use on a day-to-day basis, more frequently than anything, is Cain's *4RIP3*. The 4 R's are: to have a **R**outine, to **R**ecognize your current emotional state (probably the most difficult part for a collegiate student athlete), to have a **R**elease (what they really have to practice) and then to be able to **R**efocus, which is usually some type of visual or verbal cue. The I in *4RIP3* is **I**magery, standing for visualization.

The three Ps are: being in the **P**resent moment (not living in the past, not thinking too far into the future) allows people to stay as a part of the **P**rocess, focusing on the things that we can control in the here and now. The third P is **P**ositive. Bruce Brown is an incredibly positive person and that's someone I've learned a lot about from interactions with books and CDs and seeing him speak live. Mark Brew, our head coach here at Lee, is a very positive leader and leads by example. It's a faith-based institution at Lee, so everything we're trying to do with our guys is centered around being positive role models for them. That certainly is ingrained and starts with the Bible, which is nothing but positive literature there.

What is the *Inverted U of Energy*?

Dedman: This is a concept that I learned from Brian Cain. Take a U and turn it upside-down and put it on a graph, so you've got an x- and a y-axis. The x-axis would be performance, as you travel to your right, and the y-axis is energy. The lowest end of energy might be Eeyore, the kind of guy who has a 'Thanks for noticing, oh it's a great day, baseball's hard, I'm not good at this,' kind of attitude. That person's not going to have any success. It's going to be very random and full of luck.

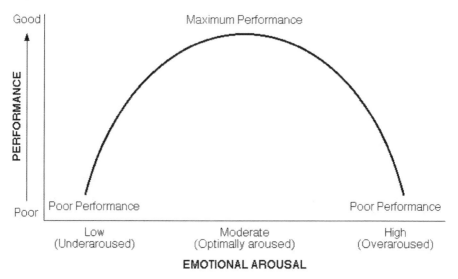

The person who gets more energy, in the middle of the graph, is consistent in energy, not overbearing or off the charts or overexcited. That's where the greatest level of energy is going to be. You're focused, you're intentful, and you're providing some passion. That's where you're going to have your greatest level of success.

Then as you travel further along the graph, the performance goes back down. You're going to have somebody who might more aptly represent the Ultimate Warrior or somebody snapping a bat over their knee at the end of an at bat. That level of energy is not going to be conducive to long-term success.

We want our guys to be engaged, passionate, and full of energy, but there's usually a quiet confidence, to steal a Schlossnagle-ism, to their energy. We talk to our guys about the Clint Eastwood stare. If you ever see an athlete with the Clint Eastwood stare, where they've got that piercing look in their eyes and they're kind of squinting, unless they're looking into the sun, they're probably going to have a lot of success. That look usually has a lot of concentration and focus and is giving energy. If you see real big eyes or a drooped face, often those facial expressions are the result of poor energy. They're too far to the right or the left.

You had the opportunity to meet Brian Cain years ago at the ABCA Convention. Do you make an effort to attend this event every year?

Dedman: Of course. I wouldn't miss it. I met Brian Cain there when I was working at Ole Miss. Cain has been a life changer for me personally. He's spurred me on to work into a lot of different areas, personally and professionally. He has helped me more than he knows. I'm very appreciative for it. I told our head coach about him before the last convention Cain was speaking at and said, "You're going to love this show." Cain was up there on stage bringing the energy, eating fire, breaking boards and all sorts of great stuff. He is extremely engaging and makes it easy to understand. The most valuable part of his system is that he makes it useful in a repeatable way.

For more great content from Coach Dedman, visit MentalGameVIP.com/JustinDedman

Exclusive Content & Free Resources

For additional content, audios, videos, links, training tools, social media and more, visit:

MentalGameVIP.com

GAME TIME
Q&A

Pre-Game Prep for the Mind & Body

Many competitive baseball players participate in between 50-162+ games each year. What are some of the most effective techniques or routines to prepare the mind and body for competition on a daily basis?

Afremow: First of all, stick to your basic personality types. Don't try to be someone you're not. If you like to joke around with the guys before the game, then stick with that approach. If you like to be in your own little world and visualize what you want to have happen on the field that day, keep doing it. There's no right way, there's only your way.

A good one is walking meditation. I recommend doing things on game day a little bit slower than you usually do. When you're walking to the park or the field, when you've parked your car and you're going to the field, walk a little bit slower than you usually do, but be mindful of your feet on the ground as you're walking. That helps anchor you to the present moment, slows you down, clears your head, and gets you into a good frame of mind. Usually we're thinking about what we want to do today, what we want to accomplish, or worrying about things that are totally unrelated to baseball. Walking meditation is great and slowing things down on game day is important.

Dixon: We're all wired differently. We all have different routines, we all do different things to get us ready. Some listen to music and some don't think about the game because if they think about it too much, they're probably going to screw it up.

That's a problem with the mental game. Some people overanalyze. They think they have to be in this Zen-like moment to be successful. That doesn't exist on a baseball field or in any athletic arena. It's never a perfect scenario, so we have got to learn to deal with failure and to be comfortable being uncomfortable. The breath, music, journaling, reading a book, there are many different ways.

I was a visualizer. I would always visualize scenarios. There's a left-handed hitter with a runner on first base. I want to get him to roll over, so I'm going to throw a fastball away, a little 4-6-3 double play. When you visualize, you are as detailed as you possibly can be. You engage all of your senses, see it, smell it, hear it, taste the sweat. Get as detailed as you possibly can, because your mind doesn't know the difference between perception and reality. If you just play it and play it in your mind, success, success, success, that's what your body is geared towards. It could be the day before, the night before, or the hour before.

Many people think with the mental game that you have to be locked in for three hours straight. That doesn't exist. It's all about short bursts of focus. Each pitch is around five seconds. I have to be locked in and focused for about five seconds, then quick adjustment, quick evaluation, what's next, next pitch, boom, go. It's a sequence of pitch to pitch, inning to inning, out to out, game to game.

We look at 162 games for a professional baseball player. That is overwhelming. You go one day at a time, you compete to the best of your ability, and you evaluate it. You have to have a short-term memory in baseball. You can't really look at results, it's got to be the process, because the game of baseball is cruel if you think about it. You can do everything wrong and get great results, or you can do everything right and get bad results. It's a cruel game, so you have to have the ability to not worry about hits, strikeouts and ERAs. You've got to think about what it takes to be successful: relationship to practice, attention to detail, and being committed and present one pitch at a time.

Gordon: I'm a big believer in visualization and thinking about your success that week, the great play you made that week, several of your great plays and your best hits. Visualize those, because if you did it once, you can do it again. We know that when you see it, your mind is almost acting as if you were actually doing it. It's very powerful to visualize. It's very powerful to have positive expectation and optimism.

It's very powerful to be in the moment, but sometimes when you're thinking too much about the play or too much about hitting, fear comes in. 'What happens if I can't reproduce it?' You have to make sure you're doing these strategies with the mindset, that I'm really focused on playing in the present, being present and not worrying about failure, not allowing fear to sabotage it.

Springer: The key word is routine. It's about getting in a routine, not a superstition, whether it's getting to the yard at a certain time, eating the same meal, or going out stretching at the same time. Both big leaguers and twelve-year-olds will benefit from learning how to show up one day at a time. Yesterday is over and tomorrow is not here. It's about today. It is a choice. Am I going to choose to be confident? Am I going to choose to play for the team or am I going to let yesterday's 0-for-4 get in the way of today? If I go 0-for-1, in my mind I'm now 0-for-5.

We are all taught all of the clichés. It's about today. Make today opening day! I give them a big picture to give them a little bit of freedom. It is not only about today, it's about the next ten years, getting great at showing up with your confident guy.

Jaeger: I feel strongly about the foundation of what you need to do. That is always going to be the core. When it comes to imagery and visualization, they're both incredibly powerful.

I would do something like inhale 1, exhale 2, inhale 3, exhale 4, and try to count to 100. That would be a powerful way to incorporate your breath in some form of concentration.

Imagery and visualization are great ways to access the right brain. They are great ways to associate very powerful images that can really get into your neuromuscular system. I am a huge fan of it. Doing that on the fly or taking some breaths is great, but can you imagine if you spent 10-12 minutes really clearing your mind, and then inputting some images or visuals? That would have a lot more staying power on a very quiet, clear mind.

When I teach meditation and we get into imagery and visualization, I have had my students spend 2 or 3 weeks only on breathing and clearing their mind. I don't even want them getting into imagery or visualization until they first learn how to clear their mind, because the imprint factor in imagery and visualization can be much more powerful if the mind is first cleared.

One of the main benefits of meditation is the ability to be neutral to thoughts that are about the future. Thoughts usually are pretty distracting, right? If we sat there with a tape recorder and played them back, we would be shocked at what our mind is thinking about. One of the most important benefits of meditation is that you're sitting there, breathing, you're getting nice and relaxed, and then some thoughts start coming up about some bills you have to pay, you should have done this, you should have done that, or you're starting to think about an argument you had with your girlfriend. Before you know it, you're gone, just spinning on this wheel.

What I love about the practice of meditation is that, at its core, it's about learning to hear that stuff but not buy into it, not engage it, not have a conversation with it. You have to develop a powerful skill of concentration, of just being present. Learn that the stuff going on around you or in your head is just there. It's not good or bad. Can you keep bringing your attention back to this presence of your breath, your concentration, or eventually just being in a relaxed state? When you're in a relaxed state, you're just being. It's like a great movie or a great song. It's just happening, and you're in it. Anything you can do to help discipline, focus, and concentrate the mind, to have more real presence and attention—it's powerful.

Brubaker: I am a big fan of imagery. It has been known not just to help athletes but to cure cancer. I'm a big fan of the concentration grid. Because we are in the age of distraction, we need to practice mono-tasking, being focused on one thing.

My favorite technique to prepare my mind and body is to get your mind ready for what your body is about to do. That is actually self-talk. I will talk to myself and say it out loud. It is one thing saying it internally, hearing it in a completely different tone, and absorbing it in a completely different way, and a whole other level when you're saying it out loud.

One example is the marathon I ran. If you met me in person, you would look at me and say, 'He is not built for speed or distance,' but I managed to finish this marathon, due in large part to what I told myself. I just kept telling myself, when things got tough, training on an 18-mile run, on hills, whatever, I told myself, 'This is easy. You've got this.' When you say it out loud, you hear it in a completely different way.

Focus on talking, not about the outcome, but about the process.

You convince yourself, through your thoughts and your words, of the correct actions. The cool thing is that, before Bluetooth technology, if you were talking to yourself, people thought you were nuts. Now everybody is walking around with headphones in their ear, so you fit right in.

Margolies: The first thing I teach an athlete is how to effectively relax their body and mind. I primarily use progressive muscle relaxation to do that. An athlete is so in touch with their muscles, and the greater their self-awareness level is, the more they're going to be able to perform when they can learn to relax their body.

The next step would be imagery rehearsal. I don't care what you want to call it, mental practice, imagery rehearsal, visualization. In textbooks you might even see it referred to as visio-motor behavior rehearsal. The more we actively engage our imagination in very specific ways, the better off we can be, using concentration or focus exercises.

Gap training or mindfulness training is really important and easy to use. If you're on a long bus ride, you can learn how to quickly get in the zone. Because it's a skill, the more you practice getting into the zone, the easier it is, when you step up to the plate, to step into the zone.

Maher: It's an up-and-down rollercoaster ride for most players. We emphasize perspective first, to really understand your values. Why are you doing this? What's important to you in your life? Where does this fit in? That's perspective.

The second thing we emphasize is 'mental parking', being able to put away from your current situation things that don't do you any good. We emphasize putting on the role of player, then taking off the role of player, leaving it at the ballpark, then putting it back on when you come.

The third thing is using a journal to keep track of your feelings and thoughts, things that you can go back to during the course of the season. You may note a particular day when you really locked in, when things were going well, how you felt, what happened during that time. Those would be the three things: perspective, mental parking and keeping a journal.

Rickertsen: Routines are actually one of my favorite things to teach, and baseball is all about that. I don't even play, and I realize it's a grind. It's a long season, and in order to be where you want to be when you need to be there, routines are a huge part of that. The reason that I like them so much is that they're such an individualized approach. For one person the emotional piece is going to be really important. Someone else is going to need to work on their attention, maybe through concentration grids or meditation. Other people may need to be doing energy management, some deliberate breathing or imagery. What I love about them and what makes them so cool and so helpful to athletes, is that they are so individualized. The ability to work mental and physical pieces into that routine, and understanding what the routine is doing for you, is going to be very important.

It's great to have a routine, and it's definitely helpful to get yourself to where you want to be when you need to be there, but there also needs to be a little bit of flexibility. For example, you're running late and you don't have time to go through your whole routine. What are your go-to pieces that are going to get you to where you need to be? When I help athletes create routines, I have them go through the list of skills that they want to put in that routine, and then we pick out the absolute must-haves. Just in case you don't have the time, or something else happens, you have those go-to pieces that will help you get there without having to go through the whole routine. I could make a case for all of the skills that I teach being in a routine, but it's not necessary for every single person.

Dehmer: We always talk about having different hats you wear throughout the day. When you're at school, your job is to get an education. When you transition from student to athlete, putting on your uniform, your cleats and all that, now it's time to be an athlete. Once you're done, as you're taking your uniform off, you're also taking that performance off, whether it was amazing or one of the worst games you had that season. It's over, and now you're putting your uniform in the laundry, it's done. It's a symbol, something that kids are actually doing instead of just a thought process or a mindset. it's something physical that kids can do. You can start tying physical things that players do to the mental side of the game. A good connection can be made for these guys, instead of just talking about the mental game, which coaches do a lot.

The other thing we used to do at practice, that I talk about on my audios, part of the *1PitchWarrior* system, is what I call 'clear the water'. We would have guys close their eyes, all in the dugout, very quiet, and I would talk them through a scenario of someone filling up a glass of water. That water is very cloudy, with lots of bubbles, you can't see through it. They're slowly coming into focus and thinking about these next two or three hours of practice. I need to think solely about being a baseball player, and putting all my effort into making sure I'm the best baseball player I can be, regardless of what happened at school, at home, or at work. Now it's time to be a baseball player. I talk them through this imagery. At the end, we say that the water is clear and our thoughts are where they need to be. Everything else is gone and we're putting that aside for now. It's time to get focused on the task at hand, and nothing else matters except this two or two and half hours of practice or game, whatever it is that we're partaking in that day. I always found that was a good way to start practice. You never know what the guys are bringing to practice, the baggage that they're bringing, maybe a fight at home with Mom and Dad or girlfriend or a terrible day at school. All kinds of things can happen, and sometimes we overlook that as coaches. It's just a good way to hit the reset button and start fresh and say 'here we go.'

Bell: Don't look at your stats, don't look at the scoreboard, and don't judge yourself. We get into this constant performance mode, 'How am I doing, how am I measuring up, how are we doing?' The baseball has no idea what your average is and no idea when that base hit is coming. We've got to be able to let that stuff go, that's the biggest thing. Batting average is meaningless because it makes no difference on the most important pitch, the next one.

If you talk to any Hall-of-Famer, they all say the same thing. 'I never imagined I would be a Hall-of-Famer. I wanted to be great. That was my goal.' They never say, 'I always pictured myself being here. Never in a million years did I ever think I would be a Hall-of-Famer.' It really got me thinking, what were the memories that all of us had? The memories on the bus, in the dugout, in the locker room, and between games are the memories that really stick with us, the relationships we have. It is all the more important to let everything out on the field. When it's done, it's done. It's over.

How can we keep connecting with others? How can we help other people? The best way to get confidence in ourselves is helping other people. We can't keep it inside. There is no secret, it's just talking to one another. It's funny how the guys that are batting .200 hang out with one another, and the guys who are on a roll are hanging out with another. I don't think that's a coincidence. It's creating this positive feeling towards one another and then being able to share it. 'Hey, this is what I'm doing, this is what I see that's going on.'

There are techniques, always something simple, that a great athlete's going to change if things aren't going so well. This is what has worked for me. I coached every athlete that I've worked with on this. You're getting ready for that big moment. You don't know when it's coming and it's going to make all the difference. Are you going to believe in yourself, or are you just kind of hoping that you're going to be ready? There's a big difference between knowing you're going to be ready and hoping you're going to be ready. That's the thing I always coach people on.

Take somebody who is in a 0-for-16 slump. It's not a good spot to be, but it happens. Hey, your moment is coming. Are you going to focus on the most important pitch, or are you going to lose that confidence in yourself? That's what differentiates people who are great ones from the people who just do OK. It's that belief. Capture those 'hinge moments.'

Question Review

Many competitive baseball players participate in between 50-162+ games each year. What are some of the most effective techniques/routines to prepare the mind and body for competition on a daily basis?

Afremow: Stick to your basic personality types. Don't try to be someone you're not. If you like to joke around with the guys before the game, then stick with that approach. If you like to be in your own little world and visualize what you want to have happen on the field that day, keep doing it. There's no right way, there's only your way.

Dixon: Some people overanalyze and think they have to be in this Zen-like moment to be successful. That doesn't exist on a baseball field or in any athletic arena. It's never a perfect scenario, so we have got to learn to deal with failure and to be comfortable being uncomfortable. Many people think with the mental game that you have to be locked in for three hours straight. That doesn't exist. It's all about short bursts of focus.

Gordon: When you see it, your mind is almost acting as if you were actually doing it. It's very powerful to visualize and have positive expectation and optimism.

Springer: It's about getting in a routine, not a superstition. Yesterday is over and tomorrow is not here. It's about today. Make today opening day! Get great at showing up with your confident guy.

Jaeger: Imagery and visualization are both incredibly powerful. The imprint factor can be much more powerful if the mind is first cleared.

Brubaker: Get your mind ready for what your body is about to do.

Margolies: I use progressive muscle relaxation to effectively relax the body and mind. Then it is imagery rehearsal because the more we actively engage our imagination in very specific ways, the better off we will be. Mindfulness is really important and easy to use to quickly get into the zone.

Maher: Perspective, mental parking and keeping a journal.

Rickertsen: Routines are individualized and needed to be where you want to be when you need to be there.

Dehmer: You wear many different hats throughout the day. When you're at school, your job is to get an education. When you transition from student to athlete, it's time to be the best player you can be. Talking the players through imagery can also be a very powerful tool to clear the mind and focus on the task at hand.

Bell: Your moment is coming. Are you going to focus on the most important pitch or are you going to lose that confidence in yourself?

It's All About Your Process

In the game of baseball and life in general, there are so many external circumstances that are completely out of one's control such as what happens when the ball leaves your bat/hand, who is in the lineup, what the weather is like, who is watching you, etc... but we live in a society that is focused on results, batting average, ERA, etc. How does a player shift their focus to the process and the controllables?

Maher: There is a constant indoctrination and education about being able to 'let go of the self'. The self identifies with results, proving themselves to other people and all those things that are outside of their control. Get back into the moment, deal with things that are important, that matter, that they can influence, and the numbers will take care of themselves. The numbers are going to fluctuate, and that's true for everybody in the game. The more they focus on the results, the more they identify with themselves, the more they get frustrated and their self-esteem enters into it. It's a constant reorientation, because the natural tendency as a player is to look at the results and what people think of you. What does the front office think of me? What does the coach think of me? It's ongoing, and some players are able to make that adjustment more quickly. Others have to fail before they start picking it up.

Rickertsen: This is probably the hardest thing to do in the sport and, for athletes I've worked with, a constant struggle. Especially in America, we're driven by results, and live in a result-driven culture. That becomes very important, especially when they're working for scholarships, to be drafted, for their starting position, or whatever it is. The results are what drive them, so it's understandable that it's a challenge. At the same time, there definitely are some skills that can help.

There's a place in our mind called working memory, and this is what we're currently paying attention to in the moment. Anything that you are consciously paying attention to right now is what we call working memory. There's a very limited amount of space within that working memory, because you can only be paying 100% of your attention to so many things. When a player starts thinking about things like results or the weather, when you start filling that very small space in your mind with aspects that you can't control, your brain can't focus on what you need to be doing. In that case, your performance is going to suffer, because you're not paying attention to what you want to be doing. While a lot of athletes do it with the best of intentions, what they don't realize is that they're filling up that really small space in their minds with information that's not helping them in that moment.

The most important thing when going out for a performance, whether it's your next at-bat or making a play in the field, is to identify your target. Figure out what the most important thing is to pay attention to. Simply by doing that, you're priming your brain to notice those aspects. As a pitcher, maybe it's my release point, my breathing or timing. I don't know what the most important thing would be for that person, but you pick out whatever that most important thing is, and just by doing that, your brain is going to focus yourself on that piece.

Another skill we can teach to help athletes is to develop cues. Especially when you're in situations that tend to be high-pressure, or where you have trouble maintaining your attention, develop cues for that, as well as a routine. It may be deliberate breathing to help activate your parasympathetic or bring your energy back down. There are several different techniques. You have to figure out what works for each individual person, but the problem is that you're filling up that tiny little space in your mind with information that's not helping you. Figuring out how to direct your attention to performance-specific information, as opposed to results, is one of the hardest things to learn.

The research talks a lot about shifting your attention vs. splitting your attention. Maybe you do need to be paying attention to four different things, but when you fill your brain with all these different things coming at it at once, your brain can't decipher all that information that quickly. The idea is to have your performance automated by that point. You pick one thing to focus on, and then the rest of it's going to follow. That's why we practice and then we play, right? If you go through practice not doing it exactly like you would in a game, not picking out that one thing, you're not going through the process of your routine. You're not working on automating your behavior.

When you go to perform at the game, it's not going to be there. You really need to have the one thing picked out, your foot, or your release point, or whatever it is, just pick out your one thing and really practice it. The goal is to automate the behavior so you don't have to be thinking about it. It is more effective to pick out just the one thing; splitting your attention is not going to be beneficial at that point.

Dixon: We're so distracted as a society. When's the last time you got home and your parents asked how your process was today on the mound? They don't. How many strikeouts did you have? How many hits did you give up? How many runs did you give up? The newspaper says this guy has this ERA, this batting average, this many RBIs and this many home runs. We're a results-oriented society, and if you allow it to distract you, it just sucks the life out of you.

Working with people, I like to figure out what they have the ability to control. For a pitcher, it's executing one pitch with 100% commitment. Once a ball is out of your hand, the only thing you can do, if it's hit to you, is field it properly. You can't control whether the umpire calls it a strike, whether your catcher gets it, whether the hitter hits it and whether your defense plays defense. You can't control the weather or the mound conditions. None of that stuff deserves your energy. Your energy needs to be focused on the one thing, doing your best to execute that one pitch at a time. It's so much easier said than done, because baseball is such an emotional game. Especially as a pitcher, you're on the bump in the middle of the field, up above everybody. Everyone is looking at you. You're a hero or a goat, and you get caught up in the emotion of it.

I had a player tell me several years ago, 'A game is easier for me, not easy, but easier for me when I can take the emotions out of the game.' That's brilliant. If you have the ability to do that, it will change everything, but it's hard. We all want success. We all want to win and we all want results. If you focus on what you have the ability to control, being committed and being present for each moment, the results come along with it.

Springer: It takes time. If you don't go 1-for-20 thirty times, you didn't play long enough. It's not only about hitting, it's about defense also. If you can't play good defense, then you're not playing in the big leagues nowadays, unless you are a David Ortiz-type of guy with huge power who can hit.

It always goes back to getting great at showing up with confidence. When Abner Doubleday said you have to get it by 8 guys, right then, the mind screw was invented. If he would have said, 'Success is when you hit the ball hard and you win,' they would have to move the mound in ten feet. If every single player would walk onto the field with 100% confidence 5 times a night in the big leagues, the ERA would be about 4.9 and the average in the league would only be about 7, but we don't do it. Big leaguers are better at it than minor leaguers.

I get emails and tweets from kids needing help to get out of their own way. Eighty percent of big leaguers don't know what I know. That's the beautiful thing about my CD. You don't know what it's going to do to them. Ben Zobrist got my CD when he was 25 years old in AA. Two years later, he was a Major League Baseball all-star. I talked to him when I met him at Christian retreat. He couldn't believe I was there. He said that changed his whole thought process.

The whole thing is about playing one day at a time, having fun and playing for the team. When you play for the team, you have guys helping you. When it is all about you, you're on an island.

Afremow: Self-awareness is the key to change. If a player is starting to feel mentally stressed or physically tense, he's probably also worrying about expectations and outcomes that will get him into trouble. Those are the uncontrollables that you need to let go. The best way to get results is to not think about them. A player should use any negative state as a cue to refocus on the purpose at hand. I like using F.O.C.U.S for Focus On Controllables Under Stress. Players can write this acronym on their glove or on their cap to use as a positive reminder on game day.

Bell: It's focus, getting an understanding of what's in your control and what's not in your control, because all you can do is locate your spot and commit. That's it. With hitters, you get a good pitch to hit and make contact. It's being able to evaluate the process. If a pitcher goes out there and wins, but he gave up five earned runs, that's not really a good outing. The process didn't match with the outcome. He was focused on the outcome. Other times, maybe you lost 2-1 and walked two guys, gave up earned runs, but you had seven or eight quality innings. That's a good start, that's the process. It all equals out in the end if we stay focused on the process and not on the results. I've known a lot of people who had great seasons, but their process wasn't good. They hit a bunch of home runs but the process wasn't good. It was outcome. It's evaluating ourselves on quality at bats, quality starts and quality innings, really buying into that process.

What helps is when coaches buy into it, so all they emphasize is the process. It's a lot easier for players to focus on the process when the coaches are dialed in that way. That's what the best coaches do. I know that's what Tim Corbin at Vandy does. All he focuses on is process, guys running on and off the field, moving guys over in situations, and winning the little battles.

Brubaker: You need to look at it like a marathon or a sprint. When you think about what's happening right now, the media, the scouts, whatever it might be, you're focusing on something that you either have no control over or that doesn't really relate to or help your performance.

You need to focus on the fact that you are going to win some and lose some. You're going to fail, that's part of the process. Do we want to succeed more than we fail? Absolutely, but understand that with adversity and failure, there is going to be feedback. The biggest thing takes time. You know it's not going to happen overnight, and that's part of what my book, *Seeds To Success,* is about. It takes time for a tree to bear fruit. It takes time for an athlete to improve to the point where he is a contributing member and impact player on the team. The coach and the athlete have to understand that it doesn't happen overnight.

We've been so brainwashed in a society that is focused on results. We've become this microwave society where we demand instant results. It used to be that when you needed to find something out, you walked to the library, looked in the card catalog, went and got the book and looked it up. Now, you just Google it on your phone. You don't even have to get off of your couch. We've become very spoiled with this instant, on-demand society, and we think that translates into every aspect of our life. It doesn't. That will never translate into sports.

Go back to focusing on the controllables, not the results. The ideal outcome is to hit a home run. What we need to do is see the ball, hit the ball. You're not always going to be able to control where it goes. Just see the ball and hit the ball.

It's the same thing in the workplace. There are so many variables to a sale or whatever you're doing. This is what I love about baseball players in the sales environment. They understand it's a game of failure and you're going to fail more than you succeed. Once the pitcher throws the pitch, you let go of it. The second you let go of it, you've let go of control. What happens, happens. You've got teammates backing you up and you're going to respond. You have to understand that we can't control everything. Literally, here's what I can control, here's what I can't. Write it down.

We sometimes convince ourselves in our minds. Our minds are our worst enemy. We think we can control things we can't. All the more reason to write the uncontrollables down. Stephen Covey does the circle of control. The things that are outside of the circle are those you can't control. This is a great exercise for athletes.

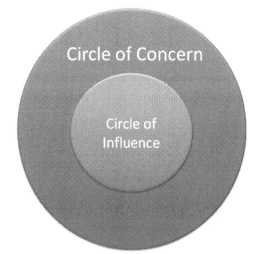

Dehmer: The *1PitchWarrior* system is literally measuring the process. We're not hanging stats on the bulletin board about who's hitting what and what their average is, what their on-base percentage is, what are their slugging percentage, ERA, wins and losses, who has the most strikeouts. None of that is important to us, and we make that clear from day one. This stuff is out the window.

You can hit the ball hard four times in a day and be 0-for-4. Most kids are going to look at it that way too. If you don't give them a Quality At Bat average, and they're left to have their own perspective on it, they're going to do what they see on ESPN, in the newspaper and online. That's the stuff that they think is important. There are many ways a guy can have a Quality Team At Bat that are very, very productive for the team. In the media's eyes or in the newspaper the next day, it is going to say 0-for-4 or 0-for-3. We wanted to give them a better perspective about those at-bats and a different mindset about it. That's really what the Quality At Bat system does for our guys, and that's what we show them throughout the year. This is what matters to us, and if you want to get in the lineup, be one of the top nine or ten guys, you're going to have a really good shot at making the lineup.

Toole: That's the hardest part of the game. When people look up baseball players to see how a guy's doing, what's the first thing they look at? Batting average. That's one of those things where you can do everything right, get a good pitch, take a good swing, hit it right on the screws, and it's a line-drive right to the center fielder and counts as an out. When you look at batting average, it's not necessarily a tell-all of how you're doing.

We try to worry about things we can control, such as hitting the ball hard. In college we did a lot with Quality At Bats. Guys are on second and third, less than two outs, we're trying to move runners over and get one in. If they're on first and second, no outs, you're trying to bunt them over, trying to move them over, things like that. I was fortunate enough growing up to have my Dad as a coach. Everything I was taught was team-oriented. I've found out that when I put the team first, moving runners over, making plays, and things like that, success tends to follow.

You don't know if you're going to be in a line-up that day, if it's going to rain, if the umpire is going to make a bad call, if your teammate is going to give you a good throw, you don't know any of that. You've just got to control your attitude and your effort, the two things that you can control. If you have a good attitude and put forth good effort, good things are going to happen.

Jaeger: First, have a daily mental practice. Without a daily mental practice it's very hard to change your programming long term, although it doesn't mean you can't. After 10 to 15 years of programming, your mind might default to that. It doesn't mean that people can't have a great ability to come back to the moment without ever doing any mental practice. I'm not saying that's not possible, I'm just saying that you greatly improve your percentages, and for some people, it's absolutely a game changer.

Practice having stuff coming up, not buying into it, and coming back to the moment. If a hitter said to me that his process was to see the ball well and hit it hard, we know what his process is. I've had this conversation with hitters and pitchers before. 'Look, it's your process, not mine. Would you agree that if you saw the ball well, and hit it hard, and nothing else entered your mind for the next five years, you'd be the best hitter you could possibly be?' Of course they say yes.

What it comes down to is identifying your process. For most people, it's very simple to identify it. It then comes down to being great at it. The way to be great at it is, when stuff comes into your mind that's not your process, to be great at coming back to the process right away.

Here's the catch: if your mind has been programmed for 10 or 20 years to think about the consequences, the results, your batting average, your ERA or who's in the stands, then of course it's going to be tough, even with great advice, for you to come back to your process quickly or efficiently. Compare that to the player who has spent 20 minutes every day not just relaxing his body, clearing his mind and working on his focus, but has also gotten really good at not buying into stuff coming in the mind, being neutral to it.

Maybe the process is to see the ball well and hit hard. In meditation, maybe it's to come back to your breathing. Come back to being quiet. Come back to getting in touch with your ankles because they are touching the ground. Whatever it is, you build this strong practice to keep coming back to your process. In your meditation, it may be your breathing, your body or just being peaceful in the game. It might be seeing the glove and attacking it, or seeing the ball well and attacking the inside part of it, whatever makes you tick as a player.

It would be nice to advise everybody, 'Look, at the end of the day, just come back to your process, no matter what.' That's right, but I don't know how much weight that's going to carry to somebody who doesn't have a practice in place. The old program may have a lot of momentum and strength from many years of thinking about who's in the stands, what the count is, who's on base, your batting average or what the coach is thinking. There is just not as much teeth in that advice versus if you and I, every single day, talked for 20 minutes in the morning.

If I took you through deep relaxation, a deep breathing session, and you started learning that, then when thoughts came into your mind, you could get really good so that it just didn't matter. 'I'm coming back to my breath, I'm coming back to my breath.' If we did that every day for three months, then during batting practice, if guys start talking about your batting average, and you start to hear that noise going, you can say, 'You know what, it doesn't really matter, guys. Even at batting practice, I just need to see the ball well and hit it hard, and I really want to master that, because that's the process I need to rely on in a game.' All of a sudden you're practicing it.

Bring your meditation away from the meditation hall. Now you're becoming aware of the thoughts in your head, the judgments in your head, what other people are saying, and you're starting to hone in on your process all the time. Maybe at your first game after doing this for only two or three days, you're a little better at your process, but there's a Kansas City Royals scout in the stands. It still kind of gets you a little. You're 0-for-2 going into your third at-bat and you're pressing a little bit because you really need to get that hit. Boy, that's a great one. You really need to get that hit, so now you're still vulnerable to your old programming.

Let's speed this up a month. We have done this every day for a month. You're more aware of it at practice, in your classroom, when people are talking to you. You're more in the present moment. Maybe it's not your baseball process, but you're starting to get better at honing into a 'process of coming back to the present moment' rather than getting caught up on tangents in your mind. We have done this for three straight months and you've been locking into this idea of your process, your breathing, seeing the ball well and hitting it hard.

Now you're in the on deck circle and you have the most important at-bat of the season coming up. You're still human, so your mind may go to some old programing and talk about 'big at bat', but BAM! Three months of practicing a new programming has got a lot of momentum. 'You know what, I have learned that all that matters is to master my breathing, seeing the ball well and hitting the ball hard. Obviously it's better if I'm relaxed, which is awesome. I have been doing this relaxation every day, and my breath now represents me feeling clear-minded and relaxed.'

If you're in the on deck circle and I call time out and say, 'Hey, what's your process?' You say, 'See the ball well, hit it hard, and take a deep breath.' I say to you, 'OK, here's what I want you to do. Take a deep breath. Man, all I care about, I don't care what happens, just see the ball well and hit it hard.' Can you see how much more teeth my advice has to you three months later, from all the practice you have done away from the field and at the field as well?

Versus if we've had a couple of meetings in the clubhouse as a group, we've talked about the breathing, we've talked about staying in the moment, we've talked about the same principles, but we've never done any mental practice together. I've told you try to do some breathing exercises, try to do some visualization. Can you see the difference of who you are after three months of just pounding this process? Your adjustment period can be very fast and maybe, as important as anything, you're just so consumed by your process that the thoughts about a 'big at bat' or anything else, they seem a lot further away in your brain.

One of the things I've been talking about recently is this idea that the more you meditate, the clearer you get. The more you relax, the more you become consumed by your process. Think of it as if the sun is getting hotter and hotter and hotter, and if you get closer to the sun, it's just going to get hotter and hotter and hotter. That's symbolic of your process, getting hotter. This is where the term 'locked in' comes from. It's just so hot that everything else around it burns up.

I love that metaphor: the more you meditate, you get to this hotter and hotter state, the more the thoughts aren't right there by your temples. They start to feel like they're a couple hundred yards away. You still may hear them, but they feel very distant and they don't feel like they have a whole lot of pull with you anymore. That's changing your default through mental practice. Your default now is more like the sun, versus the 10 to 15 years of previous programming.

It's nobody's fault. When I say this, I'm not making people feel bad or saying you should feel guilty. We're all a byproduct of this 10 or 20 years of programming. Whether it's television, the social media, the draft, recruiting, it's part of our culture. Coming back to your process, the teeth come from your practice, changing your program so the default can click in right away. You're more consumed by your process than by years of non-process conditioning.

Question Review

In the game of baseball, and life in general, there are so many external circumstances that are completely out of one's control, such as what happens when the ball leaves your bat/hand, who is in the lineup, what the weather is like, who is watching you, etc… but we live in a society that is so focused on results, batting average, ERA, etc. How does a player shift his focus to the process and the controllables?

Maher: The self identifies with results, proving themselves to other people and all those things that are outside of their control. Get back into the moment, deal with things that are important, that matter, that they can influence, and the numbers will take care of themselves.

Rickertsen: Working memory is anything that you are consciously paying attention to right now. When you start filling that very small space in your mind with aspects that you can't control, your brain can't focus on what you need to be doing. Identify your target and focus yourself on that.

Dixon: We're so distracted as a society. When's the last time you got home and your parents asked how your process was today on the mound? They don't. We're a results oriented society and if you allow it to distract you, it will suck the life out of you. Nothing out of your control deserves your energy. Your energy needs to be focused on the one thing, doing your best to execute that one pitch at a time. If you focus on what you have the ability to control, being committed and being present for each moment, the results come along with it.

Springer: It's about playing one day at a time, having fun and playing for the team. When you play for the team, you have guys helping you. When it is all about you, you're on an island.

Afremow: The best way to get results is to not think about them. F.O.C.U.S. = Focus On Controllables Under Stress

Bell: It's about focus and getting an understanding of what's in your control and what's not in your control.

Brubaker: The coach and the athlete have to understand that it doesn't happen overnight. We've been so brainwashed in a society that is focused on results. We've become this microwave society where we demand instant results.

Dehmer: You can hit the ball hard four times in a day and be 0-for-4. If you don't give them a Quality At Bat average, they're going to go to what they see on ESPN and online. That's the stuff that they think is important.

Toole: When I put the team first, moving runners over, making plays, and things like that, success tends to follow. If you have a good attitude and put forth good effort, good things are going to happen.

Jaeger: You need to have a daily mental practice. It is simple to identify your process, but it comes down to being great at it. When stuff comes into your mind that is not your process, work on coming back to the process right away.

Create Feelings of Fun and Relaxation

A survey with some of the nation's best collegiate baseball players revealed that they perform at their best and experience their highest levels of success when they are relaxed and having fun. For most players, feeling relaxed and having fun follows success. How does a player create those feelings prior to having success?

Cain: It depends on the players' perspective of what is fun and what is relaxed. When you talk about 'Hey, you've got to play the game relaxed,' a lot of players fall into that 'I'm too cool' phase, where they just carry themselves like they're too cool or they're too relaxed. When I think about relaxing, I'm thinking about sitting by the pool. There was never a day in my career as an athlete where I actually felt like I was relaxed when I was performing. The term I like is that you have to be in control of yourself.

A lot of athletes get out of control when they compete. Physically, they try to do too much. They get out of control emotionally and mentally. They want it too bad. You see this when a pitcher's front side flies open when he's throwing. Most people think it's a mechanical breakdown. Well, if the guy does it in the bullpen all the time, it's not a mechanical breakdown. If the guy stays closed in the bullpen, then flies open in the game, it's not a mechanical breakdown. He's too wound up, too geared up, out of control in the mind and it's manifested in the front side of his body opening up, manifest meaning showing up physically. The stress or pressure that player is feeling, wanting it so bad, is opening up his front side and causing him to rush. The mental game is leading to that mechanical breakdown.

You can say, as a coach to that pitcher, 'You're flying open, you're flying open, you're flying open,' but it's like me saying to you, 'Hey, you've got a headache. Take some Advil.' Until we take the nail out of your head, the headache is never going to go away. Until we fix the mindset of that player to be in control, the front side is going to keep flying open.

Players have fun because they're focused on the moment and on the process. They have increased awareness and attention. I had dinner with Alan Jaeger and Andy McKay a couple months ago in Scottsdale, Arizona. Alan said something that totally threw me for a loop, that I thought was genius. He said there's a difference between thinking, awareness and attention. Jaeger said,

'Thinking is always about the past and about the future. When you're in the moment, you're using awareness and attention.'

Right now, take your mind's awareness and attention and put it on your feet, then your ankles, your calves, your knees, your quads, your glutes, and to your hands. When you're doing what we call a body scan, you're not thinking. You're having awareness and attention for that moment. When players are playing at their best, they're not thinking, they're relying on awareness and attention in the moment.

As a hitter, you can think when your feet aren't in the box. When your feet are in the box, though, it's got to be awareness and attention. As a pitcher, when your feet are on top of the rubber, it's awareness and attention. When your feet are off the rubber, you can think about the last pitch or the next pitch, but when you step on the rubber, you've got to be committed to this pitch, and you have to trust your awareness and attention to be able to execute that pitch.

Some use the term relaxed, I say self-controlled and in the moment. You can say having fun, not concerned about the past or the future because that creates stress. It's being locked into the moment and engaged in this pitch. People who don't know the words to use might describe the moment or sensation of that performance as relaxed and fun. From the research and the experience that I have with it, I say it is connection to the moment, awareness and attention, and engagement in that moment. It is to not be concerned about the results, about the past, about how this at-bat is going to impact my draft status. It's about, 'I want to see this baseball and hit an absolute rod right past this guy's ear.'

Dixon: It's all about your relationship with practice. Playing on Friday night in front of 4,000 fans, that game is not won or lost on Friday night. That game is won or lost with your preparation and your relationship with practice prior to that game. People call it 'flipping a switch' or just playing better during games. I don't believe in that. Your relationship with practice has to be intimate, specific and detail-oriented, and it's got to be better than anyone you'll ever compete against. It's so important because we practice so much more than we play. We have got to close that gap. It's the finest details, those itty-bitty details that create the foundation for greatness. To be successful and to have the chance at success is all about preparation and your relationship with practice.

Hanson: Most important by far is the player's perception. If they perceive it honestly, if they think it's fun, if they have that Wiffleball mentality, even though everyone around them is very serious about it, and the whole environment is trying to get them to see it as a stressful thing, if they can maintain the perception that, 'You know what? This is fun, this is really fun. I love this,' then they're fine. Derek Jeter has a lot of mental game techniques that he uses, but I didn't teach him any. If you perceive it as fun, then you're awesome. Who chokes in Wiffleball? So the biggest thing of all is to stay connected with why you play.

We're working on *Heads-Up Baseball 2.0*, and one of the things we talk about is keeping your pleasure greater than your pressure. If you have the target, 'Let me stay connected with why I play and what's fun about this,' that's going to keep you the loosest of all. That's like 'inner umpire training.' You're trying to upgrade your inner umpire to say you're safe when you actually are. You know you're just playing a game of baseball. You really are safe. It's not do or die, but when you perceive that it is, it causes tension and distraction, your two big enemies as a player. If you want to extend your arm, but you have tension in your bicep because you're nervous, that muscle is working against your tricep. That's why we say that guy's stiff. He's stiff because he's tight, because he's perceiving his situation as a threat. His fight-or-flight is kicking in—the biggest thing of all.

If you give me an hour to work with a player, I'm going to spend 50 minutes working on his belief system, clearing things out of his past. I'm going to spend 10 minutes working on what I would consider cognitive-behavioral stuff, which is from *Heads-Up Baseball*. Have a routine, take a breath, use a focal point, the standard stuff for the baseball mental game. It's great. I teach it a lot, but to me that's the tip of the iceberg. What's below the iceberg is how a guy perceives it.

I would use a routine. I have my ABCs, which I've found to be easily adopted by people. I made it up for 8 year olds, but I use it for corporate executives. I work with Fortune 500 executives, business CEOs, leadership development in major corporations, and I'll teach them my ABCs.

A is **A**ct big. Physically carry yourself head up, chest up, and 'big easy', I call it. It's not like a military kind of stiff, 'I'm in control, dominating.' It's big easy. There's an ease about it.

B is **B**reathe big. You're taking a nice breath. Why? Because the lizard brain is kicking in the fight-or-flight, and it shuts off the breathing. If there's a rustling in the leaves, you want to stop breathing. Any movement and somebody is going to see you, that's why you stop breathing. You want to counteract that with a deep breath.

C is **C**ommit big. As a pitcher: 'This ball is going right there.' See it, feel it.

D is **D**o it. Act big, breathe big, commit big, and then do it. You can see how fast I can teach it. Then I have someone stand up and do it, and you can do it in moments. It's best if they practice it, but again, everything goes back to the underlying belief system and how a human being is designed. You've got to upgrade his belief system, then teach him the skills. Nobody's going to be immune from perception of threat. It's still going to be there. You want to have routines that will help in the moment, but as you perceive yourself as safe, the less you need any of the stuff we talk about in sports psych.

Springer: Make it about the team. Too many players play this game like it's a three-hour time out, like they're in trouble, instead of a three-hour game. Give yourself a little bit of freedom. It's not about you, it's about you helping the team and having fun. There's a little bit more freedom for your abilities to come out. I want you to get three hits today but that doesn't mean you're going to get three hits.

I need you to be the best competitor on the field, with an attainable goal to hit the ball hard and help your team win. I have told Paul Goldschmidt that a thousand times, and he said that connects the dots and makes it makes sense. I never asked them to get three hits, because I know that's not an attainable goal. We get caught up in goals that aren't attainable.

We feel that we need to be perfect, but we're not perfect. All of a sudden, here comes that non-confident guy creeping in. Get great at showing up with the confidence to help your team win. That guy's going to play a long time. It's about getting great at showing up with confidence. That's what we have to get great at. It's not about getting the hits, where my hands are, where are my feet are. Get great at showing up with confidence and help your team win.

Jaeger: You tend to have a lot more fun throughout your day when your mind is clear and your body is relaxed. There are other potential huge benefits from mental practice or meditation. It's one thing to say that to be more relaxed, I need to key into my breath. That is a great thing to do. However, the foundation is still going to be, what did you do for 15 or 20 minutes before you left your house? What did you do for an additional 15 or 20 minutes in the clubhouse when you had that break before you went back out to the field, or before you were supposed to show up for your game or practice that day? That's what I want to know, because that's the practice.

Would you go out and perform in a game if you hadn't taken batting practice for 6 months? You might, but how are you going to feel? There needs to be mental practice away from the field, dedicating time and awareness to clearing your mind, relaxing your body, getting into the moment, learning how to deal with distracting thoughts, learning how to oxygenate your body better, learning how to be more connected and intimate with yourself. If you study peak performance, you're very intimate with your body and your surroundings. You're very connected.

All of these great things that come up when you're in a 'peak state of mind' are things you can practice, but it needs to be dedicated practice away from the field. To be in tune with your breathing on the field would be a huge plus, even if you didn't ever do any mental practice, but you can see the strength and power of having a 20-minute session before you went to the field. Imagine if you did that every day for three months. How valuable and powerful is being in tune with your breath going to be with three months of 20-minutes-a-day in the bank?

That's my theme if anybody wants to talk about the mental game. We can talk about the process, we can talk about staying in the moment, and we can talk about react and don't think. I can spend hours talking about that stuff. At the end of the day, if you don't have a mental practice in place as a player, and if the coach doesn't have a mental practice in place every day, you're kidding yourself. The mind has had a lot of programming. The future, the past, who's watching, what's my batting average and what's at stake. It hasn't had a lot of practice learning to stay in the moment, to tune into the breathing, into what's important now, what's my process, what am I committing to now. My thoughts are not relevant right now, because I'm too focused on the now. These themes and principles start to get ingrained from having a dedicated practice. Unless you have that practice in place, it's hard to expect athletes to go out there and stay in the moment and tune into their breath, even though they know to do that, without their mind defaulting back to some old programming that they may have practiced for 10 or 15 years.

Maher: Relaxation can't be forced. If you start forcing something, you're going to work against yourself. We encourage our players to focus on the process of playing the game: what they do before the game in their routine, how they compete and stay in the moment and how they deal with their results and make adjustments. The focus is on the process. If they can key into that and lock in, they are able to embrace the game, to become more consistent, to relax and pay attention to what matters. That's easier said than done with some players. We teach the players to recognize drift, when they start thinking about things that they can't control and get agitated. This gives them a way to get themselves back into the moment.

Afremow: The goal is to play with your own ideal mental state, whatever you think and feel at the top of your game. For most athletes, having fun with a purpose, 'intense fun', is the ideal mental state. However, some baseball players perform best when they have an angry edge, what I call being 'mad decisive.' A pitcher might be thinking, 'I'm going to blow this by you.' a hitter might be thinking, 'I'm going to tear the cover off the ball.' The best way to relax and clear your mind is to try all the different great techniques that are out there and find the one that works best for you. Deep breathing is a good place to start, because we're all breathing throughout the day, but under pressure and stress we tend to hold our breath or we breathe more shallowly with the chest, instead of deeply through the belly.

Gordon: The greatest thing you can do is focus on the moment. I love this game! I'm thankful I get to play this game! Practice gratitude and breathing.

I call these the 3 F's: focusing on Fun, Faith and Fearlessness. I'm going to have fun, go out there and be my best and enjoy the moment. I'm going to have faith, expect great things to happen. If something bad happens, I expect the next play to be great. What has happened is in the past. I'm going to believe that the next play is going to be great. I'm going to be fearless. I'm not going to be worried about the outcome. All I'm going to do is give my best in the moment. It's all I can do.

I am going to control what I can control. The three things you can control are your attitude, your effort and your actions to be a great teammate. If you focus on those things that you can control, you're going to have more fun and enjoy the moment. I don't worry about the outcome, so I can be my best at the moment. I give everything I can to win, but I'm not going to worry about winning. I'm going to give everything I have in the moment so I can be my best. That's the key.

Weintraub: I use John Wooden's definition of success: 'Peace of mind in knowing you did your best.' Doing your best is different from trying hard. You have to try hard to do your best, but to do your best you also have to do three things.

It took me awhile to come to this diagram of what it would take to give your best effort, but it's all-inclusive and doesn't leave anything out.

1. Create an ideal state.
2. Commit to your plan of attack.
3. Focus.

A lot of people wait to have fun and be confident until things are going well, but that is not the thinking pattern of the greatest athletes in the world. Tony Robbins says you can change your state in an instant by changing your thoughts and your body language. When you control the direction of your mind, you control your attitude. When you control your body language, a huge piece can be changed in an instant by controlling your physiology.

Rickertsen: Being relaxed and having fun are emotions we're always striving for in performance. If you want to perform at your best, you want to be enjoying what you're doing. Recently, I've been reading research on the ability to prime your emotions prior to performance. What's being seen in the research is that you can perform up to 17% better simply by priming your emotions. Learning how to do it is important. Look at times when you were feeling very relaxed and having fun. What did that look like, and how did you get there?

It's not always about what we're feeling, but how we're interpreting what we're feeling. The difference between practice and performance, for a lot of baseball players, is feeling uncomfortable, butterflies in your stomach. You're nervous because you've never done this before or because the last time you did it, it didn't go well. How you interpret those feelings either leads to a pressure-filled, uncomfortable anxiety, or looking at it as a challenge and develop that piece of it.

Having the ability to pick what emotion you want, priming for it, is a skill that you can learn. Another piece is, once you're feeling a specific way, how are you interpreting those feelings? Are you using them to your benefit, or are you letting them be a detriment to your performance?

Bell: I coach my athletes on how to be relaxed and why it is important. Tell me about when you are relaxed, and it always gets back to confidence. The athletes who are relaxed and having fun do it because they believe in themselves. It's a game and they're supposed to have fun doing it, but they believe in themselves. They know that if they go 0-for-3 one night, it's not going to impact the next night. It doesn't mean that there's anything wrong, they just go back, look at minor adjustments to make. Got it. Let's go play.

Confidence is the most important mental skill, because confident athletes have to learn it and confident athletes do relax. It's so much fun when things are going well and when we are relaxed, trusting that it's going to work out. We need to understand that it all works out in the end, and if it hasn't, it's just not the end. We all have a moment coming up that's going to make all the difference, and we don't know when that moment's coming.

Brubaker: Think about the last thing you did off the field, that you were doing really well. You were in the zone—what were you thinking? You probably weren't thinking about anything. You were so wrapped up in the moment that you were present and just enjoying it.

You create those feelings so that, when your coach is yelling at you, in the heat of battle towards the end of practice, that's when your conditioning kicks in. It isn't always fun. Sometimes it's a grind. The way you create those feelings is to celebrate small successes. It's easy to celebrate the wins. After you win, everybody celebrates, but how do you celebrate the small successes? The little battles win the war.

A great book by Harvard researchers Teresa Amabile and Steven Kramer, *The Progress Principle: Using Small Wins to Ignite Joy, Engagement and Creativity at Work*, talks about the key to job satisfaction for people in the workplace. It's the same in athletics. Managers thought it was recognition or monetary, but for the workers, it was small daily progress towards their goals. It wasn't the big win, winning the game. It was winning the pitch, winning at the bat, winning the top of the third inning. It's about finding those small successes. When you do that, you start a little winning streak and you build momentum. In the game of baseball, you know how important momentum is.

Tully: You have to take your mind off your mind. Baseball can grind you down. A family psychologist once sold me on the idea to just look up at the sky. If you find yourself looking down at the ground, that means you're too into yourself. If you're walking and your head is down, look up at the sky. The sky is infinite. It's got all sorts of possibilities. That's one thing you can do.

Years ago, Earl Weaver, the manager of the Baltimore Orioles, had a tomato garden outside the right field fence. What does that mean? Let's remember why we were in this game. Pick up some dirt from the infield and feel it in your hands. Get out there in the sun and remember the first time you picked up a bat in the summertime. Remember how fun it was. Try to feel the fun of the game. Breathe. There's nothing more immediate, nothing that can do a better job of keeping you in the present, than breathing.

I ask the players on my team, how long could you go without food? You could go a long time without food, water or sleep. How long could you go without breathing? There's nothing more immediate than breathing. There's nothing like breathing that can bring you into the present. Feel the dirt under your feet, feel it in your fingers, look up at the sky, have an activity that takes your mind off your mind.

Another great technique is affirmations. The year that Phil Mickelson finally won a major, he had an affirmation on the last day at Augusta. He kept saying to himself, 'Today is my day.' When he made a shot, 'Today is my day.' When he missed a shot, 'Today is my day.' When he went ahead, 'Today is my day.' When he fell behind, 'Today is my day.' He finally made about an 18-footer on the 18th to win his first Master's. I give a lot of credit to his affirmations. Fun and relaxation are the way to go.

Question Review

A survey with some of the nation's best collegiate baseball players revealed that they perform at their best and experience their highest levels of success when they are relaxed and having fun. For most players, feeling relaxed and having fun follows success. How does a player create those feelings prior to having success?

Cain: Players have fun because they're focused on the moment and on the process. When players are playing at their best, they're not thinking, they're relying on awareness and attention in the moment.

Dixon: It's the finest, itty-bitty details that create the foundation for greatness. To be successful and to have the chance at success is all about preparation and your relationship with practice.

Hanson: Stay connected with why you play. Keep your pleasure greater than your pressure. It's not do or die, but when you perceive it like that as a player, you create tension and distraction. The cognitive behavioral skills are the tip of the iceberg. How a player perceives all of this is what is below that. I teach the same Big ABC's to 8-year-olds and Fortune 500 companies: Act Big, Breathe Big, and Commit Big.

Springer: Give yourself a little bit of freedom. It's not about you, it's about you helping the team and having fun.

Jaeger: There needs to be mental practice away from the field, dedicating time and awareness to clearing your mind, relaxing your body, getting into the moment, learning how to deal with distracting thoughts, learning how to oxygenate your body better, learning how to be more connected and intimate with yourself.

Maher: The focus is on the process. If they can key into that and lock in, they are able to embrace the game, to become more consistent, to relax and pay attention to what matters. We teach the players to recognize drift, when they start thinking about things that they can't control and get agitated.

Afremow: The best way to relax and clear your mind is to try all the different great techniques that are out there and find the one that works best for you. Deep breathing is a good place to start, because we're all breathing throughout the day, but under pressure and stress we tend to hold our breath or we breathe more shallowly with the chest.

Gordon: The three things you can control are your attitude, your effort and your actions to be a great teammate. If you focus on those things that you can control, you're going to have more fun and enjoy the moment. It's about the 3 F's: Fun, Faith and Fearless.

Weintraub: When you control the direction of your mind, you control your attitude. When you control your body language, a huge piece can be changed in an instant by controlling your physiology.

Rickertsen: If you want to perform at your best, you want to be enjoying what you're doing. It's not always about what we're feeling, but how we're interpreting what we're feeling.

Bell: It always goes back to confidence. The athletes who are relaxed and having fun do it because they believe in themselves. We all have a moment coming up that's going to make all the difference, and we don't know when that moment's coming.

Brubaker: It's about finding those small successes. When you do that, you start a little winning streak and you build momentum. In the game of baseball, you know how important momentum is.

Tully: If you find yourself looking down at the ground, that means you're too into yourself. Look up at the sky. The sky is infinite. It's got all sorts of possibilities. There's nothing more immediate than breathing.

Clear Your Mind

What are your best techniques to relax and clear your mind?

Springer: I talk about breathing and keeping your heartbeat between 60-80. You're going to be your best athlete there. Loose muscles are quick muscles. When you get tense, that high-testosterone guy, you're not as quick. I talk about breathing and getting energy up in the chest. Hitting is controlled violence. It's not violent violence and not controlled control. It's controlled violence, attacking the inside part of the baseball.

Dixon: The breath is a huge thing. Taking a big, quality, deep breath automatically gets you into the present. There is not a specific time, it's throughout the day. In the morning, if you just have five minutes to reflect, take a deep breath and focus on what you are going to accomplish today. We worry so much about what's happened or what's going to happen that we really forget about what's happening. To really be in the present is valuable, and we're disconnected from that. That breath is the one tool that will instantly get you into the present moment, and when you're in the present moment you have clarity. That clarity makes you more conscious of what you're thinking about and what you're doing, giving you a better chance at success. If you can only do one thing, redefine your relationship with your breath.

Maher: If a player has 10 or 12 seconds to turn himself around, we tell him something very efficient is to get in touch with his breathing. We emphasize learning how to breathe deeply, diaphragmatic or belly breathing, because it will always be helpful if they're willing to do it.

Weintraub: It's all about finding a routine that works for each individual athlete. Mental skills training is about understanding these truths and thinking patterns that work.

Where the rubber meets the road is actually doing it. Everybody's personality comes out on the diamond, but we have the ability to identify and change bad habits. It's not easy, but that's what mental toughness training is about, finding a routine that works. It's all about paying attention like a scientist would to what works and what doesn't, what's useful and what's not. There are two sides to every coin, so we have to practice finding the thoughts and images that are most useful.

Find the things that are most useful to you to get relaxed, such as stretching before games. These routines are a combination of things to do, power things to say, and images to vividly imagine. Put those three strategies in your pregame routine, the pre-inning routine, the pre-pitch routine, the pre-at bat routine, and then a post-routine when something is off track, what I call a gathering routine. We want to design these routines very carefully. If you don't have a plan, how are you going to know if it was a good plan or not? Certainly, a deep breath is huge.

There is an exercise in my book called 'Dialing It Down.' It uses strategies within the things you do, power phrases you say to yourself, and things you imagine. Ultimately it's up to each individual to find the key that works for him, whether it's Evan Longoria staring at the top of the left field foul pole or thinking back to your Personal Past Peak Performance. It can bring that calmness and confidence from that time in your life, whether it was a month ago or four years ago, bring that state to this moment with imagery.

Jaeger: I'd have to say, over the last 30 years, I probably meditate anywhere from 330-365 days a year. It's part of my morning routine. It's usually anywhere from 15 to 40 minutes, and a part of my life. The idea of not doing it can really throw me off, or make me a lot more sensitive to stress, overthinking, worrying, and all the things that you don't want to get into. Without going into great detail, it involves more breathing, being in the present moment, and learning to let my mind think what it wants to think but not attach myself to it. Practice being neutral and quiet, going to 'the zone'. When you're in the zone, you're in this quiet, non-thinking, purely instinctive place. You talk about fun and relaxed, that's a peaceful place to be.

A lot of my meditation practice revolves around that word 'peace', being quiet, peaceful and relaxed, letting my mind's thoughts run their course.

Learning how to do it is as easy as a button in this day and age with Google and YouTube. I would encourage everybody to look into it. You don't have to make it complicated. You can start with very simple breathing exercises, but eventually it is part breathing, part being quiet, part learning to be neutral to thoughts swinging around in my mind, part yoga. The idea is to take that meditation with you into your day. It's not like I'm going to the meditation hall, meditate, then leave it there. I'm going to go to the meditation hall and hopefully have that fill my day.

Rickertsen: A lot of people have been calling it 'the third wave of sports psychology', the idea of mindfulness or meditation, the ability to have non-judgmental awareness of what's going on in your mind. In my office, we've been taking 20 minutes every day to work meditation into our day. That way, we have experience with it when it's time to go and teach it.

To be honest, I struggled a lot working with mindfulness and meditation, just sitting and being aware and focusing on my breath, bringing it back to the breath. I was struggling with it quite a bit. A colleague in my office mentioned an app called Binaural Beats. You have different brain waves. Beta waves are when we're conscious, understanding what's going on and thinking about specific things. The brainwaves of meditation or mindfulness are theta waves. These binaural beats push your mind into a meditative state. This can really help people who are beginning meditators or struggling with it. It really helped me.

We've been building up the idea of mindfulness, and working that into what we're doing. A lot of athletes are finding more success with the mindfulness approach. It's individualized, so I know it's something that requires practice just like everything else we teach. It has been really, really exciting for me to research that and have it as another technique to teach to athletes. Something that's working for them better than other skills has been really exciting. The theta brain wave is the one for beginning meditation. It encourages the brain very strongly into a meditative state. You don't have to be trying to do it, it will happen naturally. For me, that was a great way to start.

Brubaker: The best way to relax and clear your mind is to take small steps towards doing that. The toughest thing I have to do, when I coach executives, is to get them to unplug from technology and try to sit still, relax and clear their mind for 15 or 20 minutes. You would think I was asking them to split an atom. Athletes are so type-A competitive, hard and in charge, but you need to slow down to speed up. You are going to get a better result when you take that break to meditate or even just stop and take a rest.

Let me give you this example. I was training for a marathon two years ago. One of my friends is a highly competitive tri-athlete ultra-marathoner. I asked him to give me his best piece of advice. I can't do everything he does, it's my first race. I was not trying to win it, I just wanted to finish. He said, 'The best thing you can do is, when you come to the water station, don't try to drink while you're running, even besides the fact that you're going to dribble Gatorade all over yourself. Just stop and take your drink, even if you just slow to a walk. Take your drink, hydrate, throw the cup away and get back after it.' I said, 'So, what's that going to do?' He said, 'You've got to slow down to speed up. You're going to have a better time on your next mile by taking that little micro break.'

It's a great metaphor for the game of baseball, for any athlete to relax and clear their mind. You don't have to sit Indian style on a yoga mat on the floor for an hour. Take three minutes. Once you can do 2-3 minutes, work your way up to 5. Take some deep breaths and try to think about nothing. Go to a place in your mind where you're at a beach, and just visualize successfully performing whatever you have to do next. I don't want to over-complicate it.

It is something I do to start my day. It's a habit I set. You want to practice it. Set a timer on your phone, every hour on the hour, take two minutes and just do it. Start the day, and then start and end the day with it. It's the little things, making it a habit.

Question Review

What are your best techniques to relax and clear your mind?

Springer: Keep your heartbeat between 60-80. You're going to be your best athlete there because loose muscles are quick muscles.

Dixon: Taking a big, quality, deep breath automatically gets you into the present.

Maher: We emphasize learning how to breathe deeply, diaphragmatic breathing.

Weintraub: Find the things that are most useful to you to get relaxed. A deep breath is huge.

Jaeger: When you're in the zone, you're in this quiet, non-thinking, purely instinctive place. You talk about fun and relaxed, that's a peaceful place to be.

Rickertsen: For beginners, the Binaural Beats mobile app is a great place to start. The theta waves help push the brain into a meditative state.

Brubaker: Athletes are so type-A competitive, hard and in charge, but you need to slow down to speed up. You are going to get a better result when you take that break to meditate or even just stop and take a rest.

Slow The Game Down & Win This Pitch

In the heat of battle, how does a player slow the game down and get back to the present moment?

Cain: The number one thing to help yourself engage in the moment is to take a deep breath. The player has to have an awareness of when the game starts to speed up or the garbage is hitting the fan. As Ken Ravizza would always say, 'The garbage is going to hit the fan, let's be ready for it.' You've got to go to a release, undo the batting gloves or knock dirt off your spikes.

Whatever your release is, you have to do something physical. You've got to take a deep breath and a verbal. The verbal I like to share with people is 'So what, next pitch.' It's the title of one of my books. Everyone says 'Hey, you've got to have a release!' Well, what is that? There are three parts to it.

You've got to do a physical to help you let go of the frustration. You have to take a deep breath to physiologically slow yourself down and bring oxygen back in the system. You have to have a verbal of 'So what, next pitch!'

When the ball doesn't go your way, say 'So what, next pitch' and get reconnected to the moment. Ravizza said this on day one of class in graduate school. 'Brian, the heart of the mental game is developing awareness, knowing where you're at mentally and in that moment.' So many times, we are stuck in the past for two or three pitches, and then we're walking back to the dugout after striking out saying, 'I don't even know what pitch they just threw,' because we were thinking about two or three pitches ago.

Probably the biggest challenge athletes have is to be able to play one pitch at a time. Everyone talks about it now, it's a buzzword. Watch the World Series, and people are saying, 'One pitch, one play at a time, try to trust the process,' but what I try to bring to the table is exactly how to do that.

Brubaker: I like to drop one big four-letter word every time I make a mistake or something goes wrong: NEXT. That's my four-letter word, the only four-letter word I recommend for a student athlete.

After you make an error or strike out, what just happened doesn't matter. It goes back to what you can control and what you can't. You can't control the fact that you just made an error. If you just struck out on a nationally televised game in front of a huge audience, you can't control what you just did. What can you control? You can control your response. You can control what you do next. The beauty of that is that you've got stimulus. There is what happened and your response. In between, you get to choose how you respond when everyone's watching.

One of the beauties of this age of distraction is that we have so much media and there is so much going on, people forget what you did pretty quickly and move on to the next thing. The cycle in the media is so quick, things are forgotten by the public pretty quickly unless it's some major disaster. The public tends to forget about it faster than we forget about it after we make the mistake. We are our own worst enemy between the ears. They move on and we need to move on.

Weintraub: The first step of any gathering routine is to accept that it's needed. If you just swung and missed at a pitch that you thought was fat, if you're pissed off at the umpire, that's a pretty good warning signal.

The next step is to learn these signals that I am off track. The more subtle my awareness, the better I'm able to coach myself and make great adjustments. The further off track we are, the more time we want to allow for changing our thoughts and our body language.

A really good gathering routine might look something like this: I disengage from the action by turning my back or stepping off the rubber. I take a deep breath. I think of why I am grateful for the opportunity that's right in front of me. I think back to my PPPP: Personal Past Peak Performance. I take another deep breath and then I focus on what's important now.

When we can bring attitude and confidence from that past performance, then get ourselves dialed down with a deep breath and focus on what's important now, which is the way to win, then there's a pretty good chance that we're going to be back to where we want to be.

The last aspect of the gathering routine is learning how to flush it. Certainly, we know we want to let it go. The way to flush it, when simply saying 'flush it' doesn't work because you're pissed, is forgive to forget. Why? Nobody is perfect.

If you're thinking like a scientist, making educated guesses and paying attention to the results, you're going to become intelligent. Intelligent is simply being good at guessing.

We preplan our gathering routine and use imagery to rehearse it so we don't skip something that we think is a good idea when we get in the heat of the moment. Then we go out there and practice it, paying attention to our results and adjusting our plan based on what we observed. It's about controlling the controllables, having a plan and holding yourself accountable for executing your plans. That's what it's all about.

Margolies: In baseball, success is getting three out of ten hits. In major league baseball, that almost puts you in the hall of fame. Failing seven out of ten times is OK. They have to understand what their job is, what the expectations are and that failure takes place in the future.

At bat, they can only be thinking about that one pitch, not what's going to come three pitches later. Yes, there are strategies that are involved. You have to recognize that, just as the pitcher is playing games with the hitter, the hitter is playing games with the pitcher. If you're not focused on that one pitch, you're not going to hit it. If you're worried about striking out, that's in the future. You can't focus on the future and the present in the same time.

We do exercises that keep them focused on that one pitch. They are focus or concentration exercises that help them stay focused on the present.

Toole: I have a very good routine when I go up to the plate. I like to take ownership of the box. I like to mess the dirt up a little bit, touch home plate, things like that. When there's a pitch that's a strike or if I take a pitch, I always step out, re-do my batting gloves, and get the sign from the coach to step back in. I was always taught to release it, let it go, flush it. That's what I do at the plate if something doesn't go so well, because you can't hold on to things.

The last pitch might have been a bad pitch or you might have taken a bad swing, but that doesn't mean that this next pitch is going to be bad. That's where a lot of people get into the snowball effect. You take one bad swing and then it snowballs into another one and another one. Before you know it, you're out. Just because you took a bad swing before doesn't mean you're going to take a bad swing this next swing.

In the field, I like to use focal points. Playing on a dirt infield, you'll find little rocks and pebbles. When I feel my mind wandering and I need to snap back to the present, or if I make a bad play, I'll try to find a little pebble on the ground and focus on it, then toss it to the side. If I can focus on a little pebble on the ground, it's going to make it easier for me to focus on the big white ball when it's hit to me.

Question Review

In the heat of battle, how does a player slow the game down and get back to the present moment?

Cain: The number one thing to help yourself engage in the moment is to take a deep breath. The player has to have an awareness of when the game starts to speed up or the garbage is hitting the fan. 'So What, Next Pitch!'

Brubaker: I like to drop one big four-letter word every time I make a mistake or something goes wrong: NEXT.

Weintraub: A gathering routine includes disengaging from the activity, taking a deep breath and focusing on what's important now.

Margolies: You have to understand what the job is and what the expectations are and that failure only takes place in the future.

Toole: Release it. Let it go. Flush it! Use focal points to snap back to the present when you feel the mind wandering.

The 'It' Factor

Some athletes just seem to have 'it'. What goes into the mind and makeup of the player who has that contagious personality that everyone loves to be around, that brings relentless positive energy every day and seems to be fueled by something much bigger than himself?

Brubaker: You should thank the parents. There is an old expression coaches use, 'If they don't bite on their pups, they probably don't bite.' That is in reference to how aggressive the kid is on the field. If he wasn't like that when he was little, he's not going to be like that as a college athlete. I also think it is something learned through role models during the athletes' formative years. The athlete has carried that with him onto the field as a high school and college athlete. You want to tap into that and shine a spotlight on that, because attitudes are contagious, for better or for worse. Is yours worth catching?

You want to look at a team like you're on a seesaw. You've got your whole roster on a seesaw. There's that negative guy on the one end, and there are a couple of those good locker room guys, those positive leaders, on the other end. In the middle is most of your team. Those positive leaders need to try to shift the balance, to get more of those guys over to their end of the teeter-totter, before Mr. Negative, the close-minded guy, starts to infect some of his teammates. The ones in the middle could go either way, depending on the influence that is exerted on them.

It is an every day battle. Coaches are fighting the war every day in terms of attrition and injuries, just trying to keep the team healthy. You're fighting that same war in terms of their mental health. Whose influence in the locker room is swaying the guys in the middle who could go either way?

Weintraub: Great parents. The answer to the question is great parents. Can someone who was not empowered as much, who doesn't have self-esteem from his early years of life built in, learn that? Can they learn it? Sure, but I do think the biggest cause for leadership and that sort of personality is their parents, the home life.

There was a study done looking for the answer to that question, and it's the foundation for some books like *Outliers* and *Acquisition of Talent in Young*

People. Fran Pirozzolo is a friend of mine and was a part of this project. He was the mental skills coach for the Yankees when they won four World Series in the 1990s and early 2000s. He said they were looking for these common traits in young people, but what they found was not commonalities in the young people but commonalities in their parents. Parenting is the toughest job in the world. It is absolutely a difference-maker. If you're a coach, recruit families. We can try as coaches, and we should work to be sure everyone becomes empowered, but ultimately what leads to the 'it' factor is great families.

Janssen: All coaches would love to have a lot more of those players. Sometimes you're fortunate to have one of those guys. They may have had some great parenting or great role models that they could learn from. They probably had parents who had high standards, who loved them and treated them well but had high standards for them.

Those guys have a huge love of the game. There's a respect for the game, and they love to play the game itself. It's an innate thing. They don't need little rewards or a lot of external stuff, there's this intrinsic love for the game, and that's why they do a lot of the things they do. It's that passion and that purpose that ends up driving them. They don't need a lot of extra stuff to motivate them or somebody checking up on them and making sure they're getting things done. They understand that, 'If I'm going to be successful in this situation, I've got to take control of my own training and take the initiative to get better, and respect and love the game as much as possible.'

Afremow: That takes a lot of maturity, and that comes from experience, good parenting, and good coaching. But the key for all players is to get out of yourself and get into the team. It really is a shared destiny, and all behaviors must be for the greater good. I would recommend to all players to be the player that you would want on your team if you were the coach.

Dehmer: As a coach, you can't even take the credit for that. A lot of that has to do with what that player has been taught at home, the environment he's grown up in, and what he's seen in other teams he played for before he got to you. A lot of credit goes to parents or coaches who have had an opportunity to coach that kid beforehand. Obviously, they get it for a reason, so there's someone who's made an impact on them well before they stepped foot in your program.

Rickertsen: In that person, I tend to see a 'growth mindset'. Carol Dweck talks about this a lot in her book about a growth versus a fixed mindset. It doesn't matter what the challenge is, they're going to go after it. They see that success comes from effort being put in. They take feedback and use it for their next performance. That individual has the perspective, 'I can get better, I can always get better, and I am going to do everything I can to get there.'

I separate attitude, skills, and gifts. Everybody is going to have a different set of gifts. I am very tall. Other people are very muscular, or they have different God-given talents that make them naturally good at a sport. You can have all sorts of different gifts. But the skills and attitudes are the pieces that can be developed and make you different. When I see athletes who are like that, they tend to have already adopted this mindset. It's great because they're going to go further and keep getting better because of that attitude or mindset they've adopted.

The good news is that those folks who tend not to be a growth-mindset person can become one by learning from those around them who are, by slowly approaching challenges instead of avoiding them or taking small steps to improve that attitude or mindset. That is the biggest piece as far as success goes. Yes, we're going to have different gifts, but what are you doing to get the most out of the gifts that you've been given?

Bell: When I talk to great athletes, the ones who just have that unquenchable thirst and that relentless pursuit, they have had a hinge moment early in their life that gave them the perspective that they were going to do whatever it took. It looks different for everybody. Ray Lewis' father wasn't around. He would do push-ups and sit-ups until he couldn't do them anymore. That was a lot of pain he was dealing with. For others, it was losing a parent. For some, it was striking out with the bases loaded in the state championship game. That fired them up, because they never wanted to experience that again. They knew how bad that hurt, so their mess became their message and their tests, the stuff they went through, became their testimony. They found a purpose greater than themselves that drove them further, above and beyond, to where a coach would say, 'I want nine of those guys.' They had a hinge moment early on.

Jaeger: A lot of it is nature. Some people are going to be born, maybe it's part of their DNA, maybe part of their social upbringing or their parenting. There are all kinds of different strokes and folks out there, right? It's just part of nature.

If you study that person, some of the things you would find is that there is a lot of selflessness and awareness of the excitement of the whole and of the group. Probably some good egolessness there. Not that there is anything wrong with having an ego, but those are the people who have an appreciation of the group.

Appreciation, one of my favorite words, is one of the most important words in the human vocabulary. You just appreciate a nice day, being out in the field whether you had a good day or not, you appreciate your teammates and your coaches who are trying to help you, even if they yelled at you that day. The common qualities of those kinds of people are a high level of appreciation and a sense of selflessness where they're really into the whole.

That's why they get along with everybody and inspire everybody. They are probably very optimistic and positive people.

If they have a negative thought, they're the kind of people who go back to meditation. They probably are very neutral, and they probably discount those thoughts very fast because they're consumed by the process of appreciation, enjoyment, excitement, and inspiration. They are contagious because they're open to the whole. They're those great glue guys, open to everything. They're also probably not very judgmental.

Cain: It is a great perspective. What are intangibles? People would say toughness, effort, great teammate. Those aren't intangibles, those are controllables that need to be taught and emphasized. I don't think there are any intangibles. What goes into the championship player and the person who's fueled by that is a burning passion and a mission for why they do what they do.

I'll use the examples of Brian Holliday, a catcher at TCU in 2010-2011, and Matt Carpenter with the St. Louis Cardinals. What makes those two guys so special? It's not their physical abilities but their passion, their energy. I watch those guys play and I want to go be a baseball player, because they bring so much passion to what they do. There are players like that all over the country in different sports. Those are the guys who have the passion and the talent.

There are a lot of players who have passion and no talent, or talent and no passion, and they're just marginal guys. When you have the player who's really, really good, and really, really passionate, they're a game changer. If you're a coach, you're lucky to coach a few of those guys in your career.

Maher: They endure. Those players are what I call 'good separators'. They've learned to separate themselves as a performer from themselves as a person. They're able to keep things going and not get caught up in the results, the last pitch, the last at-bat or the last game. They're able to wipe away the emotion from one game, good or not so good. They move on and enjoy the process of getting better, of development and improvement. They say to themselves, 'There's no limit to what I can do, and I'm going to step up and take the challenge.' They are the opposite of players who are always trying to identify themselves with the numbers, or prove themselves to somebody else, by things they can't control.

Dixon: Those kind of guys are special, the ones that you want to be around. They look at the big picture, and they understand. I'm a big proponent of surrounding yourself with people who are better than you. I want to be the dumbest man in the meeting, the least talented person in whatever I do. When you have someone like that who's just got it, you can't really understand it. They've got that certain energy, they've got that certain vibe. You let those guys go, don't mess them up. You get out of their way and let them have success. If they start to fail, you're there for them.

A lot of times, coaches get in the way of their players' success, because they've got to 'make them mine' or they feel they have to constantly be working on them. When you've got a guy who's locked in mentally and he's physical, you just let him go, let him have fun. Those are the guys who are fun to watch. It reinforces why this is so important, but they're few and far between. There's that fight, that inner fight all the time of 'This doesn't work, that doesn't work,' because we ride that emotional roller coaster. Baseball is filled with emotions, but when you've got that guy who's even keel, it's really fun to be a part of.

Hanson: It's their belief system that causes them to see things that way, in part just their disposition from birth. People are talented or not talented in the mental game, just as they are talented or not talented in the physical game, from birth. Then it can be developed or squashed by parents from ages one through five. After age six, it can be coaches, other experiences, or a book, but we're 95% run by our unconscious programs. That's the under-the-water part, the belief system, the whole lizard brain stuff. That's where I put my attention.

Someone gets what they get from their upbringing and their experiential influences. One guy's going to think the world's safe and he's safe, so he can be open, expressed, and positive. The reason we're so negative is the same issue. It's about survival. We're trying to survive. If that guy got killed over there, what happened? How did he do it? Why do you want to know that? So you don't do it. Why are we rubberneckers looking at the negative? Why does the negative sell, why is it on the news? We're wired to look for that because of survival, to make us feel safe. 'I am going to survive, now I can be more openly positive and expressed.'

Springer: He is fun to watch, as a scout or as a coach. You want that guy on your team. When you treat people right, you treat your teammates right, you are pulling for each other, it is just more fun. When you get that frigging idiot on your team, a 'me-me' or an 'I' guy, trust me, his teammates don't even want him to have success.

It can be taught. When some kids come in, it's all about them. Instincts are created when you're 11 to 14 years old, playing with your buddies. I've also seen some 17 or 18-year-olds who sign without baseball instincts. They are not going to be 21-year-old big leaguers but if they have work ethic and aptitude, they will get better. In the computer days that we live in now, it's hard to see young kids playing out in the street like we used to do.

Margolies: Let's put it in the bottle and sell it to everybody. That individual has mental skills for handling pressure, for being positive, for having that great attitude, and for being really motivated. He somehow learned those skills while he was growing up, and not everybody's been fortunate enough to have it. That person leads by example. If a coach is working with a team with one or two people like that, they can point out his ability to stay calm in the face of adversity. It's a skill and you can develop that skill also, you don't have to be born with it. We used to think that the guys who played under pressure, who didn't worry about anything and played with great confidence, were born with this stuff. I didn't have it, so I was never going to get it. That's why I kept quitting. Everybody falls along that continuum.

The coach can point out that you might have these skills and they are skills. If you want to learn how to be calm in the batter's box, I can teach you that. If you need to learn how to focus, I can give you some exercises that will help you focus better, so you can see the ball bigger when it's being thrown at 92 mph at chin level.

If we said that it all came down to the parents, then we'd also have to say the opposite and blame them when somebody doesn't have that, right? I don't want to do that, so instead I would say that it's everybody: parents, coaches, family members, and teachers in school.

Let me ask you a question. Are you a great artist? Can you draw? If I'd asked you that question five or six years ago, when you were in high school, what would your answer have been? Usually no. Now, what if I had asked you that question when you were in preschool? Somewhere along the line between preschool and now, you lost the ability to draw.

That happens to us in all sorts of things. It can be something simple like a teacher saying you can't draw or you're a terrible artist. It could be something like that Little League coach who doesn't know what he's doing, who is in competition with his own son and tells him, 'You're not a very good hitter.' That kid takes it personally. My big one is the coach or parent who says you should be ashamed of yourself for striking out. That carries over for the rest of their careers. They get into certain situations and they're afraid of failing, because of something somebody said to them ten years before. You can have really positive parents that help develop these kinds of skills in people, and you can have a couple of bad coaches and send that person in a completely different direction.

I've just started working with a client with parents who are really good positive people and this kid, only ten years old, is afraid to fail. Somewhere along the line, he had a coach that just hammered him that if you're not your best all the time, then you should be ashamed of what you're doing, because you're not working hard enough and you're not trying hard enough.

Toole: A lot of it is competitive nature. I don't know too many people who don't want to be the best at what they're doing. If you don't worry about being the best or you don't want to be the best, you usually don't last very long in what you're doing. I've got 24 teammates on my team, and all 24 of them are among the most competitive people I've ever met. When it comes to self-improvement and getting the best out of yourself, I look at sports psychology and the mental game as what I can do to bring the best out in me when it matters the most. When the lights shine the brightest, when the game is the biggest, a high school state tournament, a college national championship, or the World Series, what can I do to bring the best out that I have every single day, so that when I get to that position I don't have to change anything and I don't have to worry?

A lot of kids think they can just flip a switch or roll through practice. 'It's just practice, it doesn't matter. It's just a non-conference game in high school, or just a weekend scrimmage.' The best players in the world take those as if they were Game 7 of the World Series. They take practice very seriously. That's the thing that separates the best players in the world. The people who just get it are competitive and want to bring the best out in themselves. Through the mental game that's possible.

Gilbert: Just read Frank Bettger. Don't worry about the mind, worry about the actions, because you might not be able to change your attitude, but you could change your actions. You might not be able to change your emotions, but you could change your motions. You might not be able to change your moods, but you could change your movements. Action changes attitudes. Motion changes emotions. Movement changes moods. You could act yourself into it. If you are going to ask me what the most important axiom or quote in sport psychology is, I would say, 'Act as if it were impossible to fail.' How good a hitter could you be if, every time you go up to bat, you were acting as if it was impossible to fail?

Back when Pete Rose was chasing Ty Cobb's record for most number of hits in a career, every newspaper in America used to have the Pete Rose Countdown. How many hits did he need until he broke the record? I think he needed 14 hits to break the record. Rose was a lifetime .300 hitter. One day a sports writer said, 'Pete, you need 14 hits to break the record. How many at bats do you need to get the 14 hits?' Pete said 14. Even though he had 20 years of being a .300 hitter, in his mind he was a 1.000 hitter. Act as if it were impossible to fail.

Tully: You thank God you have guys like that on your team. If you have that kind of player on your team, let your life and your team be enriched by it. I'm not sure where it comes from.

The great unanswered question in performance psychology is in people who never give up. Where does that come from? No one really knows the answer to that question. Anyone who can find the answer to that and bottle it is going to make a lot of money and have a great life. Thank God for people who have great attitudes.

As a coach, you want to impart to your athletes on and off the field that all of life is a decision.

Brian Taylor, the first overall pick for the New York Yankees, found himself in an altercation one night. He fell on his arm and never pitched in the major leagues. Decisions led him there. On the other hand, a guy like David Eckstein couldn't even talk his way on as a walk-on. David Eckstein hit until his hands bled, made the major leagues, and one day was MVP in the World Series. Your decisions are your destiny. I tell my players that all the time. Don't tell me how big, strong, fast and agile you are, tell me what your decisions are, and I will tell you your destiny.

Dedman: The guys who are ready for that have built up a lot of trust in other people and have a lot of self-confidence because they have worked very hard and they trust their own preparation. The elite, the top 5% of guys that any program would have, are willing to buy in and maybe teach some of the other guys what it is and why it's important. They've come from great experiences and great relationships, or they've had enough perspective in their lives to see past negative experiences that they've had. Everybody's been burned and everybody deals with it differently. The people who show the most resilience and relentlessness and have some perspective are going to have more trust and be more willing to dive in.

You've got to have some of those guys, from an athletic standpoint in coaching. You have to recruit those people whether they're going to be your best player or not. You've got to try and get as many of those guys as possible. You're just not going to be a very good team otherwise. You might have a lot of talent, you might even have good skill, but you could be a very average team because we're not coaching an individual sport in baseball. When teams aren't flowing together, not believing together, and don't have a singular heartbeat, it definitely shows. There's a lot of scatterbrain and lack of trust between players. When you can get everybody at least close to on board, that's huge, but you've got to have some players who are leading the way, who are not just buying into what the coaches are talking about but are living it with them.

We talk with our guys a lot about how the mental game is not a baseball thing, but a life skill. In order to have great awareness and be able to recognize where your mental state is, you have to be thinking about it. When you get distracted taking that calculus exam, or some pretty girl sends you a note and now you're all distracted, or you're at the line in a restaurant and there's really bad service, you need to be aware of your emotional state and understand how you can change that and take responsibility.

Mike Bianco certainly made me very aware, when I coached with him at Ole Miss in 2010, of the times I would transfer blame or not take full accountability for thoughts I might have. It was a great opportunity for me to reevaluate the way I was talking and communicating, and most importantly, thinking. Whatever we think, we're going to say, and whatever we say, we're probably going to do. People judge us on what we do, so it all goes back to how we're thinking. We have to practice thinking a lot more intelligently.

Tony Robbins has been talking a lot about what we surround ourselves with. Brian Cain talks about the five people that you surround yourself with. The cumulative effect of those five people and their cumulative energy, attitudes, and thought processes are going to be the way you think and act and live. That's true for books and television and radio. If you're listening to awful sports talk radio every morning and watching Sports Center highlights, and movies where they're cursing all the time, you're going to have more bad habits and be more negative than you would be if you were making different choices. We all have choices and it begins with our thoughts, no question.

Question Review

Some athletes just seem to have 'it'. What goes into the mind and makeup of the player who has that contagious personality that everyone loves to be around, that brings relentless positive energy every day and seems to be fueled by something much bigger than himself?

Brubaker: You should thank the parents. It is something learned through role models during the athletes' formative years. You want to tap into that and shine a spotlight on that, because attitudes are contagious.

Weintraub: Great parents. They were looking for these common traits in successful people, but what they found was not commonalities in them but commonalities in their parents. Ultimately, what leads to the 'it' factor is great families.

Janssen: All coaches would love to have a lot more of those players. Sometimes you're fortunate to have one of those guys. They may have had some great parenting or great role models that they could learn from. They probably had parents who had high standards, who loved them and treated them well but had high standards for them. These guys have a huge love of the game and don't need little rewards or a lot of external stuff because there's this intrinsic love for the game, and that's why they do a lot of the things they do.

Afremow: That takes a lot of maturity which comes from experience, good parenting, and good coaching. But the key for all players is to get out of yourself and get into the team.

Dehmer: As a coach, you can't even take the credit for that. A lot of that has to do with what that player has been taught at home, the environment he's grown up in, and what he's seen in other teams he played for before he got to you. A lot of credit goes to parents or coaches who have had an opportunity to coach that kid beforehand.

Rickertsen: In that person, I tend to see a 'growth mindset.' It doesn't matter what the challenge is, they're going to go after it. They see that success comes from effort being put in. They take feedback and use it for their next performance.

Bell: When I talk to great athletes, the ones who just have that unquenchable thirst and that relentless pursuit, they have had a hinge moment early in their life that gave them the perspective that they were going to do whatever it took.

Jaeger: A lot of it is just nature, maybe part of their social upbringing or their parenting. There is a lot of selflessness and awareness of the excitement of the whole group. That's why they get along with everybody and inspire everybody. They are probably very optimistic and positive people and are very neutral. They probably discount those negative thoughts very fast because they're consumed by the process of appreciation, enjoyment, excitement, and inspiration. They are contagious because they're open to the whole.

Cain: That person is fueled by a burning passion and a mission for why they do what they do. They bring so much passion to what they do. When you have the player who's really, really good, and really, really passionate, they're a game changer. If you're a coach, you're lucky to coach a few of those guys in your career.

Maher: They endure. Those players are what I call 'good separators'. They've learned to separate themselves as a performer from themselves as a person. They say to themselves, 'There's no limit to what I can do, and I'm going to step up and take the challenge.'

Dixon: Those kind of guys are special, the ones that you want to be around. They look at the big picture, and they understand. I'm a big proponent of surrounding yourself with people who are better than you. They've got that certain energy. They've got that certain vibe.

Hanson: It's their belief system that causes them to see things that way, in part just their disposition from birth. It can be developed or squashed by parents from ages one through five. After age six, it can be coaches, other experiences.

Springer: He is fun to watch, as a scout or as a coach. You want that guy on your team.

Margolies: That individual has mental skills for handling pressure, for being positive, for having that great attitude, and for being really motivated. He somehow learned those skills while he was growing up, and not everybody's been fortunate enough to have it. I would say that it's everybody: parents, coaches, family members, and teachers in school.

Toole: A lot of it is competitive nature. If you don't worry about being the best or you don't want to be the best, you usually don't last very long in what you're doing.

Gilbert: Act as if it were impossible to fail.

Tully: You thank God you have guys like that on your team. If you have that kind of player on your team, let your life and your team be enriched by it. Your decisions are your destiny.

Dedman: The guys who are ready for that have built up a lot of trust in other people and have a lot of self-confidence because they have worked very hard and they trust their own preparation. Brian Cain talks about the cumulative effect of the five people you surround yourself with. Their cumulative energy, attitudes, and thought processes are going to be the way you think and act and live.

Get That Negative Guy to Buy In

Every team has 'that guy', the negative, closed-minded guy that is too cool to invest time into improving his mental game. How does a coach get that player to buy in to the system he is trying to implement?

Hanson: The biggest thing is safety, and that has to do with trust. Does he buy in? Does he trust you? The year before I was full time with the Yankees, I did a project working with all their minor league managers with a leadership development program. The first thing that came out of it for them was, 'I need to get a guy.' I said, 'What do you mean by get a guy?' They meant get respect, get connection. It can't be something that's forced or pushed, but it does require intentionality.

What you give energy to expands and grows. This negative, closed-minded person is, in effect, interference. Remember the equation Performance = Potential - Interference. If he is on your team as a big source of interference, and you give him a lot of attention, it's just going to expand and become a bigger deal. I would do my best to neutralize the negative effect he could have, and focus on what I want to have happen rather than what's not happening with him.

Jaeger: At the end of the day, coaches are the captains of the ship. You don't want to force somebody to do it. I would say, 'Look, you have a choice. You can either buy in as a team, just like we all practice at the same time, and we all go to study hall. For some reason, if you want to not buy in, I'm not going to get mad at you. You can go outside the clubhouse until we're done, or you can just sit there in the corner as long as you don't distract us.' Without guilting the player, you have to have a heart-to-heart with the player and say, 'Look, even if you just sit here and count to 100 while we're doing this meditation, just do something to work on your mind.'

If they're still too cool for school, I don't want to pass judgment on that player, but what is the team about? A team is about everybody getting on the same page and pulling a rope together. So that guy, whether it's meditation or study hall, is saying, 'Look, I'm an individual. I don't want to.'

I don't want to put it on people that they have to do what everybody else does, especially against their will, but you have two options. One is that you recruit players who are into everything you're going to teach, not just the physical parts, and you let them know up front that we do mental practice as part of the daily thing, and if you have a problem with that, maybe you would not be a good fit here.

Or you work with the player to understand how this can really help them. If they don't want to do it, you give them options and say, 'Look, you can sit here while we're doing it as long as you don't distract us. You can go outside.' You may have, out of 18 guys, 3 guys who were lukewarm and not buying in. What do you think happens after the other guys start playing and looking more relaxed and giving feedback to the other 3 guys like, 'Man, I have never felt better in my life!' You can hope to win them over that way as well.

Gordon: You can't drive anyone else's bus. You've got to make sure that you're empowering them to drive their own bus. You can encourage them, uplift them, inspire them and give them a book to read. You've got to help that person get a vision of what they want to achieve. Once they've got a vision, the goal of the coach is to connect them to the vision, help them to see it and not forget it, to reinforce it and live it. If you can connect them to a vision, something they really want to work towards, that's the key.

Cain: Of all the mental game skills, the underlining one in my life is what I can control and what I can't control. If I'm the coach and I have a player who's not buying in, what can I control? I can control how I teach to this player, the examples I show this player, my relationship with this player. If I have all those things in place, I have the best chance for getting them to buy in.

Why do people not buy in? The reason they don't buy in is that they don't understand, they're not educated enough on why they should buy in, or they don't see the pleasure and success that will come if they do buy in. What they see is the pain of, 'Well, why would I want to do this? I have to change and this is going to be uncomfortable for me. I don't want to do it.' When people don't buy in, it's because their coach or teacher has not educated them enough as to why they should buy in.

We also haven't tuned into radio station WIIFM, 'What's In It For Me?' 'Hey, this is what's in it for you. This is how this concept or principle I want you to buy into is going to take your performance from where you are to where you want to be.' If you can't educate and communicate clearly to get that point across, they're not going to buy in. If the player doesn't see how what you're teaching him is going to help him get to where he wants to go, because it's all about what's in it for them, then they're not going to buy in.

You have to agree to disagree, understanding that everybody may not buy in. There are going to be some players who are super-talented who aren't going to buy into what you're selling. As long as they're not a cancer to the team and pulling the team down, that's OK. You run into trouble when you have a player who doesn't buy in and they try to sabotage you. That's when it becomes unacceptable. They try to get other people not to buy into what you're selling. If you don't believe in what I'm selling, we can agree to disagree, as long as you don't become a distraction or a cancer to pull other people down. They can say, 'Hey, I see where that works. I can see the validity in that. It's just not for me.' Great, but don't try to tell other people it's not for them either. Just let them do their own thing and you do your thing.

Sometimes we try to get everybody to be the same, and we run into trouble with that. By the same token, you've got to have a very, very clear identification of what your program is all about and your set of core values. Certain things are negotiable: hitting techniques and strategies may be negotiable. We're not making cookies here. We're making champions. But when you're talking about the championship culture of a program, that's a non-negotiable.

At Ole Miss, their championship culture is being relentless, being committed to excellence, having belief and being selfless. If they're not willing to do that, then you have to set what I call the 'train 'em or trade 'em deadline'. It's a strategy I learned from a friend of mine, Bruce Brown. He says, 'You've got to set the train 'em or trade 'em deadline.' This is who they're going to become. If they aren't willing to do that, or they're not capable of doing that, then you have to trade them to someone else, because you don't need them anymore.

My message to athletes here is, 'Hey, you guys are special men. You're special human beings, but the game is going to go on without you.' There has to come a time where you realize that the game is bigger than all of us. If I were to die today, the game will still go on. College baseball programs are going to find someone to come in and coach their mental game. When you realize that everyone is dispensable and everyone can be released, you go at it with a bit more humility and tenacity because you realize your window of opportunity is very small. You can be replaced and you have to go out there and enjoy the battle.

Springer: I don't get too many negative responses. However, what I teach is easier said than done, because we all want to get hits. There's no truer statement on my CD. You want to have fun and get hits—I get it. There's no better feeling in the world, but the perfectionist has a hard time grasping it. You can't be a perfectionist and play baseball—it will kill you.

We are playing the biggest self-esteem-destroying sport in the world. You don't get a hit when you do everything right. It's just a bad feeling. This is why I talk about changing your definition of success. I give you permission not to be perfect, not to get three hits today. That frees up their mind right there, but everything's great because they just talked to me. They hit three balls hard and go 0-for-4, and the next day they do nothing right and go 0-for-4. Then they'll be in a panic mode, 'I've got to get a hit.' You lose it that quickly, especially when playing pro baseball. In pro baseball, you're getting five at bats a day every day, whether you want them or not. Baseball doesn't care what you feel. You're getting your five at bats.

Gilbert: You cut him, even if he's the best player on the team. One of my students asked one of the top high school coaches ever in New Jersey, 'What's the biggest problem you ever had?' He said the biggest problem any coach will ever have is when your best player has the worst attitude. When your best player has the worst attitude, you have to treat him like a cancer. You have to cut him out and get rid of him, because sooner or later he's going to bring the team down.

The best thing is when your best player has the best attitude. Back in 1958, Pete Dawkins went to West Point. He won the Heisman Trophy in football, he was an All-American hockey player and the number one student academically. Like the saying, a rising tide raises all boats, he made everybody else on his hockey and football teams better. He made everybody else in his class a better student. He brought everybody up. A player with a bad attitude, no matter how good he is, will bring everybody down.

I grew up in Boston, and maybe the greatest athlete who ever lived was Bill Russell. Whenever there was an elimination game, whether it was a Game 7, the Olympics or the NCAA, Russell never lost. Bill Russell made everybody on the court better when he was on the court. That's what all of us want to do.

I wrote a story about two guys who were high school athletes together. One was the superstar of the team, and one was just an average player, but he was voted captain. The superstar of the team couldn't believe the other kid was voted captain, so he went to the coach and asked, 'How come they voted for him and not for me?' The coach said, 'You're the best athlete I've ever coached. You're the best player *on* the team, but he's the best player *for* the team. You want to be the best *player* in the state, but he wants to make us the best *team* in the state.' So, are you the best player *on* the team, or the best player *for* the team? Hopefully you're both, but if you had a team where everybody wanted to be the best player *for* the team, the team would be unstoppable.

If you have somebody who's that divisive, and his attitude is destructive, just get rid of him. If you're coaching him in high school or college, you're not the first coach who ever had this problem with him.

Dedman: I have made the mistake of trying to force the issue. If we're trying to force the issue with someone who is this cool, not ready or not wanting or he's too good for it, we need to dig deeper and have open conversations with them about what we notice in them. We need to give them our perspective and converse with them about why it is important.

My experience is that the people who are not ready or willing to buy in either have had some really negative experiences in trusting male role models or authority figures, or they just don't have a whole lot of confidence in themselves and are showing a lack of willingness to change. Change can be really scary and painful. 'Perception of pain', as Tony Robbins puts it, 'is often greater than the reality of pain.' Each player is going to have their own history that is going to dictate how they evaluate whether they want to do it or not, and at what level they want to do it. We've got to get to know our players, to understand where they've come from and who they are, and that takes time.

We introduce the mental game to them in one of our first meetings so we'll know within the first couple of weeks who's all in, who's half in, and who has no interest. You need to spend the majority of the time with the people who are on the fence. If a kid shows up in the cage early to hit, you don't have to ask them to go hit, they're going to show up. You need to explain to the others why it's important and why you value it. Ultimately, you have to build up a relationship of trust before they will listen to anything you're going to tell them.

Weintraub: It's a challenge. If the player doesn't experience failure, why should they listen? If they're hitting .500 standing on their head, I'm OK with that because they do have mental skills. What they're doing is working.

When I was younger, I was asking people the same thing. How do you get someone to be coachable when they're not? The answer I consistently got is that you don't, because they have to experience failure before they become open to the adjustment.

I'm an optimist, so I don't find that answer completely satisfactory. I certainly think that people like Brian Cain, Tony Robbins and hopefully myself, are able to motivate someone to change, to show them that they want to change and that they can have what Brian Cain calls 'inexpensive experience' instead of 'expensive experience'. You can have an inexpensive experience by learning from someone else's mistakes. If we can illustrate why they would want to change, and it's about motivation, then there is a chance. Ultimately, they have to really feel it at a deeper level. It's a good question and a tough battle. You may be the greatest coach in the world and still not be able to get anywhere until that athlete experiences a failure. I'm certainly in favor of trying different ways and staying enthusiastic and optimistic about it.

Rickertsen: I struggled with this when I first got into the field because in almost every team there is at least one who thinks he knows better. I used to get very wrapped up, pouring a lot of my energy into that individual. The fact of the matter is that if they're not ready to hear it, they're not going to hear what you have to say anyway.

Unfortunately, with guys like that, you have to let them come to it on their own time. Seeing the benefits it has on their teammates and the success that they're having with those skills can expedite the process. With that particular individual, it's something they have to come to on their own time. You can teach them the skill, but unless they're willing to practice it, they're not going to get much out of it anyway. I've had to be careful with myself, take a step back from those players, and teach them the skills so they have them when they're ready to use them. I find they often come around pretty quickly when the people around them are seeing success with those skills.

Janssen: It's not always possible, but you try to screen out that guy in the first place who doesn't have that buy-in, that attitude or commitment. Your best approach if you have the opportunity to be selective is to screen those people out, understanding that this person may not be a good fit with your philosophy, your core values and the culture you're trying to create. The best time to fire someone is before you hire them or bring them on your team.

If you've already got such people, invest the time to talk with them one-on-one, to convince them that these intangible aspects are going to be really important for their success. A lot of times these people are influential and there are people who follow what they do, so they have that impact on others. Even though they may not want to do it for themselves, you can talk to them about how it's going to have a ripple effect on other people as well. If a guy is pretty stubborn, as a coach, you can get them to do things at what I call compliant level. 'You may not be fully bought in 100% and leading the way, but we at least need you at this minimally acceptable level so you don't become a distraction or a bad example for the rest of the guys.'

If a person continues to be resistant and not on board, you let the person know, 'We need you at least at this level, and if you're not going to be at this level, then I can't give you the playing time that you want or the status you want to have in terms of captain role or anything like that.' If it becomes too much of a distraction or an issue, at some point you may have to decide that this is not a good fit. 'There may be another program philosophy that fits with you, but here's where we're trying to go, here's why we'd love to have you involved, but if you can't be at least at this minimal level, then this may not be a good situation for either of us.'

Brubaker: Athletes in baseball in particular, which has long season, talk about it being a marathon and not a sprint. Baseball has a long season, and a lot of athletes start to turn a blind eye to their coaches. The athletes are not hearing the coach's voice because it's the same person telling them the same thing over and over and over again. The power of bringing in an outside voice is hugely important.

I see this a lot with my kids, as a parent. I tell my daughter to make her bed every day for six years, and every day it's a challenge to get her to do it. She goes to horseback riding camp. Her horseback riding instructor explains to the campers, who are eight-year-old kids at the time, how you do everything. 'If you want to become a better rider, you need to start paying attention to detail in the rest of your life. I want you to go home and start making your bed every morning.' I never had to tell her from that day forward to make her bed. It's the power of an outside voice.

Whether it is a mental conditioning coach, a sports psychologist or a performance consultant like myself, have someone come in. That can accomplish that buy-in for a couple of those negative close-minded guys or the ones who think they are a little too cool for this. You can show them in a different way, through a new, fresh voice in the locker room or the team room. Eventually, they come around, especially when the one thing athletes want is results. You don't care about what drill you're doing if you know it works. You don't care about what play you're running on the field if you know it's going to work. If a coach can quantify how imagery improves an athlete's performance, eventually that negative close-minded guy, who's probably sitting on the end of the bench and isn't playing anyway, is going to come around because he sees it working for other people. Otherwise, he's just not meant for the program.

Afremow: First and foremost, the coach needs to buy in to mental training. If the coach is a big believer in the importance of the mindset in baseball, players will usually follow suit. However, if a player demonstrates a negative attitude to mental training, the coach must speak privately with the player to share his observations and get to the bottom of what's going on for that player. Perhaps the player has a misconception about mental training, or maybe a negative experience in the past, and that needs to be resolved. If several players appear not to be buying into mental training, it's important that the coach re-evaluate whether the team's mental training program should be revamped. Maybe it isn't a very good one. If you have a good mental training program in place, most if not all players will really enjoy it.

Dixon: We call those people 'Negative Norms.' They are victims and everyone is against them. It's tough, because they are a distraction, trying to pull people down with them and get people on their side. When they feel out of the loop, when they see others having success, they're either going to continue to rebel or give in and join. You can't waste your energy.

Some guys just don't believe in the mental game and that's OK, because we're all wired differently. There's going to come a point in their lives where they're going to say, 'OK, I've maxed out my physical ability, what next?' That's when they're going to get slapped in the face with the mental game. You could tell someone to stop smoking, but they're not going to stop smoking until they want to stop smoking. You preach the mental game and you physically and mentally partake in the mental game and you have passion for it, and those people, whether they say it or not, they're paying attention.

When they decide to do it, that's when you grab them. Or when they have failure, you grab them. Failure is the best learning moment. When things are going good, you can't tell a guy to change, because they're going good. It's when they're failing, having repeated failure, when they're on an 18-game hitless streak, that's when you say, 'Hey man, let's try this.' They're just more apt to it because they're in a vulnerable state. As a coach, when your team is failing, those are the best learning opportunities.

Goldberg: If you have an athlete who is closed-minded and thinks they have all the answers, they're a danger to themselves. If you're not open to learning, you're seriously handicapping yourself. All coaches can do is show them what they're doing wrong, show them a better way, show them that if they work on the mental game, they would improve greatly. You can lead a horse to water, you can extol the virtues of drinking water and why it's good for you, but wringing the horse's neck will not make it thirsty. There are certain athletes you're not going to get to.

Maher: That's a tough situation. Most coaches are not going to try to push anything on the player. At best, they may try to get another player to 'talk the talk' to him, but if not, they're just going to have to let it go, try not to get into a situation where they're pushing something down the player's throat. The best thing would be for that player to be desperate enough that he'd say he's got to adjust and be willing to trust. I have found, over the years, that this kind of player is just not willing to trust in other people, a coach or whoever it might be.

Bell: This is actually the biggest challenge. The coach's philosophy, what coaches expect, has a big impact. It comes down to leadership and how that leadership communicates the message. The coach can coach it up, but the leaders really impact that message and make it go. When someone is going to be a drain or an 'energy vampire', carrying around that mental baggage, they could snap out of it with those visual cues to remind. They could recognize themselves.

Sometimes, it's a heart-to-heart with the coaches. If somebody isn't going to get the process across, they're bringing other people down and not being a good leader or teammate. Being a good teammate is what it's all about. Nobody cares what your average is, they really don't, and nobody cares how you do it. They care about winning the ball game and being a good teammate. When did we learn that stuff? When did we really learn it? People get recognized individually, but it all comes down to winning the game and being a good teammate. That's what translates into real life more than any kind of talent.

Tully: There's no 'one size fits all' mental skill. I actually had this issue with one of my players, but I realized I wasn't going to force anything on that athlete. It just doesn't do any good. My way isn't going to help you, only your way is going to help you.

I once read a great story about a guy who had just been hired as a major league batting coach. His philosophy was, 'I am not going to approach anyone about hitting. What I am going to do is stand behind the batting cage every single day, and help everyone who asks me for help.' If a player doesn't think they need help, either they're going to be like Manny Ramirez and hit the heck out of the ball, or they're not going to hit the ball. If they hit the ball, they don't need what you have to say. If they don't hit the ball and they're too dumb to listen to you, you don't have any control over that. Maybe that player belongs on the bench.

There are affirmations, anchoring, visualization and breathing. There's no one size fits all, so I suggest these topics to my players, and it's funny how different ones adopt different methods, which is great. Remember, it has to work for them, that's the most important thing. It has to work for them.

Margolies: Good coaches are pretty good about getting that guy under control through external motivators. They've got the carrot, playing time, and they've got the stick, I'm going to bench you, to deal with that player's attitude. A lot of it comes down to how the coach works with the other players on a team. We all know that one person on the team who says that this is a bunch of garbage, I don't want to do this. If everybody else is on board, they're going to be more on board.

I've worked with teams where there's been that one guy. On a hockey team of 16-20 year olds with 20 guys, 19 are, on a scale of 1 to 10, 8-10 on buying into mental training and one guy who doesn't want to have anything to do with it. By the end of it, they took care of him. They took him aside and said, 'Look, you're not going to spoil this for us.' They applied pressure to him. Between the coaches and the players, it takes care of itself.

Dehmer: You kind of wear on them. You just keep giving them that information. From our end of things, it's been a real positive thing, because our best players have bought in, and they play well with it. If your best guys are doing it, it sells itself. There is always that guy who is very reluctant, 'No, it's not for me.' I call that guy on straddling the line. Some days he's in, some days he's not, he's doing the hokey-pokey on us, one foot in, one foot out. You have to keep working with them. That's where one-on-one works, telling that kid you really want him to try it. That connection where you show him you care can go a long way. If you put it out in a general team meeting, some kids are going to just do it and some aren't. That's where you have to go the extra mile, put your arm around that kid and say, 'Hey, I want you to give this a shot. I know this can be a difference-maker for you.' You keep working on them.

Toole: In college, we had a couple of those Joe Cool guys who thought the mental game was something you did if you had something wrong with you. When they think of sports psychology, the mental game or mental skills, a lot of people think that you have to have something wrong with you to work on that. That's not the case at all. Kids who don't buy into it or take the time to get into it are actually hurting themselves. If you want to become a college athlete or a professional athlete, the proof is in the pudding. You look at successful guys like Evan Longoria or Matt Carpenter, playing in the World Series, playing at the top of the world of sports. If those guys are using it, there's no reason why a high school kid or a college kid can't use it.

The biggest thing I would do to try to help a kid understand it is to use examples. There's a good video of Evan Longoria talking about routines. I've read a lot of stuff with Matt Carpenter. Everyone watches Sports Center and sees the great players. If you can use them as an example to a kid, you'll be able to get through to them. I'm trying as a player to become an example for other kids too. Just because you're talking to someone about sports psychology, about the mental game, doesn't mean there's anything wrong. It just means you want to be the best you can be.

Question Review

Every team has 'that guy', the negative, closed-minded guy that is too cool to invest time into improving his mental game. How does a coach get that player to buy in to the system he is trying to implement?

Hanson: The biggest thing is safety, and that has to do with trust. What you give energy to expands and grows. This negative, closed-minded person is interference. Remember the equation Performance = Potential - Interference.

Jaeger: Coaches are the captains of the ship. You don't want to force somebody to do it. A team is about everybody getting on the same page and pulling a rope together. Recruit players who are into everything you're going to teach, or you work with the player to understand how this can really help them.

Gordon: You can't drive anyone else's bus. You've got to make sure that you're empowering them to drive their own bus. You can encourage them, uplift them and inspire them.

Cain: Why do people not buy in? The reason they don't buy in is that they don't understand, they're not educated enough on why they should buy in, or they don't see the pleasure and success that will come if they do buy in.

Springer: The perfectionist has a hard time grasping it. You can't be a perfectionist and play baseball—it will kill you. We are playing the biggest self-esteem-destroying sport in the world.

Gilbert: You cut him, even if he's the best player on the team. The biggest problem any coach will ever have is when your best player has the worst attitude. You have to treat him like a cancer because sooner or later he's going to bring the team down.

Dedman: We need to dig deeper and have open conversations with them about what we notice in them. We need to give them our perspective and converse with them about why it is important. They just don't have a whole lot of confidence in themselves and are showing a lack of willingness to change.

Weintraub: I certainly think that people like Brian Cain, Tony Robbins and hopefully myself, are able to motivate someone to change, to show them that they want to change and that they can have what Brian Cain calls 'inexpensive experience' instead of 'expensive experience'. I'm certainly in favor of trying different ways and staying enthusiastic and optimistic about it.

Rickertsen: Almost every team has at least one who thinks he knows better. I used to get very wrapped up, pouring a lot of my energy into that individual. If they're not ready to hear it, they're not going to hear what you have to say anyway. You have to let them come to it on their own time.

Janssen: It's not always possible, but you try to screen out that guy in the first place who doesn't have that buy-in, that attitude or commitment. The best time to fire someone is before you hire them or bring them on your team. Invest the time to talk with them one-on-one, to convince them that these intangible aspects are going to be really important for their success.

Brubaker: The athletes are not hearing the coach's voice because it's the same person telling them the same thing over and over and over again. The power of bringing in an outside voice is hugely important. That can accomplish that buy-in for a couple of those negative close-minded guys or the ones who think they are a little too cool for this.

Afremow: First and foremost, the coach needs to buy in to mental training. If the coach is a big believer in the importance of the mindset in baseball, players will usually follow suit.

Dixon: They are victims and everyone is against them. You can't waste your energy. Some guys just don't believe in the mental game and that's OK, because we're all wired differently. Failure is the best learning moment. When things are going good, you can't tell a guy to change.

Goldberg: If you're not open to learning, you're seriously handicapping yourself. There are certain athletes you're not going to get to.

Maher: That's a tough situation. Most coaches are not going to try to push anything on the player. This kind of player is just not willing to trust in other people, a coach or whoever it might be.

Bell: The coach's philosophy, what coaches expect, has a big impact. It comes down to leadership and how that leadership communicates message.

Tully: There's no 'one size fits all' mental skill. My way isn't going to help you, only your way is going to help you. I suggest these topics to my players, and it's funny how different ones adopt different methods, which is great.

Margolies: Good coaches are pretty good about getting that guy under control through external motivators. If everybody else is on board, they're going to be more on board. Between the coaches and the players, it takes care of itself.

Dehmer: If your best guys are doing it, it sells itself. There is always that guy who is very reluctant, 'No, it's not for me.' I call that guy on straddling the line. You have to keep working with them.

Toole: The biggest thing I would do to try to help a kid understand it is to use examples. Just because you're talking to someone about sports psychology, about the mental game, doesn't mean there's anything wrong. It just means you want to be the best you can be.

Consistent High Performance

What are the most important aspects to consistently performing at a high level?

Cain: With the athletes I've worked with, first is to focus only on what you can control and let go of what you can't. Second is the process and what you need to do to get where you want to go. When I say process, think of a staircase: what are the steps you have to take to get you where you want to go? If you want to win the game, what do you need to do to win this play?

Control what you can control. Focus on the process and the steps you have to take to win this pitch. Be a great teammate. Whether you're struggling or you're going really good, you're going to be there for your brothers, and you're going to be a great teammate.

And the fourth one, I think, is toughness: the ability to withstand adversity and keep moving forward. There's always going to be adversity, and you've always got to keep moving towards your goal.

Gordon: It starts with knowing what you want, then working harder than everyone else. Hard work has been and always will be the key to success. Develop your strengths and make sure to build upon your strengths. You may have weaknesses, but make sure you build upon and really focus on your strengths. That is key. It's about the deliberate practice, getting better every day. See yourself as a craftsman in your sport, with the desire to master your craft. It's that mentality of mental toughness, positivity, overcoming adversity, and facing challenges head-on, being mentally tough, being positive, and being faithful through all of that.

Loving what you do is so important. If you don't love it, you're not going to work hard to be great at it. That's a big part as well. If you get burned out, then you've got to recharge and refocus. Ask yourself, 'Do I really want this?' When you fail, it's an opportunity to find out if you really want it, and then you come back stronger. We want to be the best, but the goal should be to be the best that we can be and see where it takes us.

Maher: We use an acronym: MAC. **M**indful is being able to stay in the moment, to respect the moment because that's all you have. **A**cceptance is accepting the experience and the situation in the game, not judging yourself at that time and in that moment. A pitcher may be on the mound with two outs and no men on base, and then a minute later, he's got two outs with runners on second and third. That's the situation. He's got to accept that. If he starts judging himself, 'I didn't get out of the inning. I could have had a quick inning,' he's in trouble. **C** is for commitment – committing to what you're doing. If I think a routine is very, very important, do I commit to that? If I think the next pitch is very, very important, do I commit to that? So we try to emphasize the M.A.C., the three things that give a player a better chance than not of making progress if they are willing to buy into it.

Afremow: The key is to be confident in yourself. You have to respect the opponent and what they can do, but you have to respect your own abilities even more. Then, focus—you need to live in the moment. That's when we're at our full power, so be here, all here, right now. Third is composure. Use your emotions to your advantage, rather than your emotions using you. A little anxiety is OK, a little frustration is OK, getting a little bit down is OK when things aren't working well, but you've got to use that as positive fuel to perform your best.

Janssen: The big three that we focus on in our Leadership Academies are:

Commitment: you've got to commit to putting in the work. Success doesn't just come, you've got to invest the time long-term. People talk about the 10,000 hour rule, or the ten year rule of putting in at least 3½ quality hours, 6 days a week, 50 weeks out of the year to get really good. If you want to excel at the highest levels of sport, that commitment has got to be there.

Confidence: you're going to go up against some pretty good people during that time, and you have to have that belief that you can get the job done. A lot of that confidence is going to come from the quality work and commitment that you've made, but you've got to be able to go to battle mentally with those opponents, knowing that you've got at least as much, if not more, of what it takes to handle that situation.

Composure: the ability to manage your emotions, to overcome the adversity that's going to be inevitable throughout the course of a game or season, and handle that pressure situation as well.

Commitment, confidence and composure are three of the most important mental skills and ones that we stress to our players and coaches.

Brubaker: Number one is coaching. If you look at great athletes in every sport: Roger Federer, Tiger Woods, the elite baseball players in today's game doing it naturally. What do they have in common? They all have a coach even when they don't need a coach. Michael Jordan, when he was basically running the team, didn't need a coach. He's like a coach on the court, but he wanted a coach, because a coach sees blind spots that you don't see. You can't see the picture inside the frame. They see the same situation through a completely different set of eyes, and they can show you what you need to do to get to the next level that you may not be able to see.

At the same time, we need accountability. Accountability is the highest form of love. Teammates hold each other accountable. I want to see you reach your greatest potential. If that means having a difficult conversation with you, telling you what you don't want to hear, maybe calling you out on something because I know you're better than that, they're going to do that. Without accountability, you're not going to consistently perform at a high level.

The third piece of the puzzle is focus, or refocus. In the age of distraction that we're in, we get side-tracked from the task we're on. Let's say we're doing an interview and the phone rings. You stop to pick up the call and you come back to the interview. You might be back physically, but mentally, it takes about 15 to 20 minutes to really get back into that zone. Think about how many times you're distracted over the course of a day or the course of the game, and the actual cost attached to that. We need to be better at refocusing. We're going to be distracted, that's inevitable. You might hear a little bit of what that heckler in the stands says, as much as you try and block it out. There might be something going on in the dugout that catches your eye when you're on the field. We need to get good at refocusing.

Weintraub: Harvey would say there are three levels of mental toughness. Mental toughness is all about doing your best now. It's about consistency. Everybody makes mistakes, but the mentally tough ones don't allow that negative snowball effect. You've got to want it. You've got to care. You have to be motivated. You've got to know what to do. You've got to do what you know.

Rickertsen: This relates to the idea of the 'growth minded' person, the mindset you adopt towards your performance and how you approach challenges. How do you view effort? How do you view other people's success? How do you view feedback? How are you able to learn from and use everything that you've done and seen in the past? It is the mindset that I'm going to choose to perceive everything that happens to me in a way that's productive, failure or success, whether somebody else is doing it or I'm doing it. If it's a challenge, and maybe I wasn't successful in the past, what can I take from that in order to be successful in the future? What can I take from the feedback I'm getting and apply that?

Instead of trying to avoid failure and avoid challenging situations because you're not sure you can be successful, it's this idea that you're going to approach this and not care if you fail or not. Even if you fail, that's feedback. you can adjust and make improvements. This mindset can be adopted by athletes who don't feel like they have it just yet. It's a little bit of an abstract concept, but it shows up on a daily basis, an attitude. How do you approach practice, the weight room, feedback from teammates or coaches, or your slump? How are you using the feedback you're getting? I would have to go with growth-minded for sure. How growth-minded are you? A close second would be how process-oriented you are. Are you able to separate what you need to be paying attention to from what you don't need?

Springer: It's definitely confidence. Competing with confidence is everything. It is changing what you think success is in this game. 90% of a quality at-bat is how you feel when you walk up to the plate. Do I know I can hit or am I hoping to hit? There's a huge difference in that.

Make it about the team. I know that when you make it about the team, you're going to have better success. If your job is to get the guy over, get him over, get a bunt down, play good defense.

The number one thing is to get rid of your batting average. The batting average is the biggest trap in the game. I do everything right and go 0-for-4. Why is that the barometer for everyone's success? It's a trap. It's like a mouse in an exercise wheel. Coaches need to know this so they can get rid of it in their program. I stole it from Clint Hurdle. I would be 0-for-4 but I'd see 3 Q's up by my name. Trust me, I'm in the lineup the next day, because he knows I'm having good at bats.

Just think if there was a hard hit contact or QAB award at the end of the year in the big leagues. We have the technology to figure it out. I would rather win a hard hit contact batting title than a batting title based on batting average.

Goldberg: Mentally, one thing that separates the best from everyone else is how they handle failure and setbacks. No one likes to fail. I've never met an elite athlete who likes failing, but the really successful athletes have learned that, when they mess up, it's an opportunity to find out what they did that didn't work and what they need to do differently next time. They get curious when they mess up rather than angry or furious at themselves. A lot of athletes get frustrated when they mess up, and as a result, they stop taking risks. The really successful athletes won't stop taking risks. They're not afraid to fail, because they understand that failure is an important part of going from beginner to expert.

The other is your work ethic. A lot of people think that the really great athletes have advantages over everyone else. My feeling is they want it more. They're willing to do whatever it takes. They're willing to do the extra, the uncomfortable, the sweat, and the stuff that hurts. They're more willing to do that than most other people.

Bell: That's all I talk about in *The Hinge: The Importance of Mental Toughness*, is that confidence is the most important mental skill. Then it's focus and refocus. How do we let go of mistakes? How do we let go when things are going bad and we didn't come through in that situation? How do we let that stuff go? It's the second most difficult mental skill, because we've worked so many hours at what we're doing. It's a good thing to expect success, but it's not always going to happen. Can we let go of that stuff, can we let it go and move on? How do we do it? It's confidence, focus and then refocus.

Tully: Consistently performing at a high level has to do with consistent approach. You can't control where the ball goes once you hit it. You can hit it hard, but it might go right to the second baseman. We're going to prepare consistently. I've spent about 20 years in major league clubhouses, and I guarantee that's what players talked about the most. Sports writers hated it because it sounded like a cliché. Maybe it is, but it's also true. They can't control what happens.

We call it EAR at my school. You can't control where the ball goes, but you can control three things: your Effort, your Attitude and your Response to mistakes. Those are huge because they're controllables. You can't control results, but you can control your effort, your attitude (or approach), and your response to mistakes.

My book, *The Improvement Factor: How Winners Turn Practice Into Success*, has a great story about Ted Williams. A teammate of his strikes out and he comes back to the bench. Williams says to the guy, 'When you swung and missed that ball, did the ball go over your bat or under it?' The teammate says, 'Who cares? I missed it and I'm out.' Williams says, 'Who cares? That's the only thing that matters. Knowing how you failed is the first step in making good.' Here you have two major league ballplayers. For one of them, the game is over when he strikes out, but for Ted Williams, the game has just begun when he strikes out. You have the choice of how you're going to respond to failure.

Dedman: From an individual standpoint, players have to be engaged, meaning that you trust the people teaching you, the system and the process. That's certainly the most difficult when you have new athletes in your program, which is going to be every year. You're going to have eight to ten new athletes each year. They need to be engaged.

They need to be enthusiastic. Someone said that nothing great was ever accomplished without enthusiasm, and I've experienced that to be true. You've got to be a giver. Brian Cain talks about being an energy-giver and not a taker. Be a fountain, not a drain.

If you're engaged, that encompasses a lot of things, focus, belief, trust and confidence.

Dehmer: Everybody's got to be all in. The team mindset and the 'we over me' mentality, knowing that you're fighting for something bigger than yourself, has to be the foundation of any good, solid program.

Second is a good, solid practice plan, game-like practices that are pressure-packed and more than just teaching fundamentals. Going through the skills and drills and the repetition of things can become mundane when you're in a high school setting, let alone when you're in a college or professional season that is even longer with more games. It can become very monotonous, so we want to try to keep it very game-like, keep the intensity up, knowing that kids are always being measured and evaluated, even at practice. As coaches, we were able to measure practice just like we were able to measure it at a game, and we were always giving that feedback to the players. We were holding them accountable because we wanted to 'make practice almost tougher than the game.

Third is having a good, solid foundation of mental toughness, knowing how to slow the game down, making sure that it doesn't get out of hand for you, because we know that one big inning can be the difference in a game. Typically the team that scored the most runs in one particular inning wins the ballgame.

Toole: Most important would be preparation: in the weight room, working hard, getting your swings in the cage, getting your ground ball work. That's where you start to build confidence through your routines. If I can go out and take a few ground balls every day throughout the course of the whole season, before the season is done I'm going to take a lot more ground balls than I expected, because it adds up. Growing up I was told, 'Do a little a lot, not a lot a little.' If I go out every day and take 15 or 20 ground balls, that's going to add up over the course of time, instead of going out one time and taking 50 ground balls. The more often you do something, the better it's going to help. Preparation is definitely one of the biggest things.

Focus is definitely hard. Baseball games are three hours long. You've got a pitch, and then you can kind of zone out, then you've got a pitch, then you can kind of zone out, so it's easy for people's minds to wander and it's hard to be locked in pitch by pitch for three hours. It all comes down to believing in yourself. In today's world, people tell you that you're not strong enough, not fast enough, you don't throw hard enough, you don't hit far enough, things like that. If you believe you can do something, if you put in the time and effort and have good routines, anything can happen. I'm definitely an example of that.

Question Review

What are the most important aspects to consistently performing at a high level?

Cain: Focus on what you can control and let go of what you can't. Focus on the process of doing what you need to do to get to where you want to go. Be a great teammate. Toughness to keep moving forward.

Gordon: It starts with knowing what you want, then working harder than everyone else. Hard work has been and always will be the key to success. Loving what you do is so important because if you don't love it, you're not going to work hard to be great at it.

Maher: MAC – Mindful is being able to stay in the moment. Acceptance of the experience and the moment without judging yourself. Commitment to what you are doing.

Afremow: The key is to be confident in yourself. You need to focus and live in the moment. Third is the composure to use your emotions to your advantage, rather than your emotions using you.

Janssen: Commitment to putting in the work. Confidence and the belief that you can get the job done. Composure to manage your emotions and overcome adversity.

Brubaker: To go to the next level, you need a coach, accountability and the ability to focus in today's age of digital distraction.

Weintraub: You've got to want it. You've got to care. You have to be motivated. You've got to know what to do. You've got to do what you know.

Rickertsen: It comes down to how growth-minded and process-oriented you are.

Springer: Competing with confidence. Make it about the team. Get rid of the batting average.

Goldberg: One thing that separates the best from everyone else is how they handle failure and setbacks. The really successful athletes won't stop taking risks. My feeling is they want it more. They're willing to do whatever it takes. They're willing to do the extra, the uncomfortable, the sweat, and the stuff that hurts. They're more willing to do that than most other people.

Bell: It's confidence, focus and then refocus.

Tully: Consistently performing at a high level has to do with consistent approach. Control the E.A.R.: Your Effort, Attitude and Response.

Dedman: Players must be engaged and trusting in the system and the process. They also need to be enthusiastic. If you're engaged and enthusiastic, that encompasses a lot of things: focus, belief, trust and confidence.

Dehmer: Everybody must be all in with the 'we over me' mentality. A solid pressure-packed practice plan measures practice similar to how it is in a game. A solid foundation of mental toughness and knowing how to slow the game down is also necessary.

Toole: Preparation, focus and believing in yourself.

Power of Imagery & Mental At Bats

Can a player who is injured expedite the rehab process with imagery? Can a player who is not starting mentally prepare for when their time comes?

Dixon: No doubt about it, visualization is a powerful, powerful tool. They've actually done studies with someone who is laid up in a hospital bed. Doing visualization and imagery actually stimulates the same brain areas as when they're physically doing it. Obviously you're going to get bigger, faster, and stronger from actually doing it, but you're triggering the same brain paths and the same muscles by visualizing it as when you're actually doing it physically.

Being a designated hitter in baseball is one of the hardest things you could ever do. You're out of the game, there are a ton of distractions, and all of a sudden, you're getting called off the bench to hit in the most pressure situation. If you're visualizing, locked in on that pitcher, 'OK, if I get on with the bases loaded or I get on with runners at second and third with less than two outs, here's how they're going to try to pitch to me, and here's what I'm going to do.' You go over scenario after scenario, then when you get in the box it's been there, done that. You just go and you trust. If you're not prepared, then you don't have a chance.

Visualization is fantastic. When I started visualizing, I found myself giving up home runs. It was negative. Like anything else, you've got to work at it. I don't go out there and throw a great breaking ball right from the get-go, it's a process. You get a little bit better each time. That's why visualization and the mental game is not a sometime thing, it's an every day thing. The more you work on it, the better you get, the more detailed it gets, and the more success you have.

Cain: Mental imagery is one of the most underused and most powerful training techniques. It is used by fighter pilots, the military, Olympic athletes and mixed martial arts fighters all the time. Many times as baseball players, since we play every day, we don't utilize those strategies to give us the best chance for success. What you see with mental at bats are players who are not in the lineup grabbing a bat, grabbing their batting gloves, going down to the end of the dugout and actually going through their routine. They look at the pitcher and watch the pitcher throw. They go through their stance, get their foot down, and then they close their eyes and visualize the pitch they just saw, the arm action of the guy who just threw the pitch, and see themselves hitting a missile somewhere in the yard. They're going to do that again for the next pitch and the next.

Let's say you're the starting shortstop, and I'm the backup shortstop. You get four at bats in a game and you see a total of 15 pitches. I've seen myself hit 15 missiles all over the yard while I've been taking a mental at-bat in the dugout. So when I get the chance to pinch hit, or I get the start or come in off the bench because you got hurt, I'm that much more prepared to come in and play.

The brain cannot tell the difference between what you visualize and what you physically experience. This is why imagery is such a powerful tool. If you have ever woken up from a dream of falling out of an airplane and you're about to hit the ground, you jump up from your bed, your heart's racing and you're in panic mode. You look around you and go, 'I was just having a dream' and then you go back to sleep. The reason you wake up and the reason there's a horror movie industry is that the brain does not tell the difference between what's real and what's imaginary. It's processed in the same psycho-neuromuscular pathways. Your body has a physiological response to psychological stimulus.

I'll try to have athletes recovering from surgery watch daily video of their best performances. It might be just two minutes of video a day. Visualize pitching that way for 2-5 minutes so they continue to hard-wire the neurological pathways from the brain into the body to still be able to execute that skill. After they visualize themselves pitching, the next thing is to visualize the next 200 feet, another 'Sign of Success'. Visualize the next 200 feet, the next step of the rehab. If my rehab is to be able to straighten my arm, then I'm going to visualize myself moving from 45 degrees to 90 degrees so I'm building those pathways to get there. I not only visualize winning the national championship, I visualize where I'm at, in that moment, and whatever the next 200 feet of my rehab or my performance is.

Rickertsen: Mental imagery can be very challenging to learn to do correctly and effectively, but it is one of the most powerful skills that we teach. Imagery, for healing specifically, coupled with a breathing technique, has been found to increase the rate of healing by up to 30% for a broken bone, a torn ligament, or something like that. The actual physical healing can increase by up to 30%, and I don't know any athletes who don't want that.

There are two ways to use imagery for healing. You can do what we call metaphorical. For example, you picture little construction guys in there putting everything back together. You can do literal imagery, picturing the bone fusing itself back together. Some people find one more effective than the other. Some also find one less painful than the other. If you're able, pick out which one works better for you, and couple that with a specific breathing technique. That's specifically for healing, but also use imagery as a way of keeping your mind and body sharp for when you return to your sport. The mind-body connection is so strong, and that's one of the reasons I love imagery. You can do a skill physically, or you can do a skill with very vivid imagery, and the same parts of your brain are going to be highlighted. It's like your brain can't tell the difference between performing it physically or imagining it.

The example I always use is waking up after a bad dream. You're sweating and you're uncomfortable, but you were lying in your bed and your brain couldn't decipher whether that was real or fake. You're having a physical reaction to the dream imagery. In the same way, when you picture yourself going through the hitting motion or the throwing motion, picturing that very vividly in your mind, your muscles are actually responding in the same way.

Granted, it is in a very small scale compared to doing it physically, but you can still keep that motion going even though you're not physically doing it. For some training exercises, where they're not able to train as many times as they want, using imagery is one way to keep their muscles and brain in tune to that very specific skill.

Afremow: The mental game is really important and the rehab process is no different than any other physical challenge. The key is for a player to think of rehab as their new sport until they get their game back, and they will get their game back. Some players might try to rush back and re-injure themselves, while others might just go through the motions and take that much longer to heal. It's important to stay patient and persistent. During recovery from an injury, it's crucial to stay sharp by mentally practicing one's game. Visualization is crucial. You've got to see and feel in your mind's eye running through the same practice drills. When you're watching your teammates practice, go through the same routines in your own head. During games, when you're watching your teammates play, see and feel yourself out there on the field making good plays. That will help you stay sharp, and when you return to the field, you'll be ready to go.

Brubaker: Imagery can do wonders medically to help you recover faster. I've seen it in my life. I've seen it with cancer patients. I've seen athletes use imagery to get a better result. There has been tons of research on that, I can't overstate that enough. It's hugely important.

Also, even if you're not rehabilitating, if you're the backup, you're not getting a lot of time at practice or a lot of reps. You might not be on the field anywhere near as much as you want, but you can take those mental reps.

I believe every result that we have in life happens twice. First, it happens in your mind. Then, you go there physically. You're accelerating your learning curve. You're actually accelerating your results if you consciously go there in your mind as often as possible. Whether it is rehabilitating a knee injury or trying to get more playing time, it goes back to controllables. You can control your attitude, your effort, and your level of commitment.

There are plenty of athletes who come back way ahead of schedule. Think of Adrian Peterson with the Minnesota Vikings and how fast he came back from his total knee reconstruction. He came back inside of a year, which is unheard of. You can think of others who were never the same after the injury. If you went back and looked at some of the minute details of his day versus their day in the rehabilitation process, he's not only doing the little things, but also his mindset. He put it in his mind that he was going to be back by a certain date, and he was going to be back at 100%. We need to put into our mind what we want and get out the things we don't want. A lot of that is what you tell yourself.

Question Review

Can a player who is injured expedite the rehab process with imagery? Can a player who is not starting mentally prepare for when their time comes?

Dixon: Visualization is a powerful, powerful tool. Doing visualization and imagery actually stimulates the same brain areas as when they're physically doing it.

Cain: Mental imagery is one of the most underused and most powerful training techniques. The brain cannot tell the difference between what you visualize and what you physically experience.

Rickertsen: Mental imagery can be very challenging to learn to do correctly and effectively, but it is one of the most powerful skills that we teach. Imagery, for healing specifically, coupled with a breathing technique, has been found to increase the rate of healing by up to 30% for broken bones and torn ligaments.

Afremow: It's important to stay patient and persistent during recovery from an injury. Visualization is crucial. You've got to see and feel in your mind's eye running through the same practice drills.

Brubaker: Imagery is hugely important. I believe every result that we have in life happens twice. First, it happens in your mind. Then, you go there physically. You're accelerating your learning curve. You're actually accelerating your results if you consciously go there in your mind as often as possible.

Maximize Your Potential Under Pressure

So many players underperform because they're afraid of failing. How do you effectively get them to perform to the best of their ability, meeting their full potential, with the potential of failure still lingering?

Afremow: One important reminder is that baseball is what you do, it's not who you are. You are more than just an athlete. Embrace all the roles you play in your life to feel good about yourself. Keep in mind that you really do have everything to gain and nothing to lose in sports, so go for the glory. When you do fail, learn from it, and then let it go. Move on with confidence. Move forward.

The other side of the coin is fear of success. A lot of athletes are concerned subconsciously, 'If I play really, really well, there are going to be constant demands placed on me to keep this going. Can I live up to that?' That eventually leads to fear of failure, but in the meantime, it's 'Can I live up to the demands?' and 'Do I want to live up to the demands to be that guy?' You have to give yourself permission to fail and learn from it, to fail forward, but also to be successful, that you can handle whatever comes your way. Why not you? Why not be the best you can be?

Jaeger: If it's something in the future, you are far removed from your process. FEAR is Future Events Already Realized. If someone's dealing with failure, the first thing I'm going to have them do is say, 'Well, what does failure mean?' They're going to say, 'What does the fear of failure mean?' Of course, it's always going to come back to the future: if this happens, if that happens, what if this, what if that. It just comes down to language. Your new intention has to be to default to your process. What is your process? See the ball well, hit it hard. OK, great, that's your mantra. See the ball well and hit it hard.

I'm not saying that this old programming of fear-based thoughts isn't going to creep in. When it does is where meditation is a great practice. They work on stuff coming into their minds and staying neutral. If you are dealing with fear of failure, you remind them of good strategy: to stay in the present, trust and commit to your process. They may still have some stuff come into their mind. It comes down to whether they have the awareness to start defaulting or coming back to their process. That's a practice within another practice. It all goes hand in hand.

If someone is dealing with fear of failure, and it has some pretty good momentum, guess what's the first thing I'm going to have them do? I'm going to say, 'Look, maybe we're not going to deal with your fear of failure in the batter's box while sitting on a cushion right now, but sitting on a cushion for 15, 20, maybe 40 minutes, which to me is like 20 hours of great therapy. You just spent time practicing, whether it's about your fears, about failure or about something unrelated, you're practicing stuff coming into your mind and allowing it to be, not blocking it out or pushing it away, which gives it more energy. You're practicing being neutral to it, redirecting your attention back to the present moment, back to your process.

This is where the rubber hits the road for mental game stuff. It is changing the programming, learning how to redirect your attention from old programming that has come in because maybe you're on a 1-for-20 and you're starting to have a lot of negative thoughts. Whatever it is, it's all going to come back to you. Can you be neutral to this old programming and come back, redirect your attention to where you want it to be, which is your process? To get to the root, to really change the program on a deep level, is where I believe this daily practice becomes so important.

Brubaker: They need to have the proper perspective. At the end of the day, baseball is a game. Games are supposed to be fun. Sure, you get a scholarship for it and if you get to play professionally, it is your livelihood, but it's a game.

If you're in a foxhole and you let somebody down, that could cost you and everybody around you lives at war. Keep the perspective that there are people going through far tougher things than what you are going through right now. People are going through chemotherapy, people are in a war zone.

We are fighting for our freedom to go play a game. Maybe you can let go of some of that self-imposed pressure. You know you're playing a game, and in some ways the beauty of baseball is that you're supposed to fail more that you succeed. Then you know it is pretty special when you do succeed. You're hitting a round ball with a round bat. It's probably the hardest physical activity, athletically speaking, there is.

Celebrate your success and use your failure as feedback. Success leaves clues. You cannot personalize failure. It's an event, not a human being. You are not a failure. What you just did, did not have a successful outcome. Break it down and identify what you need to do a little differently. Then go after it next time.

Brian Cain is the greatest mental conditioning coach in America right now. Every team would be irresponsible not to have his perspective poster and not look at it every day. Everybody needs to take a page out of Cain's book. If you want to change your life, you have to change your perspective. That is probably the biggest thing I learned from Brian. I consider him a mentor. Nobody does it better. Everybody should make a perspective poster.

Weintraub: I try to get them to redefine success and failure. That's an uphill battle, because our society teaches that if you're behind on the scoreboard, you're a loser.

John Wooden's definition of success is that you're a winner and you're successful if you do your best. It goes back to the three categories of strategies: things you say to yourself, images you use, and things you do to try to create that ideal state.

I say to my kids when I put them to bed at night: 'Your best effort is always good enough.' That is such a tough concept, and right on point with the personality in this question. They might say that their best is never good enough. They certainly wouldn't say that it's always good enough. It's important for them to understand that everybody has fear of failure. It's universal, inside of all of us.

Some people have more of the 'Oh no, what if I'm not good enough?' We must recognize that it's really all we can do, and we're maximizing our chances at success when we give our best effort. It makes sense that your best effort would always be good enough. It requires faith and patience to believe that. If we have faith and patience, it's not that we're going to win, that we're going to get the college scholarship or get drafted. It's that I know that if I do the right thing, I'm going to be rewarded. It might be by getting drafted but it might not. That's outside of my control, but I have faith that this good behavior, in the long run if not in the short run, is going to be rewarded.

Dehmer: Fear and self-doubt are self-inflicted wounds. As a player, I can remember times when I was worried about striking out, swinging at the high pitch or the ball in the dirt, or being 0-for-4 after already being 0-for-3. Typically I got what I was thinking of.

We have to train our players to make sure they're focusing on what they want to do, not on what they want to avoid, failure obviously being one of those. When we toe the rubber or get in the box, we're 100% ready to compete in a way that allows us to focus on what we're trying to do instead of, if I'm trying to get a bunt down, 'Oh gosh, what if I pop this up?' We train our guys that, if those thoughts of doubt and fear step into our mind, we step out of the box, clear our mind, and get back to focusing on what we're trying to do for the team, then go from there.

Question Review

So many players underperform because they're afraid of failing. How do you effectively get them to perform to the best of their ability, meeting their full potential, with the potential of failure still lingering?

Afremow: One important reminder is that baseball is what you do, it's not who you are. You are more than just an athlete. Embrace all the roles you play in your life to feel good about yourself.

Jaeger: If it's something in the future, you are far removed from your process. FEAR is Future Events Already Realized. This is where the rubber hits the road for mental game stuff. It is changing the programming, learning how to redirect your attention from old programming.

Brubaker: They need to have the proper perspective. Celebrate your success and use your failure as feedback. If you want to change your life, you have to change your perspective. Everybody should take a page out of Brian Cain's book and make a perspective poster.

Weintraub: I try to get them to redefine success and failure. It's important to understand that everybody has fear of failure. It's universal, inside of all of us.

Dehmer: We have to train our players to make sure they're focusing on what they want to do, not on what they want to avoid.

Championship Culture

What are the similarities among championship teams you have been around?

Janssen: I've been doing this a long time and I've been fortunate to see about 25 different teams win NCAA national championships. I was trying to figure out what it is that all these guys have in common. Obviously, talent is a big part of it. You have to have talented people. When you look at their culture and how they've attracted talented people and helped them develop their full potential, six things kept coming up:

First is credible leadership. Coaches and captains are strong leaders who knew what their program stood for, who modeled the way, and who didn't put up with much crap from people who were going in the wrong direction. They made sure that everyone was on the same page.

Second is a clear and compelling vision. We know exactly what we're striving for, whether it's a conference, state or national championship. Everyone is on the same page and that is driving them each and every day.

Third is core values. They understand what their program is all about. They recruit to that, give feedback to that, and eliminate people if there's not a good fit with those core values. They're very clear about what their program is all about and what they stand for.

Fourth is standards of behavior, standards that they're just not going to fall below. There are certain expectations that they have of their athletes, both on and off the field. They are well-communicated and praised when people match and exceed those standards, and coached quickly or confronted when they fall below those standards. They have very, very high and uncompromising standards.

Fifth is a committed and unified team. Everybody is bought in to what they're trying to achieve, and everybody rallies around that same cause. They have the ability to put that common goal ahead of their own interests, which is hard thing for young kids to do.

The last one is aligned systems. The whole structure of the program is fully aligned with the vision, values and standards of the program. They recruit people who are a great fit with their vision, values and standards. They do an orientation with the young people to make sure they understand their vision, values and standards. When they evaluate a game or a season, it's all done based on vision, values and standards. When they give feedback, when they decide who's starting, when they decide who the leaders are, all of those things are in alignment with their total vision, values and standards. They focus on building a program where everything is aligned towards what they want to accomplish. If something is misaligned, they get that corrected quickly because they know that it might start eroding their culture.

Brubaker: Commitment. I was guilty, when I was coaching, of hyping, 'You're playing for the name on the front of the jersey. You're playing for your institution. That number that you wore, that's a tradition rich number. So and so wore that number before you. You're playing for the alumni.'

Ultimately, kids on the team aren't playing for the university, for mom and dad or for some alumnus who is 75 years old whom they may have met once at an alumni tailgate. Ultimately, they're playing for themselves and they're playing for the guy next to them. They aren't even really playing for the coach. They are playing for themselves and for each other.

Those championship teams are filled, from top to bottom, with a roster of student athletes who don't want to let each other down and who don't want to let themselves down. As a byproduct of that, they are going to make the university look good, they are going to make the team look good, the alumni will be happy. They're going to make their parents proud. In a way, that is surface stuff. At the core, they are playing for themselves and for each other. That is the similarity among championship teams—guys next to each other really care about one another. It goes back to trust. They just don't want to let each other down. They have a common mission.

Dixon: Baseball teams and your relationship to practice are like any other relationship. If you're married or have a girlfriend, there are good times and bad times, times you love them and times you hate them. When you're dealing with 35 different personalities, not everyone is always on the same page. It's important that the majority of them are, and that's why, as a coach, you can't teach one way, because one way is not always the right way for some people. You've got to use different verbiage or go one on one. The hardest thing for a coach to figure out is, 'How do I figure out 35 different personalities? How do I get to all of them, one way or another?'

On our national championship team in '95 at Cal State Fullerton, we were blue collar, a bunch of grinders. We just loved to get dirty. We had a chip on our shoulders because no one thought we were good enough, and we had fights. We held each other to an extremely high standard. When one person didn't meet that standard, the coaches didn't have to do anything. Players would say, 'You need to pull your head out of your you-know-what and you need to go to work.' There was such a level of excellence, and anything below it was just not accepted. That's hard to come by.

It's an individual sport within a team concept, but you can only go so far as an individual. When you stop worrying about who gets the credit, it's amazing what happens. It's tough and it's a balance, because guys need to get bigger, faster, and stronger and work on their specifics. If you're pitching, work on your breaking ball versus your change-up. If you're hitting, work on this guy stepping into the bucket or whatever it is. It's individual, but there have to be moments during a practice and throughout the season where you work on the team. You work on the whole, guys coming together, counting on others, relying on others, because when it's all said and done, those national championship teams and those World Series teams and some of the best teams you'll ever see, all they talk about is team cohesion, leadership in the clubhouse. 'We're a family.' It's very, very consistent. That team concept is a necessity for success, there's no doubt about it, but hard to create nowadays.

Margolies: One of the things I see is professionalism, going about their job of playing this game in a professional way. They do their training, work on their skills, work on their fitness and their mental training, and they take it as a professional would take it. I've seen kids as young as 12 or 13 years old play like a professional. 'Professional' gets a bad rap, because we don't think you can be a professional and have fun at the same time. I'm a professional and I love working with athletes. I have a great time and lots of fun with them. Being a professional doesn't exclude you from having fun, but being a professional does mean that you go about doing things a certain way.

We have lots of examples of teams that have won the World Series where there is no chemistry, where players hate each other. The Yankees, years ago, were known for having zero chemistry. It didn't mean that if the ball came to the shortstop he was going to hesitate to throw it to first base. You do that because that's professional. The same thing happens with basketball teams. I'm not going to pass it to the open guy because I don't like him? At the professional level, that doesn't happen. In Little League, it does happen, if they're not professional. Professionalism really does carry over. It's the way you work at your skills and your fitness, and how you do your mental training. It's all focused on the goal of being the best that you can be.

Jaeger: I would say that the team chemistry and the communication among coaches and players are phenomenal. I feel like it's really a family. I know one of Butch Thompson's themes is the word Connection. Family and connection is huge. The process and that awareness is strong. I'm not saying they're perfect at it every day.

I do feel like sports psychology is becoming more of a part of culture, but the championship teams really have it in spades. I know with UCLA's team, family, connection, and presence are key. Ken Ravizza, who is very involved in that program, is great.

The family, the connection, and communication. Let's not kid ourselves. Maybe there is a time and place for more of a military, yelling, intense approach, but the culture nowadays is different. For the most part, kids want to be nurtured. Communication is vital. Whether it's bringing in Ken Ravizza or Brian Cain, the teams that are around those themes every day and working on those are the ones that seem to be successful.

Afremow: On championship-caliber teams, all of the players have bought in. All their behaviors are for the benefit of each other. They're working hard against each other in practice, but in games they're supporting each other. They're competing against each other in training, and then in competition they complete each other. They're really good at looking at everything as a challenge. If a team is up on us, we like that. Let's come back at them. If we're up on a game, let's increase the lead. On a championship-caliber team, the players have positive rivalries with each other. They're all trying to help each other get better, because everyone benefits from being part of a winning team. They really do a good job of supporting each other when that support is needed.

Toole: A lot of it has to do with chemistry. I'm playing on a team right now that's having some success. That stems from guys pushing each other. If you miss a ground ball in batting practice, your teammates will let you know that they saw you miss a ground ball. They hold you accountable for what you do. Accountability is big. If a coach and teammates start to hold each other accountable, that's a huge step towards having a championship team.

One of the things that a lot of teams don't understand, and I didn't understand growing up, is the difference between being a good friend and being a good teammate. If your best friend is out on the field screwing around and goofing off, it doesn't mean that you can't go up and say something. That's the biggest thing. In today's world, a lot of kids would rather be good friends than good teammates. It's OK to speak up. It's OK to say something. They might get angry with you, but in the long term it's going to benefit your team. The biggest thing with a championship team is going out there and having fun, doing the little things. In baseball, it's bunting people over, hitting behind runners, guy's on third base and getting him in, pitchers throwing strikes. Obviously, that wins games. When you do that, the game is a lot more fun.

Springer: My first 10 years in pro ball, we were in the playoffs every year. My AA team had Billy Bean, Lenny Dykstra and 18 other guys that played in the big leagues. We had guys that liked each other, that were pulling for each other. My last 4 years had no playoffs, a lot of individuals, no pitching, and it was not fun. Winning is fun. It takes a little time to get that chemistry with the guys. When you come in to a new position, you want to prove that you can play, and you make it about you. Make it about the team.

Gilbert: That's easy. Positive energy. You can feel that. Bruce Springsteen, in every concert, is totally energetic. In his 60s, *Rolling Stone Magazine* voted him the greatest touring rock act in the world. How can a guy in his 60s be the greatest touring rock act in the world? It's all about energy.

There was a very famous radio sports talk show, Mike and the Mad Dog that used to be on WFAN in New York. Mad Dog was really into Springsteen. One morning he said, 'Hey, Mike, I saw Bruce in Philadelphia. It was the 30th time I saw him, and my buddy got me backstage passes. I spoke to Bruce and asked him the question I always want to ask: 'Bruce, I've seen you 30 times, and every time you're better than the last time. How do you do it?' Springsteen took the question seriously. He said, 'Before every concert, I think of two things. One, tonight is the most important concert of my life, and two, it's only rock and roll.'

Everything that I want to get across in sports psychology is in those two rules. One, today is the most important game of your life, and two, it's only baseball. This isn't life or death. The more we interfere with your performance by thinking this is special, the more likely you are to mess up. The killer words are, 'This is it. It's now or never. It's do or die and there's no tomorrow.' As soon as we start doing other than Springsteen, we don't treat it as important and we make it more important than a game, we screw up our performance. What Bruce is saying is that he *plays* music, he doesn't *work* music.

Back in the 70's, Willie Stargell was the captain of the Pittsburgh Pirates, who had some phenomenal teams back then. A sports writer said, 'Willie, what is the secret to your success?' because the Pirates back then were a really tight, bonded team. He said, 'Very simple. I just listen to what the umpire says after they play the national anthem.' The sports writer said, 'What are you talking about?' He said, 'After they play the national anthem, what does the umpire say? He says, Play ball! He doesn't say 'work ball'. He says, Play ball! That's the secret. You don't go to the ballpark to work. You go to play.'

Look at all the people who make a whole lot of money playing music, acting in plays, playing sports: it's playing. What is playing? Playing isn't recreation. It's not fun fun, but it isn't serious serious. Playing is serious fun, that's what playing is. The result still matters, but 'it's only rock and roll'. It's only baseball. Don't drive yourself nuts.

Question Review

What are the similarities among championship teams you have been around?

Janssen: Obviously, you have to have talented people but it seems to come down to these 6 things: Credible leadership, Clear and Compelling Vision, Core Values, Standards of Behavior, Committed and Unified Team and Aligned Systems.

Brubaker: Commitment. At the core, they are playing for themselves and for each other. They have a common mission.

Dixon: When you stop worrying about who gets the credit, it's amazing what happens. The World Series teams all talk about team cohesion, leadership in the clubhouse, and being a family. It's very, very consistent.

Margolies: One of the things I see is professionalism, going about their job of playing this game in a professional way. It's all focused on the goal of being the best that you can be.

Jaeger: The team chemistry, connection and the communication among coaches and players are phenomenal.

Afremow: All of the players have bought in. All their behaviors are for the benefit of each other.

Toole: A lot of it has to do with chemistry. Accountability is big. It's OK to speak up. It's OK to say something.

Springer: Winning is fun. It takes a little time to get that chemistry with the guys. When you come in to a new position, you want to prove that you can play, and you make it about you. Make it about the team.

Gilbert: Positive energy. Two important aspects of sports psychology: today is the most important game of your life and it's only baseball. This isn't life or death.

Get Your Mind Right

What are some ways that coaches can be sure their players are in the proper mindset prior to competition?

Janssen: That's one of the challenges of coaching. For each guy it's a little bit different. Some guys like to be off by themselves visualizing. Other guys, if they were off by themselves, they'd get a little stir-crazy. Some guys just need to be loose, hanging out with other guys and joking around a little bit, which for some coaches can be a little bit scary, wondering if this guy as focused as he needs to be. This might be a guy who, if he starts thinking too much, ends up getting the old 'paralysis by analysis' and gets in his own way.

One of the best things a coach can do is to sit down with each of their players and help them figure out which method works best for them. Looking back at your best games, 'What your mindset was like in the dugout before the game? What was it like between innings?' helps pinpoint what that guy's mindset looks like. Once you've pinpointed that, it's a matter of helping that guy develop a pre-performance or pre-game routine that is not only physical, but also mental, starting to get him into the groove the week before, the night before, the morning of, as well as leading up to the game itself.

What are some of the things that get my mindset into that groove? It could be music or visualization, some guys might use highlight videos, whatever it might be for that particular guy. What good coaches understand is that not every guy prepares the same way or needs to be mentally doing the same thing. Each guy is a little bit different. As long as I know that each guy is doing the thing that gets him ready to go, a coach should feel good that each guy is doing everything he can to bring his A-game that day.

Cain: A strategy Skip Bertman used at LSU back in the 90s when they won all the national championships was showing highlight videos before the team went out to compete. It's also telling a story. Another thing you will see Bianco do at Ole Miss is, roughly ten minutes before the game, tell them a motivational story that ties into what the theme is for that day, what their mission is for that day. This is a very effective strategy to create the right mindset, but the mindset is not built the day of the game, the mindset is built every day. On the day of the game, you just heighten awareness about the concept of the mindset. When you go on the road into a hostile crowd, you're not saying to the players for the first time ever, 'Hey, today, make sure you guys take a good deep breath to slow the game down. Today, focus only on what you guys can control and communicate.' It is emphasized from day one. At that point it's not anything new, it's just reinforcing and increasing the awareness to what the mindset must be in that moment.

Brubaker: If you need to give them a big rah-rah moment before a game, you're in trouble. You've got problems that no speech, no pep talk, no coach or consultant can help you with, because that means your guys weren't in the right frame of mind leading up to that moment.

The best way you can make sure your players are in the right mindset relates to the one key quality that championship teams and organizations all posses: ownership. It can't always be coming from the coach. The coach can't be the one who has to make sure to babysit the kids. Make sure you're in the right mindset leading up to the game. After a loss, if everyone's joking around on the bus, it can't be the coach telling everyone to quiet down. 'Hey we just lost, you shouldn't be clowning around.' When the players own it and they police among themselves, that's when you know you have a great team.

You can have a good team when it's coming from the coach and it's all the coaches' voice, but the coach will be tired, he'll probably be sick to his stomach, and have gray hair. You'll be good, but you'll be great when the players own it.

It's like a rental car. You'll beat on that thing. Nobody washes the rental car before they return it. They certainly don't wax it. You don't care if you spill soda on the seat. When you own it and you paid for it with your own money and sweat equity, that's when you care for it. If you want your players to be in the right mindset before competition, they have to have that championship culture and chemistry. They've got to own it. When your players are teaching each other, it's a far more powerful tool than when it's just you teaching them. Whether it's X's and O's on the chalkboard after hours, in practice, coaching each other between innings, whatever it might be, when there is that mutual accountability, it takes things to a whole different plane than just working for your boss or your coach.

Tully: You have to make your practices as game-like as possible. Perhaps the greatest value that a coach has to instill in his players is that the only play that matters this year is the one that's happening right now. The one that just happened is over, and the only play that matters is the next one. You let go of what just happened except what you can learn from it. You learn from the past and you apply it to the future, but you don't live in the future or the past, you are completely involved in the present.

That's why we pick up the dirt, just to feel the infield dirt, the first time we step on a field, or we take that piece of grass and put it in our teeth just like we did when we were kids. We look up at the sky just to relax, or we breathe or say our affirmations. We work on this all the time in practice. When a player has bought into it in practice, you can tell. That means they're ready to do it in the game. It becomes a habit just like anything else. If they break down in the game, you can go to the mound or pull them aside in the dugout and say, 'Remember, we're going to stay in the present.'

Herb Brooks, at Lake Placid, after the US went ahead 4-3 against the Russians in the third period, what did he keep saying to them? 'Play your game. Play your game.' That is just fantastic coaching. Play your game.

Question Review

What are some ways that coaches can be sure their players are in the proper mindset prior to competition?

Janssen: Each guy it's a little bit different. One of the best things a coach can do is to sit down with each of their players and help them figure out which method works best for them by looking back at your best games. As long as I know that each guy is doing the thing that gets him ready to go, a coach should feel good that each guy is doing everything he can to bring his A-game that day.

Cain: The mindset is not built the day of the game, the mindset is built every day. On the day of the game, you just heighten awareness about the concept of the mindset. It is emphasized from day one.

Brubaker: They have to have that championship culture and chemistry. They've got to own it. When your players are teaching each other, it's far more powerful.

Tully: You have to make your practices as game-like as possible. It becomes a habit just like anything else.

Win The Big Game

You hear about coaches and teams not being able to win the big game and then you hear about teams that are 'clutch' in the playoffs. What factors seem to contribute to these differences?

Jaeger: I have a saying in my book, 'Nothing special, nothing changes.' The minute you make something special and important, you tend to put pressure on people and change what you have been doing. I come back to the basics, what is your process? Every day, whatever your process is, nothing changes. If you're in a regional, even calling it a regional is dangerous. You just have another game on Friday. Even calling it a game is dangerous. To me, you get a chance to go out and master your process.

Every individual has a process as a hitter, as a pitcher, as a base runner, and as a defender. We have a process as a team. You just keep crushing those principles. When you start talking about regionals, Omaha, College World Series, the playoffs and the post-season, these are all dangerous words. There are a percentage of players who are going to thrive because it's post season, and that's great! Let them be them. But, generally speaking, the idea is to keep pounding the principles. Nothing changes. Don't make it special. It's just like that Albert Pujols commercial on ESPN, 'Just keep pounding.'

Another metaphor I love is, 'Just pound the nail.' You hit the top of the nail over and over. You don't look left or right because it's the post-season, the preseason or the regular season. You pound the top of the nail because it's the most efficient way to get the nail in the wood.

Cain: The best strategy for the final push to the big game late in the season is the same strategy you use the first day of spring training, the same strategy you use the first game of the year. A game is a game. A run in the first inning is worth as much as a run in the ninth inning. It's worth one run. It is what it is.

Look at Augie Garrido, the head coach for Texas. He's won five national championships in four different decades, over 1900 wins. He finished ninth in the Big 12 in 2013, ninth out of nine teams! They didn't make the Big 12 conference tournament. It may have been the worst season in Texas baseball history. What did he do the next year? He goes to Omaha in the Final 4. What's the difference in those two years? Is it an amazing influx of talent? I don't think so, they just play better. Maybe they were a little more consistent. It's the compound effect of being a little bit more consistent in your routines, a little bit more consistent in your daily habits. That's all going to translate into how you perform and how you live your life, the success and results that you get.

If a team is going to be clutch, it's about being able to manage the moment and play the way that you play. You're not going to step up in the big game. The step up has to happen every single day. Ole Miss and TCU aren't trying to step up when they get to Omaha. They're trying to manage the moment and play it one pitch at a time, the same thing that they've done all year. There is no difference.

There's a difference for the fans. There's a difference because there are TV cameras. There's a difference because in Omaha you play every other day, unlike the rest of the season. There is some management that has to happen of the surroundings, but mostly, the only thing you can control is not what goes on around you, not what happens to you, but what's going on inside of you. Championship teams and the players who are 'clutch' simply have an awareness of what's going on inside of them. They are able to manage the moment better than those who crack under the pressure.

Maher: A lot of it is the presence or the stance of the coaches and the team manager. How do they deal with failure, with the string of six losses in a row, with situations that are very, very important because they have to win this game but they don't want to put it like that? How they present themselves to players, how they interact with them, is very, very important because the players are going to take their cue from that. Secondly, players who have quite a bit of experience can naturally take the lead with other players, talk to them. Show them how things have to be done, particularly when the playoffs or championships are on the line.

Springer: Get good pitching! It always goes back to pitching. Good pitching will shut down good hitting for the most part. It's getting 25 guys pulling the same way. Everyone's got two players in him: the confident guy and the non-confident guy. You want confident guys showing up to the yard. You want to make it a 25-man roster, not a 50-man roster. Get 25 guys showing up with confidence to help the team win. Get guys buying into that, and you're going to win a lot of games.

Rickertsen: I love the idea of the 'big game'. It's an idea that's created by individuals, right? It's the same game, the same distance from home plate to first. Everything's the same, you're doing everything the same, but we add this element of pressure that we interpret to make it a big deal. It becomes this idea of the 'big game'. It goes back to working memory. Instead of what you were focusing on when you were performing so well, in the 'not-big games', in the games throughout the season, now you've filled that little small spot in your brain with this big pressure element of 'I need to be successful here.' You start abandoning all the things that were working for you in the past. What is intriguing to me and to a lot of athletes is, how can we bring what's been working for you in the past to this game?

We know our brain is going to respond to very specific information, so let's be very selective about what we're putting in there. Because of all the build-up to this big game, you're thinking about all sorts of different things that you weren't thinking about before, and that's filling your attention. Once your brain is filled with these high-pressure elements, that this is a 'big game', that this is a must-win, that scouts are going to be there, whatever it is, your physiology is going to follow suit. This can lead to faster heart rate, sweating, discomfort, butterflies and all sorts of different feelings. We interpret those as not a good feeling, or not helpful, so it begins to snowball. It always starts with attention. What are you allowing your brain to pay attention to, and are you able to bring it back if it ever leaves that attention point?

Brubaker: There's no magic bullet. Some people say they're game day players who show up for the big games. Either you're trained, or you're untrained. There's no 'I'm tough on game day.' You're either trained or you're untrained.

The teams that can't win the big game, that aren't clutch in the play-offs, are the same teams that probably haven't committed to the mental game year round. So much of it is mental in the 'big game' or a 'big clutch at bat'. You need to take the extraordinary and make it ordinary. The way you do that is through training. Are you practicing the way you're playing? Are you making practice as big as the game?

A game can't be bigger than what you do every day, because you get out of your comfort zone. It seems like something foreign to you. Muhammad Ali said, 'You train like you fight. You fight like you train.' Not winning the big games says they're probably not winning the big practice. If they're not clutch in practice, you know they're not going to be clutch a game. It gets back to how you do anything is how you do everything. When you look at some of the under-performing teams on game day, go look at how they practice.

I always thought it would be interesting, whether it's baseball or any other sport, if coaches on game day couldn't talk to their team, couldn't communicate with their players. You would see, even more than you do now, which teams practice really well. For student athletes, it's the same thing in class. Here is the lecture and then there is exam day. If you were engaged and involved and the teacher was teaching well in the lecture, you're going to do great in the exam. You won't need to ask anybody questions, you won't need anybody to tell you the answers, you won't need to look it up in the book, you know it because you're trained. I would love to see coaches not being able to communicate with players during the game.

Tully: First, keep it as normal as possible. You don't ever want to draw attention to what the standings are. This is why some teams don't like to look at the scoreboard. It has to be all process. You can't think about what anyone else is doing. You can't think a minute ahead or a minute behind, you have to stay in the moment.

You need full engagement, full effort, full commitment, full buy-in to the fact that every pitch matters. Every pitch is a battle.

Question Review

You hear about coaches and teams not being able to win the big game and then you hear about teams that are 'clutch' in the playoffs. What factors seem to contribute to these differences?

Jaeger: I have a saying in my book, 'Nothing special, nothing changes.' The minute you make something special and important, you tend to put pressure on people and change what you have been doing. 'Just pound the nail.' You hit the top of the nail over and over. You don't look left or right because you know it's the post-season, the preseason or the regular season. You pound the top of the nail because it's the most efficient way to get the nail in the wood.

Cain: The best strategy for the final push to the big game late in the season is the same strategy you use the first day of spring training, the same strategy you use the first game of the year. A game is a game.

Maher: A lot of it is the stance of the coaches and the team manager. How do they deal with failure? Secondly, players who have quite a bit of experience can naturally take the lead with other players, talk to them, show them how things have to be done.

Springer: Get 25 guys showing up with confidence to help the team win. Get guys buying into that, and you're going to win a lot of games.

Rickertsen: Everything's the same, you're doing everything the same, but we add this element of pressure that we interpret to make it a big deal. It becomes this idea of the Big Game.

Brubaker: The teams that can't win the big game, that aren't clutch in the play-offs, are the same teams that probably haven't committed to the mental game year round.

You need to take the extraordinary and make it ordinary. The way you do that is through training. Are you practicing the way you're playing? Are you making practice as big as the game?

Tully: First, keep it as normal as possible. It has to be all about the process. You can't think about what anyone else is doing. Every pitch is a battle.

Mental Training vs. Physical Strength & Conditioning

Does mental training compare to physical strength & conditioning in the weight room?

Gordon: Oh yes! We need to build mental muscle as much as physical muscle. The best and the rest are separated in the mind, by what you believe, what you think, and the confidence you have. If you don't have confidence, it doesn't matter how strong or how talented you are. If you don't have confidence, you're not going to play very well. We need to train our mind and build that mental muscle as much as physical muscle.

It's not found at each level of the sports world as it is in the Olympics. It's becoming more popular, but I hope we give enough attention to it. We need to focus on it. It will help people overcome fear and help them focus better. We need to help them stay positive, to overcome their challenges and adversity. We also need to give them tools to perform at the highest level.

Cain: You have to do a little, a lot. You walk into the weight room, you lift weights today, and you're not going to necessarily notice the strength difference tomorrow. You get on a strength and conditioning program so you can be stronger 4-7 months from now when the season comes around. It's the same thing with mental conditioning.

You've got to train a little bit, a lot. This is the use of *The Daily Dominator*, and of all the audio I create for the teams I work with. They have to do a little, a lot to train and hard-wire that peak performance and that champion's mindset. Here is the difference between strength conditioning and the mental game. Let's say tomorrow, you're playing in the NCAA National Championship. We're not going to get any bigger, faster, stronger, more technical, more mechanical between now and the national championship. However, if you change your focus from 'having to win' to 'wanting to win', from 'we have to win the national championship' to just 'win this pitch', you can have a dramatic difference in your physical performance.

Although you want to condition it consistently, like you do in the weight room, the mental game can transform your performance in an instant.

The best team's not going to win, it's the going to be the team who plays the best. The mental game is a difference-maker, as it is in college baseball or any sport.

Brubaker: Everybody looks at your mindset or attitude as a trait that people have. 'He's got the mental toughness gene.' No, he doesn't. He's trained. Your attitude is not a trait, it's a muscle. When you're in strength and conditioning, if you don't train that muscle for 48 hours, it starts to atrophy. But when you do train it, you train it to fatigue, then you rest it and it grows stronger.

I talk about teams being battle-tested. We each need to have our resilience muscles tested, fatigued to a certain extent, to grow back stronger. It's exactly the same as physical conditioning. So many people neglect the mental game because they're so worried about the physical game, and that's why they don't get to the next level.

Physical conditioning will take you so far. As Yogi Berra said, "90% of the game is half mental." My question is, 'How are your mental reps?' Everybody is so focused on the physical reps, they forget about the mental reps. Are you blocking off time to train your mind, to train your attitude, like you're blocking off time to go into the weight room? The earlier you begin to practice that 80 to 90%, the better it will serve you later in your career.

Margolies: There is Yogi Berra's, "Baseball is 90% mental and the other half is physical." I'll ask that question to the audience, and invariably people will say that it's 70-90% mental, but when I ask them how much time they spend on that part, they say almost zero.

If you think about mental training as you would physical training, weight training, aerobic training, speed training or even technical training, working with an individual coach on your hitting or throwing or even running the bases, the one thing that they have in common is that they're skills. The one thing I really want to get across to all athletes is that the mental things that we're talking about are skills. They're no different. If you don't work on them, you're not able to use them. If you don't keep working on them, they become latent. It's as if you were to take off six months from hitting, the first time you step into the batting cage you're probably not going to hit all that well, right? It's the same thing with the mental skills.

If you're not using skills on a weekly basis to help you deal with stress or to keep you focused, and then I put you in facing a really tough pitcher, how are you supposed to be able to do those things at the drop of a hat? If you're not practicing these things, you're not going to be able to use them.

That's a lot different than thinking of them as some kind of developmental psychology, where they're just latently there and if all of a sudden you're in a situation, they're going to snap right in and you're going to be able to use them. It doesn't work that way. You practice these things, then you get in and you can perform. It's just like weight training or skills training. It all has to do with what you are prepared to do, how practiced are you at it, how much you understand it, so that you can then apply it.

Jaeger: It would compare in that they're both about discipline and dedication, putting time aside to develop a part of you in the weight room. Of course it's going to be something physical, and really to some degree you're going to get some mental benefits too, right? When you're working hard, you have to have some perseverance, patience and discipline, so there are mental benefits there too. They're both a practice, something that you work at as opposed to hoping that it works out without putting the time into it to do it.

Rickertsen: They are very comparable! As I work with athletes or soldiers, we spend so much time perfecting the physical, the strength, the plays, the mechanics, it's hard for me to understand why the mental conditioning piece is not as important to some folks. I strongly believe that they work together to develop each other. You can use mental training while doing the physical training, and if you can, then why not?

You're always going to have the mental pieces, whether you can perform physically or not. Maybe you're having the best physical day of your life, but if the mental pieces aren't there, you're not going to be able to perform at your most authentic and optimal level. I definitely see how they're both very important to performance. I see how they can combine to help one another in a lot of ways. It makes it easier for athletes to understand when you're working so hard on the physical piece. Then you ask them, 'How much of your game or your performance do you think is mental, and what are you doing to build that piece?' Then there's an 'Aha!' moment where they're like, 'Yeah! I would say a good portion of my performance is mental, and I'm not really doing a lot of work on that on a daily basis.' For a lot of athletes, that can be eye-opening as well.

Springer: There are 40 rounds in the draft for a reason. It's why some first rounders can't get out of A ball and some guys that don't get drafted spend 10 years in the big leagues. It's not physical, it's mental.

The mental side is probably the most underrated tool. There are some really good people teaching the mental side, I'm not the only guy. The mental side is everything. The greatest draft pick in the history of the game is when the Boston Red Sox took a 5'7" below average running second baseman in the first round. His name is Dustin Pedroia. This guy is a gamer who knows how to compete. This guy is a team player, and that is what it's all about. Having all the tools is great, but if your mental game is not really, really good, then it's a waste of tools.

Tully: Mental skill and mental toughness is just like any other skill. It can be developed and strengthened with practice. Just like any physical skill or physical strength, if there's not enough practice, it can slide backwards. Peter

Ueberroth, the former baseball commissioner's favorite saying was, 'In life, you're either moving forwards or sliding backwards, there's no such thing as standing still.' These mental toughness skills have to be practiced at every single opportunity.

Question Review

Does mental training compare to physical strength & conditioning in the weight room?

Gordon: We need to build mental muscle as much as physical muscle. The best are separated from the rest in the mind, by what you believe, what you think, and the confidence you have.

Cain: You have to do a little, a lot. The best team's not going to win, it's the going to be the team who plays the best,. The mental game is going to be a difference-maker in the national championship as it is in college baseball or any sport.

Brubaker: Your attitude is not a trait, it's a muscle. So many people neglect the mental game because they're so worried about the physical game, and that's why they don't get to the next level.

Margolies: They're both skills. If you don't work on them, you're not able to use them, and if you don't keep working on them, they become latent. It all has to do with what you are prepared to do, how practiced are you at it, how much you understand it, so you can then apply it.

Jaeger: It would compare in that they're both about discipline and dedication, putting time aside to develop a part of you in the weight room.

Rickertsen: I definitely see how they're both very important to performance. I see how they can combine to help one another in a lot of ways. It makes it easier for athletes to understand when you're working so hard on the physical piece.

Springer: There are 40 rounds in the draft for a reason. The mental side is probably the most underrated tool. Having all the tools is great, but if your mental game is not really, really good, then it's a waste of tools.

Tully: Mental skill and mental toughness is just like any other skill. It can be developed and strengthened with practice.

Goal-Setting vs Process

How important is goal-setting and envisioning the future in comparison to a focus on the process of doing what is most important today?

Cain: You've got to know where you're going, or you might end up climbing the wrong mountain. The last thing you want to do is be working hard to climb a ladder and figure out the ladder is leaning on the wrong wall. If you're running 100mph, but going around in a circle, you're not going anywhere. You have to set goals and you have to know where you want to go. The biggest challenge I see with people setting goals is that they don't set the bar high enough. They also set an outcome goal, but they don't create a process to get there. The image I'll leave you with is that of a staircase. At the top of that staircase is your outcome goal and what you want to achieve. What are the steps you have to take to get there always coming down to what your daily plan is. I am big fan of a lot of the concepts of that Tony Robbins teaches. One of the programs I went through was his program on time management. The biggest take home from that for me was that most people live by a to-do list to figure out what their day's going to be. He says that's the backwards approach. The thing that's missing from most people's daily focus and goal setting is:

Tony Robbins' RPM – Rapid Planning Method

R: What's the **Result** that you want?

P: What's your **Purpose**? Why do you want it?

M: What's your **Massive Action Plan**?

People want to start, before setting goals, saying, 'I want to be 195 pounds.' OK, now let's see why. Why do you want to be 195 pounds? What do you want, why do you want it, and then how are going to get there is the key things to goal setting. Most people will set an outcome, but they don't come up with a purpose. There isn't that fuel and that passion behind why they want to accomplish that so they lose motivation after three weeks or three days, as most people do with their New Year's resolutions. New Year's resolutions usually don't have a big enough reason why, and then they lose motivation after a few days because they don't have the fuel behind it to keep them going.

Gordon: I'm not a huge believer in goals in that way. Goals are all about outcomes. I'm all about the process and being in the moment. John Wooden, the greatest basketball coach of all time, never focused on winning. He focused on the process that produced winning. The goal is not to win a championship. The goal is to become a champion. I want people to become champions and focus on that. If you focus on becoming a champion, you're going to be the kind of person who makes plays that win championships.

I do believe in visions. I believe in having a big-picture vision of what you want to achieve. Not goals, but more of a big-picture vision of seeing your best self, seeing you play at your highest level and knowing the potential you want to reach. I had this vision of speaking in front of a large arena when I was really young. It wasn't a goal, just a vision I had. Several times I have seen that vision come to fruition when I'm speaking now, but it wasn't a goal. I never said I wanted to be a New York Times bestseller. I want my books to be read. I want to have an influence, make a difference, and write something that was worthy of impacting others. If you do that, the outcome will take care of itself. *The Energy Bus* took about 4 years to be a best seller. I was never about the outcome. I just felt that if it reaches people, great. If it doesn't, that's OK too, as long as the books have an impact but it was never a goal to be a best seller.

Janssen: Most people need that kind of long-term vision and that purpose for what they're doing, because they know there's going to be a lot of drudgery along the way with the training, and the lifting, and the conditioning, and all that. They need that big carrot out there that keeps them inspired and they know that there's a purpose for all the work they're doing. That work is not a sacrifice, but it's really an investment in that long-term vision or goal that they have for themselves. I'd say a good 90-95% of people probably need that long-term goal to provide some reasoning and rationale for all the grunt work they've got to do to give themselves a chance to get there.

I do think there are a few people out there, and I'll give you an example. Leah O'Brian Amico was a person I worked with when I was at Arizona with their softball program. She was one who never really set the goal of being an Olympic athlete, but just each and every day worked the process. She was one of the hardest workers, she had a great attitude in what she did, and she was one of those people who understood that if I really invest each and every day, something special could happen down the road. Something special happened for her three times. She was a three-time Olympic gold medalist for the USA softball team. She was one of those 5%-ers that didn't always have that long-term goal driving her, but just understood that if I take care of the process, and that was something that worked well with Mike Candrea, their coach, that philosophy was something he has always preached, that if you take advantage of each and every day, you're going to set yourself up to have some pretty special things happening in your future.

Rickertsen: When I go through goal-setting with athletes, I go through both pieces, because you have to be able to see where you want to be, what's your overall goal, then envision yourself completing it. That is very important. In a lot of ways, it becomes a self-fulfilling prophecy to be able to picture what you want and to be able to picture yourself at that point. Once you've picked out what your goal looks like, and you're able to envision yourself at that point, come back to the day-to-day. Research talks about the idea of mental contrasting, which I do with athletes. This is the idea of, 'What's one obstacle that I'm going to encounter when coming up against this goal? What's one benefit of achieving this goal?' Then you go back and ask what's another obstacle and another benefit? Going back and forth is what creates energy to accomplish your goals.

Dwelling on the obstacles is not likely to be very energizing. If we focus just on the benefits, we're not going to see how hard we're going to have to work in order to reach that goal. The idea of going back and forth creates this balanced energy just prior to beginning or working towards that goal.

The other piece is breaking it down into smaller chunks. Break it down into where you want to be in a month, then where you want to be the month after that. Where your nutrition needs to be, where your fitness needs to be, where your mental game needs to be. Break it down, and then, what do I need to do tomorrow? It almost turns into an upside-down tree, where the big goal is at the top and it trickles down from there. You need to be able to envision what it looks like and how you feel after accomplishing that goal to really understand if it's something you want to work towards. Both pieces are really important when it comes to goal setting.

Brubaker: People get so focused on goal setting and envisioning their future. It might be such a distant future that they're not committing themselves to the process in full measure each day. I like to look at it this way: you look at your goals and your future through a telescope. It's important to get a clear picture of your ideal future, what it's going to take and clarity around it. At the same time, you want to step back from that and look through the microscope, to focus on the process, on what's most important today, what's important now and how we are going to go about tackling that. The whole concept is drilling down on that microscopic level, looking at the very next activity this hour or this day, versus the quarter, the fiscal year, or what your five-year-plan is going to look like. You need to be aware of both, but I'll take action in the moment over planning to get ready to get ready. I'll take action any day over that.

Tully: You have to be really careful with goal setting. If you set yourself a goal of hitting .320, every time you don't get a base hit, you feel stress. In *Think Better, Win More: How Sports Psychology Can Make You a Champion*, we say never think about winning, because winning brings stress. The minute there's an injury, the minute there's a setback, you say, 'Uh-oh, I'm not winning!' Now your mind is on your mind. If you put the emphasis on full effort, the by-product of that is winning.

Let's look at that again. Thinking about winning is stress, the by-product of total effort is victory. So which one are you going to do? Of course you're going to do full effort. If you want to break it down, you don't want to hit .320, you want to hit the ball hard.

As a baseball player, sometimes the pitcher gets you out, you don't get yourself out. You've got to tip your cap to that guy. He's not out there for no reason at all. He can spin it, he can throw it hard, it's hard to hit that, but you've got to make sure that he gets you out and you don't get yourself out. No swinging at bad balls. No swinging in the wrong counts. If you have an honest, good at-bat and you hit the ball hard, things are going to tend to come out all right.

Question Review

How important is goal-setting and envisioning the future in comparison to a focus on the process of doing what is most important today?

Cain: You've got to know where you're going, or you might end up climbing the wrong mountain.

Tony Robbins' RPM – Rapid Planning Method

R: What's the **Result** that you want?

P: What's your **Purpose**? Why do you want it?

M: What's your **Massive Action Plan**?

Gordon: John Wooden never focused on winning. He focused on the process that produced winning. The goal is not to win a championship. the goal is to become the champion. I believe in having a big-picture vision of what you want to achieve. Not goals, but more of a big-picture vision of seeing your best self, seeing you play at your highest level and knowing the potential you want to reach.

Janssen: Most people need that kind of long-term vision and that purpose for what they're doing, because they know there's going to be a lot of drudgery along the way.

Rickertsen: I go through both pieces, because you have to be able to see where you want to be, what's your overall goal, then envision yourself completing it. Dwelling on the obstacles is not likely to be very energizing. If we focus just on the benefits, we're not going to see how hard we're going to have to work in order to reach that goal. The idea of going back and forth creates this balance of energy just prior to beginning or working towards that goal.

Brubaker: People get so focused on goal setting and envisioning their future. It might be such a distant future that they're not committing themselves to the process in full measure each day.

Tully: If you put the emphasis on full effort, the by-product of that is winning. Thinking about winning is stress and the by-product of total effort is victory.

Exclusive Content & Free Resources

For additional content, audios, videos, links, training tools, social media and more, visit:
MentalGameVIP.com

MILLION DOLLAR QUESTION

What do you know now that you wish you knew then?

Cain: The importance of a day and the importance of a book. One day can change your life, one book can change your life, and that one book for me was *Heads-Up Baseball*. I read it on July 4th, 2000. That book changed my life and I'm hoping some of my books, whether it's *The Leadership Clock* or *The Mental Conditioning Manual* or *The Daily Dominator*, become that book that changes your perspective, so that it changes your life. The value of a day and the value of having successful habits of excellence, and you become what you do on a daily basis, the importance of surrounding yourself with quality human beings and people that have a bigger vision than you do, and that you become the average of the five people you hang out with most. Most people will think that there is no point in doing this or that. That's why there is a term called average. Most people are average: the best of the worst and the worst of the best. I think the importance of finding a mentor, finding people to share ideas with, who are going to be expanders and challenge the way that you think is very important. Sometimes you have to work really, really hard, and look really, really far to find some of those people that can help you to do that. Ultimately, one of the greatest places to get them is through books. I'm an avid reader. I really hated reading when I was growing up. I thought it was boring. I wanted to go out and be active, and now I can't get enough. Every time I work out, it's an audiobook. When I'm in the car it's an audiobook. At night when I get in bed, I'm reading a book. You can really tap into some of the elite minds in the world through reading, or through listening to podcasts and things like this.

What do I know now that I wish I knew then? I wish I had known the power of a day, the power of mentors, the power of reading. Make sure you find your mission, that you take the time to step back from the daily grind and the fast pace of everyday life, put down the cell phone and ask yourself, 'What is it that I really want?'

At 35 years old, I have finally gotten clear on what it is I really, really want and some people never really answer that question. It's a difficult question to answer, but one that must be asked.

Hanson: I spoke at my high school thirty-year class reunion. I said, 'Raise your hand if you regret what you did more than what you didn't do.' Nobody. 'Raise your hand if you regret what you didn't do more than what you did do.' Everybody. Why didn't you do it? Because you were afraid of what other people would think.

What if I could get that earlier, that what other people think really does not matter? What matters is my own integrity, my own principles, if I am acting consistent with what I believe to be right and good. If so, then go for it. If I'm trying to avoid looking bad, that's a waste of time.

I talked to a big league guy in the clubhouse during a big league game. When you're going good, what are you doing? When you're going bad, what are you doing? I was building some self-awareness. Self-awareness is knowing yourself and is fundamental. He said, 'I'm at my best when I look middle-away. In my off years, I look in.' Why would you look in? Why would you want to get beat by a fastball, break a bat, look bad? Really? But he's human, run by safety, and he didn't realize it until I had asked him about it. When you say it out loud, you think, how could someone think that? He's a major league player, but if you're not aware of how you operate as a human, then you don't make the changes that you need to make.

Springer: Get rid of the batting average. That's the main vein in my speeches. Your career starts when you say 'I don't care what I hit.' That is going to give you the freedom to walk up to the plate with confidence. I can speak to 100 10-year-olds or dads. Dads need to know these kids are playing the biggest self-esteem destroying sport in the world.

A friend asked me to approach his seven-year-old's travel ball team. I said 'So, do you know you're coaching the biggest self-esteem destroying sport in the world?' He asked, 'What do you mean?' 'Your son makes a mistake and he wants to cry. The other team's cheering, the coach is yelling at him, and that is normal. Then, on the ride home with you, the kid wants ice-cream after the game, and for one little error, you're beating him up for the fourth time.'

Two months later, I see the guy. He walked right up to me and said, 'You changed my life. When you told me my son is playing the biggest self-esteem destroying sport in the world, you hit me right between the teeth. I was so embarrassed that I couldn't even talk. Thank God we got interrupted. Two months later, I'm the most positive coach on the field. When I hear another coach yell at a kid, I cringe. I get my son ice-cream after the game because that's what he wants. My ex-wife wants to re-marry me!' We love our kids so much, but how do we tell them?

These dads who are coaching, God bless them. If they can get one of the kids on their team to play in college, that would be great. They are not all going to be college players, and not all are going to be pro players, but they're all going to be men. We have to build them up, because this game will break you down.

I don't need my coach doing it, my teammate doing it, or my parents doing it. This is what I love about the academy I started, *QualityAtBatsAcademy.com*. I have over 30 3-minute videos. Kids can download their swing and take a look at it. I do podcasts twice a month. Interviews with coaches and players are archived, all aimed to help dads and kids. For the first month, it's free. If you don't like it, you can get out on day 29. But we are not having a lot of guys get out, because it's like a baseball community and it costs only $30 a month. Parents spend $60 for a half hour flip session once a week. I've got something for $30 that would change the way you think, which is the most important part.

Gordon: When I played lacrosse at Cornell, I was so outcome-focused. If I didn't play well, I was miserable. I always worried about making mistakes. I didn't truly enjoy the game. If I was to go back and do it again, what I wish I had known was that it was about the process, having fun, giving your best, and God will do the rest. It's about fun, faith and fearless. I wish I had known that my identity is not wrapped up in myself as an athlete. It's what I do, not who I am.

The goal of sports is to make you a better human being. I can see how sports changed my life. Playing Division 1 lacrosse changed my life. Now I work with all these athletes that are a big part of my life. Sports have the opportunity to change our lives if we are open to learning from it. The life lessons we take from it will be incredible. If I could go back and do it again, I would have done that. I also would not have allowed distractions to get in the way of being my best. Distractions are the enemy of greatness. I always tell the young athletes now, 'Twenty years from now, you're not going to say, 'What if you had spent more time on Facebook or Instagram or Snapchat.' You're going to say, 'I wish I would have devoted my life to be the best I can be.'

Afremow: All of us are in a quest to be our best, and the main lesson I've learned is don't be too proud to get help from special people with special skills. Most of us, especially men, especially athletes, want to be self-reliant. It is actually a sign of strength rather than a weakness to reach out for guidance and support. Others have been there, done that, and we can learn a lot from them. For players, don't think that you already have to have all the answers. Sports psychologists, sports nutritionists and other professionals can help you get to where you really want to be.

Jaeger: The simple answer is meditation. Even going back to high school, I felt like I was a typical person with a lot of worries, stress, and a lot going on around me. I was caught up with a lot of the consequential outcome stuff.

The second answer is that I wouldn't want to change anything because it all brought me to have to get tuned into this world. I feel like the mental game or lack of it cost me a chance to see how far I could have gone in the game. I went through a very difficult time then and I didn't have any tools.

A simple answer would be that I really wish I had been more aware of meditation and Yoga. My goodness, for someone who's not quite ready for hard-core meditation, you want to soft sell it a little bit. Yoga is amazing, because with Yoga, you're getting the benefits of meditation, mental work, physical work, stretching, flexibility, balance, strength, endurance and mind-body connection. It's just an amazing, amazing art form.

Weintraub: All of it. Like many, I was an immature kid who thought I had a lot of answers. When you realize that you don't have any, you start getting better faster. People have to be in the right place in their life to receive certain lessons.

I was in college when I read Harvey's book, *The Mental Game of Baseball*, and that was really when I was ready to start understanding discipline. That's one of the reasons that his writing had such an impact, because it caught me at the right time. The more we're around great people the better. It has a positive effect.

When I was in high school, going to all these camps was not a normal thing, but certainly if I could go back and attend more baseball camps and be around some really great baseball minds, maybe some of that would have rubbed off on me and I would've grown up a little bit faster.

One of the reasons I'm a good mental skills coach now is because I messed up so many things in my life. I certainly am still making mistakes, but hopefully at a slower rate. Get the chance to be around good people. Whenever and wherever it is, try to take advantage of that opportunity.

Janssen: I knew culture was an issue, but until probably the last two or three years, I didn't really see what a pervasive issue it was and how many things it impacted. You just assume and hope your culture is going to be good, but it takes time, forethought, and constant managing.

One of the coaches I talked with about this used the garden analogy. It's constantly tending and tilling your garden, fertilizing it and pulling the weeds out. If you can create a good culture, then a lot of these issues tend to take care of themselves. Lou Gerstner, the former IBM CEO, said it took him until age 52 to really understand that culture isn't just one aspect of what you do, it's everything. That's been an eye-opener for me, after doing this for several years, to see just how important that culture factor is, and how important a coach's job is to create that culture, champion that culture, and be a caretaker for that culture.

Maher: I've been in this since 1987, so it's been a number of years. What I wish I knew then, from a professional provider's standpoint, is how to slow down, not push something on someone and, most importantly, listen to them. In the area of sports psychology, people are rushing through things, pushing their product or theory, and they want to hear their voice, not the voice of the player. I have found over the years, with professional players in particular, that if you take the time to build a relationship and listen to them, they're going to tell you what they need and what's important to them. That's what I wish I knew when I started out.

Brubaker: Two things really stand out. If you're not paying, you're not paying attention. It's the old expression that you've got to have skin in the game. As someone out in the working world now, looking at bottom line expenses, profit and loss, you pay much more attention and you want to get much more value out of the things that you are paying for out of pocket.

We are very fortunate that when we were college athletes, a portion of our tuition was subsidized by scholarships, grants, loans or parental support. Many student athletes are getting, if not a free education, a deeply discounted one. When we're paying, we pay a little more attention, we want to squeeze every last dime out of our experience and get as much benefit as we can. I wish I would have realized that a little earlier. I might not have taken some faculty mentors I had for granted. I knew their value, but I didn't realize just how much wisdom they were imparting to me at the time, that I would be paying top dollar for if I were an entrepreneur hiring them to help me later in life. Having skin in the game definitely changes the value of things.

The other big piece is realizing that life is the curriculum, that we're all students, and that everybody you meet has a lesson to teach you. This is the principle behind my book *Seeds To Success*. Realize that everything is a learning experience. It might seem like adversity or failure, but the whole point of it is to help you become better later.

Rickertsen: Awareness. I didn't consciously think about it when I was a competitive athlete, but so much of my athletic performance just happened to me. Especially from a mental standpoint, I was a victim, for lack of a better word, of what was going on in my brain. If I had a bad day at school, or at practice, then I was going to continue to have a bad day. I just wasn't aware that I had control of those pieces, that I wasn't just a victim to my own head, that I could take control and I could have the performance and the mindset that I wanted. Now I can apply that even to my job and say, 'These are the skills that I know now. Even though it's not a sports performance, how can I add that into my performance? It's understanding that how you think is not permanent, it's just a habit that you've created, and you can create any type of habit you want. Looking back on my career, I know that I was very much a victim of my own brain, and I didn't use it all the time to my advantage.

Knowing that I can create a habit of thinking just like I can create a physical habit would have been very, very impactful in my sport career.

Bell: The biggest thing is routine. I never had a routine growing up and I never had one in college. I never understood the importance of it. Even the pros I work with, sometimes their routines are just bad. What's a good routine? Anything that gets you dialed in and focused on this pitch. More and more, sports psychology, mental training and mental coaching has made its way into the high profile of elite athletics. That was the biggest thing I never got. I never understood how crucial breathing was, although it's something so important. The cleansing breath and that refocus can make all the difference. I never got that stuff. I just love helping so many athletes with basic things like that, then going deeper and working on that confidence issue. I never knew there was going to be that one moment that made all the difference, and it does. It's true and it's real.

Dixon: It's J-bands, Alan Jaeger and his long toss program. I coached it for ten years, and I saw what it did to hundreds of kids. I could only imagine if I had that as a player where would I have been. I had some success, but with J-bands, with today's technology and video analysis, it's just so much more advanced. The one other thing would be to be in the present more.

Gilbert: I know exactly what I wish I knew back when I was younger. Back when I was younger, growing up in Boston, I wanted to be the third baseman for the Red Sox, I wanted to be a great student, and I wanted to be a superstar musician, but you know what happened? Other kids had more athletic talent than I did. Other kids were smarter and more musical than me. That's what I thought when I was in the fifth, sixth, seventh, eighth, ninth and tenth grades. Now I realize that the kids who I thought had more athletic talent, they trained harder than I did, practiced more than I did. The kids who I thought were smarter than me, they studied more than I did. The kids who were more musical, they went to more lessons and practiced more than I did. Nobody had more ability than me. They just used better strategies. They just trained harder. Anybody can be trained to do anything.

Suppose we were walking on a hot summer day and we see three bodybuilders wearing muscle shirts walking towards us. You say, 'Hey, Dr. Gilbert, God bless these young men with great bodies.' I would say, 'What are you, nuts? These guys work out like maniacs and take steroids. They take drugs. They train.'

The thing I know now that I wish I knew then is that anybody could be trained to be a great athlete, anybody could be trained to be a great student, anybody could be trained to be a great musician. I know, of course there is the kid at school who never studies and gets all A's, but I would say, the research is showing with the 10,000 hours thing that it's all about training and not about talent.

I was in the Hammonton High School wrestling room. They had on the wall, 'Hard work beats talent when talent doesn't work hard.' What I tell myself now is, if you want to be third baseman for the Red Sox, train like Ted Williams. If you want to be the smartest kid in the school, study like Melissa Sapio. If you want to be a great musician, put in the time that Bruce Springsteen puts in.

I met some of Bruce Springsteen's high school teachers. Do you think he cared about school? All he cared about was music. I spoke to the high school history teacher of David Copperfield, the great magician. He said, 'I was teaching history to this guy who was doing these things every day under his desk with three rubber balls and this and that, and I finally had enough. I said, 'David, I don't know what you're going to do with your life, but you're not going to make any money doing little tricks with the balls.' Now if you want to hire David Copperfield to do one performance, it would cost $250,000. So David Copperfield was doing all right.

I'd say the thing I know now that I wish I knew then is that everybody has ability, all they are lacking is the strategy. People don't know this. They always doubt their ability. No, don't doubt your ability. Doubt the strategies you're using. Doubt the way you're training. Perhaps you can't hit a curve ball. Do you think you were born not to hit a curve ball? No, you were trained not to hit a curve ball, so you had better start training better.

Toole: I wish I knew more about routines when I was younger. I was always a player. I played basketball, football, baseball, and soccer in high school. I used to listen to Eminem when I was a high school student, trying to get myself all pumped up and jacked up for a game. Then I'd go out on the basketball court and do 110 mph down the court and miss a layup because I was out of control. Growing up, I didn't understand the type of person I was or the type of player I was. I was more of an energetic, hardworking kid, so in order for me to do well on the court or on the field, I had to relax before games. In college I developed a routine where I didn't listen to the music that got me pumped up, I listened to the stuff that got me more relaxed. I turned into a country music fan, because that's what gets me locked in to play.

Obviously, if you're playing football it's a little bit different than baseball. You're running down the field as fast as you can, trying to tackle people. I didn't understand what a pre-game routine was growing up. I was always thinking, "Oh, it's a Friday night football game, I'm going to get as jacked up as I can.' I'm going to run out there and just go crazy. I carried that over into basketball, then into baseball. If I had a better understanding of routines and getting myself locked into play, I would have had more success in other sports. Routines are huge and I didn't understand that as much as I do now.

Tully: That's easy. I wish I had known that the only thing that matters is the present. There was a study done a couple of years ago in the United Kingdom that said most people spend most of their time focusing on the wrong thing.

The first sentence was: 99% of the people spend 99% of their time on things that don't matter.

I would identify what needed to be done, and then make sure it got done. That means staying in the moment, working on it, refusing to get distracted when the temptation is there, just staying on it. I know an Olympic coach who says, 'Stay on it.' That's his way. Persevere in that thing that you need to do. That's all I know about coaching now. You have to identify what needs to be done, make sure it gets done, and you have to do that all the time.

Margolies: The biggest thing is that all of these things that I'm talking about are skills. If it's a skill, it can be learned. For 35 years or so, I have been teaching it this way, as a skill. I've worked with thousands of athletes, and only had two athletes in all of that time that I would classify as having real issues, where I had to refer them to a psychotherapist or a clinical psychologist for depression. One was a girl for an eating disorder. If you take the approach that an athlete cannot handle stress in the batter's box and that's a psychological disorder, then we're doing ourselves a disservice.

It's a skill, and virtually anybody can learn to handle that kind of stress. It takes practice, it takes the right understanding of what it is they're doing, but it's just a skill. I'm a very big proponent of using imagery. My research at the U.S. Olympic Training Center had to do with imagery, and I have very specific ways that I teach athletes to use it. It's one of those critical factors that helps make a success of people when they're playing. Two weeks ago, I went to the game of an athlete I had worked with. He's a professional athlete and when he saw me in the green room after the game he said, 'Yes, Mike, I'm still doing the visualization.' He had just returned from the World Cup, and he's using it at that level. Visualization, imagery rehearsal, and relaxation training are skills, and if you use those skills it will help you perform at a much higher level.

Dedman: When I started coaching, I felt like I had to prove myself to others. What I realized over time was that most of my mistakes were in fact because I was worried too much about perception and not necessarily as much about the relationships that I had and the impact I was making. When I started coaching baseball, I thought that I was coaching baseball because it was baseball. It didn't take me too long to realize that I wanted to coach baseball because I enjoyed teaching. I enjoyed relationships, helping people who were younger than me, giving them my experiences and other people's experiences and helping them learn about themselves. Now the thing I enjoy most is helping guys to trust themselves, have confidence in themselves and learn how to make adjustments. The biggest thing is that when I first started, I was way too concerned about me. Not to say that I still don't have some of that, but certainly I spend more time thinking about the people I've had an opportunity to have an impact with than I did before.

Dehmer: The mathematical side of things, the way to measure the process that I've developed along the way, has gone a long way, for practices and for games, to put a different spin on the game, a different perspective that kids are not very used to. Ultimately it becomes a great way and a great vantage point to look at the game and their performance, because we know that so many kids are going to personalize performance. If I can give them a better way to view their performance, a more positive way, what we've found is that even if a kid's hitting .300 for his batting average, his Quality At Bat average is about twice as high for those same at bats he's had all season long. It's a no-brainer to show that kid that he's hitting .600 as opposed to .300.

It's the same thing with our pitchers. We had a player, when our streak was snapped, who was the pitcher on the mound and ended up losing his second start of that season, so he's 0-2 on the season going into his third start. His body language was telling me, I'm 0-2. We went back and looked at his strike percentage, his A3P percentage, and how many Quality Innings he's had. It was phenomenal how well he had pitched. Obviously, the outcome wasn't what he had wanted, but he was giving us every chance to win the game and he was pitching exceptionally well. The statistics and the process-based measurement that we had recorded were off the charts. You would think that he would have won them, but we said, 'Hey, you just keep doing what you're doing and keep pitching the way you're pitching and good things are going to happen. We're going to make those those plays, we're going to get a clutch hit for you.' He never lost a game the rest of the season. He competed so well in the state championship game that we ended up winning 1-0 and he pitched a no-hitter in the state championship game. It was a turning point for him. It allowed us to show him something positive that he was doing, because it could have gotten in his head really, really quickly with another loss and been 0-3 and who knows where it could have gone from there.

It's ammunition on a lot of different levels for coaches and players to allow them to measure themselves. It allows coaches to make good, sound decisions about who they're going to put in the lineup instead of just thinking, 'Well, he hit good at practice, he's been looking pretty good in the cages.' When you start measuring it using criteria, it does become a lot more black and white. I'm very envious of a track coach who has to pick those four guys to run the 4x relay, because they just say, 'Toe the line and run. Whoever wins, the first four, you're in the lineup.' It's pretty easy, right? A baseball coach has a lot more decisions to make with defensive and offensive things, and there's a lot more that goes into it, but measuring it makes it a lot easier for coaches to do in the long run.

Question Review

What do you know now that you wish you knew then?

Cain: The power of a day, the power of mentors, the power of reading, and making sure that you find your mission, that you take the time to step back from the daily grind, and the daily fast pace of everyday life, put down the cell phone and ask yourself, 'What it is that I really want?'

Hanson: What other people think really does not matter. What matters is my own integrity, my own principles, if I am acting consistent with what I believe to be right and good. If so, then go for it. If I'm trying to avoid looking bad, that's a waste of time.

Springer: Get rid of the batting average. Your career starts when you say 'I don't care what I hit.' That is going to give you the freedom to show up to the field with confidence. Baseball is the biggest self-esteem-destroying sport in the world.

Gordon: If I was to go back and do it again, what I wish I had known was that it was about the process, having fun, giving your best, and God will do the rest. It's about fun, faith and fearless. I wish I had known that my identity is not wrapped up in myself as an athlete.

Afremow: Don't be too proud to get help from special people with special skills. Most of us, especially male athletes, want to be self-reliant, but it is actually a sign of strength, rather than a weakness, to reach out for guidance and support.

Jaeger: I wouldn't want to change anything because it all really brought me to have to get tuned into this world. I had to adjust my life to where I could understand why.

Weintraub: When you realize that you don't have any of the answers, then you start getting better faster. People have to be in the right place in their life to receive certain lessons. Get the chance to be around good people, whenever it is and wherever it is, and try to take advantage of that opportunity.

Janssen: Culture is everything and how important a coach's job is to create that culture, champion that culture, and be a caretaker for that culture.

Maher: How to slow down, not push something on someone and, most importantly, listen to them. If you take the time to build a relationship and listen to them, they're going to tell you what they need and what's important to them.

Brubaker: You've got to have skin in the game. When we're paying, we pay a little more attention, we want to squeeze every last dime out of our experience and get as much benefit as we can. Also, life is the curriculum, we're all students, and everybody you meet has a lesson to teach you.

Rickertsen: Awareness. I was very much a victim of my own brain, and I didn't use it all the time to my advantage.

Bell: The biggest thing is routine. I never understood the importance of it.

Dixon: Alan Jaeger's J Bands and long toss program.

Gilbert: Anybody can be trained to do anything. 'Hard work beats talent when talent doesn't work hard.'

Toole: I wish I knew more about the importance of routines when I was younger. If I had a better understanding of routines and getting myself locked into play, I would have had more success in other sports.

Tully: The only thing that matters is the present. 99% of the people spend 99% of their time on things that don't matter.

Margolies: All of these mental game tools are skills. If it's a skill, it can be learned.

Dedman: What I realized over time was that most of my mistakes were in fact because I was worried too much about perception and not necessarily as much about the relationships that I had and the impact I was making.

Dehmer: The mathematical side of things, the way to measure the process that I've developed along the way, has gone a long way, for practices and for games, to put a different spin on the game.

HOT SEAT

Bringin' The Heat!

Positive Energy

Dixon: Contagious.

Rickertsen: Contagious.

Bell: Contagious.

Brubaker: Contagious.

Toole: Dustin Pedroia.

Gordon: Pete Carroll & Gus Bradley.

Hanson: That's all there is.

Weintraub: Useful.

Margolies: Motor.

Maher: Laser-like fine tuning.

Dedman: Have to be a giver.

Tully: Love it when you see it.

Afremow: What every player should bring to the field each day.

Jaeger: Infectious. Someone that appreciates the environment.

Cain: The foundation of a championship team and a skill you must develop if you're going to become a champion.

Goldberg: Good athletes who want to be there, want to work hard, want to improve, don't complain. This is one aspect of being a winner.

Springer: Positive energy is a choice. I'm going to bring it or I'm not. It is choosing to be positive, choosing to help, choosing to give and not always take, take, take.

Janssen: Positive energy is one of those invisible forces that has to fuel you, your athletes and your team. Hopefully it's something you're trying to create.

Gilbert: This is probably the most important thing. Read Frank Bettger. We could control our energy through our actions. A-C-E: Action Creates Energy.

Dehmer: Positive energy comes from a decision you make. You can be that player who is the drain on the team, or you can be the guy who's going to uplift the guys around you. You always have a decision, and it is a choice.

Confidence

Dixon: Necessity.

Maher: Belief.

Hanson: Overrated.

Toole: Clayton Kershaw.

Margolies: Belief in yourself.

Jaeger: Inner trust. Unconditional.

Dedman: Is a choice.

Tully: Hard to build, easy to lose.

Rickertsen: Important to performance and a skill.

Gordon: What you need to be your best.

Bell: The most important mental skill, also the most difficult.

Weintraub: Controllable. Comes from the way we think about our preparation and our experiences.

Afremow: Confidence is a beautiful thing. Respect the competition but always respect your own abilities even more. Trust is a must.

Brubaker: Confidence is a choice you make moment to moment, day to day. It is not something that you can just order up. It is something that you have to choose to do.

Springer: Confidence is a choice. Sometimes, we think that we have to have success to be confident, but if you're not confident, you're not going to have any success.

Dehmer: Very, very fragile, but by the same token a decision that you can make with body language and how you act and go about things. You don't have to show that you're 0-for-4 or 0-for-10 or in the worst slump of your life, you can still act confident at any moment.

Cain: The secret to unlocking your performance success. Confidence is a choice, and confidence is made up of what Tom Hanson in his book *Play Big* talks about with the ABCs. **A**cting big, **B**reathing big, and **C**ommitting big. Those are the fundamentals of confidence.

Gilbert: You might not be confident on the inside, but you have to be confident on the outside. Train yourself to act as if you're confident. Act confident, then you'll feel confident. If you say, 'When I feel confident, then I'll act confident,' it will never happen. When you start acting confident, you'll feel confident.

Goldberg: Confidence is something that you have as a by-product of doing all the hard work. You can't tell yourself to be confident, it doesn't work that way. If you pay your dues, put the work in, work on the mental side of your game as well as the physical side of your game, then confidence will be waiting for you as a byproduct.

It's a direct result of what you focus on. If you go into performance and you focus on the right things, specifically your job and you, and not other people, you're more likely to be confident. If you go into performance and focus on opponents, then you're likely to have no confidence.

Janssen: Confidence is one of those absolutely critical aspects to an athlete's performance, but one that is extremely tenuous, a huge roller-coaster. When

I'm playing well, it's easy to have confidence, but especially in the game of baseball, if I'm 0-for-10 or 0-for-12, what's happening to my confidence right now? How do I get that back and going for me, because if I don't have confidence, I'm pretty much shot.

Championship Culture

Dixon: Practice.

Maher: System and routine.

Bell: Process, process, process.

Rickertsen: Created by athletes.

Toole: Derek Jeter. The Yankees.

Hanson: Essential to winning championships.

Dedman: Can be created, but takes a lot of energy.

Jaeger: Communication, connection, process-oriented and a nurturing environment.

Margolies: Professionalism that extends throughout the entire team.

Tully: That's the way we do things around here. The best teams in the world, that's the way we do things around here.

Gilbert: T-E-A-M: Together Everyone Achieves More, if there's a Total Effort from All Members.

Afremow: If you really want to win, you've got to buy in. Every player on the team is important and every player is trying to make a positive difference. That's what a championship culture is all about.

Brubaker: Built one player at a time. You have to get everybody's mind right. You have to get everybody moving towards the right side of that teeter-totter in a positive way to influence a culture of champions who are playing for each other, not just next to each other.

Dehmer: Comes from the top down. It has to start with the coaches and be presented by the coaches daily, continuously, and consistently, no matter what the circumstance. Obviously at that point it's the responsibility of the players and everyone within the program to uphold it.

Goldberg: It's an attitude that winning teams have where they support each other. The team is bigger than the individual. They understand the value of takings risks and failing. They support each other. They don't scapegoat each other. They don't put each other down when they make mistakes. Instead, they build each other up. It's what you find on very successful, repetitively successful teams.

Springer: Team. You've got to get 25 guys buying in. If you don't have 25 guys buying in, you're probably not going to have a championship.

Gordon: Doesn't happen by accident. It's something that you must cultivate and work on every day. You must be relentless in creating it.

Weintraub: Priorities. Excellence and enthusiasm won't surprise anybody, but I put forgiveness right up there with those two, because if you don't have forgiveness, you won't be able to maintain enthusiasm, which will therefore have an impact on your excellence.

Cain: The foundation of any team. The first thing I do when I go to work with a program is to make sure that they've established a championship culture. If you're on a team, take this test. Hand an index card to every player and staff in that program and ask them to write down the four to five character traits that are your championship culture. If not everyone writes down the exact same thing, you don't have a culture. You have 35 or 40 people with their different ideas about what the culture should be. If you're going to be a champion, you've got to get everyone on the same page about who you are, that is step number one as a head coach.

Janssen: It's absolutely essential for a team's long-term success. It's something that coaches need to consciously build and maintain, but it is often neglected until it's too late. Bruce Weber was in his last season as basketball coach at Illinois, and things were heading downhill. In a press conference after the game, he admitted that what he had done was focus too much on winning and not put in the kind of culture that would help to win long term. There are too many coaches who, after the fact, realize their main error was not focusing more on that culture aspect.

Routines

Tully: Are everything. Everything.

Bell: Dialed in. Breathe. Just hit.

Rickertsen: Builds comfort for performance.

Dixon: Find what it is and maximize it.

Maher: Purpose and commitment.

Weintraub: The way to guarantee success.

Toole: Nomar Garciaparra. When I was growing up, he always did this batting glove thing when he got in the box.

Gordon: Essential. Winning habits are what we become.

Cain: The fundamentals of consistency and the secrets of success are hidden in your daily routine.

Margolies: We have pre-game, during the game, and post-game kinds of routines. They set us up to get into the zone.

Brubaker: They make the extraordinary ordinary. It's not a big at bat. It's just the next at bat. They're all the same.

Dehmer: The foundation of making sure you can compete one pitch at a time, a huge part of being a 1PitchWarrior.

Hanson: Routines are really important, and yet they are a double-edged sword. They can work for you, and they can work against you.

Jaeger: Having the discipline to do things that are the core or foundation to being as good as you can be. They're very important.

Afremow: Routines are habits of champions and they are always under a player's control. In contrast, superstitions are always in control of the player.

Dedman: If you don't have routines, you're just grabbing at random stuff and it's very much just luck and fortune.

Springer: Routine is not a superstition, it's something that makes you good, but you also have to realize that the results might not be there. Routine needs to be the same as long as you have had enough success to know that it's right.

Gilbert: Routines, habits, rituals, that's it. My friend Mike Tully said, 'If you're watching practice, the first day of spring training or the seventh game of the World Series, the guys are doing the same thing over and over again.' So much of sports is routines and rituals, but you want to have the right routine and the right ritual. You want to make it a habit, because you want to be able to do the right thing without thinking about it.

Goldberg: Pre-performance routines are the most important way that an athlete has of staying calm pre-performance, distracting them from performance-disrupting distractions. If I have a pre-race ritual as a runner or as a swimmer, or a pre-hit ritual as a batter, I'm going to use that to control my focus, and that's going to do two things for me. That's going to keep me calm and it's going to keep my head in the game. When you don't have a ritual, you get nervous and you tend to focus on the wrong things.

Janssen: Routines are important to get the athlete and the team in the right mindset. It goes back to understanding what makes each guy tick, getting him in the groove and making sure he sets up a routine. Whether it's an exhibition game, playing for a national championship, at home or away, that routine should be something he can grab onto.

Process

Bell: Championship culture.

Dixon: The only thing that matters.

Rickertsen: The key to success.

Maher: Being in the moment.

Gordon: If you love the process, you'll love what the process produces.

Margolies: Individual things to focus on that keep you present.

Weintraub: There's no good in worrying about things that are outside of your control. So it's all about process.

Hanson: Process is essential. I'll link it in with system, and having a system is one of the absolute most important things for consistent success.

Afremow: Always trust the process to deliver the results. Have a process in place, trust it, and you're likely to get the results you want.

Jaeger: How many hours do you have? It's something that's really important to identify first and foremost, and to figure out what things you need to do to be great at it consistently.

Dedman: If you're outcome-oriented, it's going to be a grab bag, an assortment of luck. If you're process-oriented, you always have something to go back to that gives you trust and self-confidence.

Janssen: Process has got to be worked on a daily basis. That's the secret to success, whether you have that long-term vision, or whether you're a Leah O'Brian Amico and just understand how valuable it is. It's got to be something you do each and every day.

Dehmer: A huge buzzword that is overused. I almost hate that word when coaches don't back it up with things that they're actually doing. It is about the process, but if you're not measuring the process and you don't have a process that you're measuring, then it's just lip service.

Springer: Process is everything. It's about today, about the attainable daily goals and doing what you can control. You cannot control yesterday anymore, and you can't control everything. You can control right now, so get great at that.

Gilbert: Process beats product every single time. If you're always focusing on the scoreboard, you're never going to hit the ball. Focus on what you're doing while you're doing it. Don't focus on what you're going to get out of it. If you're taking a test and you're focusing on getting an A, that's going to screw up answering the math problem. Do what you're doing while you're doing it.

Tully: You're never looking for the product. You don't go out and try to win a ballgame. You go out and do everything you possibly can to win the ballgame. You get a good secondary lead, you take pitches when you're supposed to, you hit behind the runner when you're supposed to, you back up bases, you encourage your teammates. You do everything you can, you don't think about winning, you think about giving full effort.

Goldberg: Process is what makes the world go round in baseball and in any other sport. Process is staying in the now. It's about focus. You could focus on outcome, 'I've got to get a hit,' or you could focus on staying calm up at the plate, feeling quick hands and seeing the release point in the ball and nothing else. When you focus on process, you do well. When you focus on outcome, you choke.

Cain: Nick Saban talks about the steps you have to take to get to where you want to be. The process is something that's constantly ongoing, something you're always trying to understand, and what makes championship-caliber programs like Alabama football or LSU baseball. Skip Bertman referred to the process as his system. The process is what's going to make you either a failure or a success.

Brubaker: If you forget everything else, remember that you have to have a process. I will take it outside the realm of sports. I work a lot with sales organizations and sales people. It doesn't matter what their process is, but the salespeople who have a process that they employ, as opposed to just randomly going about their job, are exponentially more successful. It isn't the actual process they are using, the ABC process or XYZ or whatever it is, it is the fact that they are using one. If you can't explain what you're doing, as a coach or an athlete, as a process, I'm not sure you know what you're doing.

Controllables

Margolies: Yourself.

Maher: Letting go.

Rickertsen: Where you need to focus your attention.

Brubaker: The only thing you should focus on.

Dixon: Figure them out. Don't waste your energy on stuff you can't control.

Bell: Focus, refocus, breathing, routine, and how we respond.

Gordon: Attitude, effort and action to be a great teammate. Focus on them. Control the controllables.

Toole: Umpires, because you can't always control what they're going to do.

Hanson: Often misunderstood. I would say they're illusive. You want to focus on what you can control, and yes, I'd go with very important to focus on.

Dedman: Our thoughts are the most controllable things we have. If that's our focal point, the other things usually take care of themselves.

Cain: Everything else is a waste of time. You must focus only on the controllables, and all you can control is yourself and your APE. If you want to know what APE stands for, check out *The Mental Conditioning Manual.*

Afremow: That's where all of our energy needs to go on game day. The main controllables that come to mind are positive self-talk, good body language, great communication, and strong effort.

Weintraub: They make success happen. A lot of people try to buy into this definition of controlling the controllables and giving your best effort leads to success. What I'm saying is that it doesn't just lead to success. It is success.

Tully: That's the jackpot. You control what you can control and let everything else go. You can't control the umpire, the field, the weather, the fans or the opponent. You can control your effort, your attitude, and your mistake response.

Dehmer: It's where you need to get your kids focused the most, making sure that they're focusing on what they can do and what they're trying to control rather than the things they can't. It is a tough thing to do, but we need to understand which ones are the controllables and which ones are the things that are uncontrollable. That's part of teaching the mental game to your players.

Gilbert: Probably the greatest prayer of all time was written by a professor of philosophy at Columbia University, Reinhold Niebuhr, and they use it a lot in AA. 'God grant me the serenity to accept the things I cannot change, the courage to change the things I can, and the wisdom to know the difference.'

Springer: Controllables is everything. You can only control only what you can control. Don't beat yourself up or think you have to be perfect at everything. There's one perfect, Jesus. That's it. When you think you have to be perfect, all of a sudden your non-confident guy creeps in, and he sucks.

Janssen: Got to control them. People lose their composure over something they have very little control over. If you can live in that world of the controllables and control those, you're definitely going to have the poise and composure you need to be successful.

Goldberg: The biggest cause of stress for any athlete, in or out of baseball, is when you concentrate on things that are out of your control, like winning, getting a hit, your stats or playing time. Controllables are the things you have direct control over. If I have to face a really great pitcher, I might not be able to control what he throws, but I can control staying calm and I can control making sure I see the ball. When you focus only on things you can control, your tendency is to be a much more competent athlete under pressure.

Jaeger: Great when you're talking about things you can control, of course. But there's a trap to that word, because ultimately, if you study peak performance, the highest place you could be is in a mode of trust. Control can easily cross over into fear, perfectionism and trying too hard. Peak state is about surrender, trust, letting go and allowing.

Mind-Body Connection

Rickertsen: Powerful!

Dixon: Very, very spiritual.

Maher: Being whole

Bell: Body language doesn't talk, it screams.

Afremow: The body always wins when the mind refuses to give in.

Gordon: It's everything. The body hears what the mind is saying, so speak kindly and positively to your body.

Brubaker: You can't underestimate it. If it can help your body rid itself of cancer cells, it can help you hit a round ball with a round bat better.

Toole: You go out and you visualize. I always visualize hitting a line drive out over second base. Whenever that happens, to me, that's the culmination of the mind and body coming together.

Dedman: It has to be practiced. Awareness takes time. Most 22-year-olds are way more aware than 18-year-olds. We have to help them understand that their thoughts and approach affect their body.

Tully: It's everything. When you're in practice, you have to be mindful. In our school, we have a saying, 'You have to work on what you're working on while you're working on it.' You identify the thing you need to work on. It's just so important that you work on what you're working on.

Springer: The mind is over the body. The mind doesn't know that the body is not doing it. I can visualize myself hitting missiles for 5 minutes, then I can go take BP for 5 minutes, and now I'm hooking balls and hitting balls off the net. When I'm using my mind, I'm not taking any bad swings.

Dehmer: What goes on in the mind is what's going to be seen in the body. It's got to start with the short game, which is the six inches between your ears. If we can work there first, then we can have a pretty good opportunity to make sure the body performs at its best. I'd much rather have a guy that has a real good mental game and maybe not the prettiest swing, than the guy who has the prettiest swing and a five-cent head.

Margolies: That's really where the relaxation training and the imagery training come in. As we become self-aware of our muscles and of everything we're doing, and don't just leave it to our unconscious, as we are consciously able to make that connection and work on that skill, it's an increase in self-awareness.

Janssen: Fortunately, it's something that a lot more people are recognizing. When I first started out in this career 20 years ago, I had to spend the first 20 minutes trying to legitimize the mind-body connection with athletes. Fortunately the field has advanced tremendously, and now it's something that they're much more aware of.

Cain: Make sure those two sync up, because if your mind is somewhere else than where your body is, you're thinking too much. You're thinking in the past, you're thinking in the future, and awareness and attention is where the mind and body are always synced up. Thus the reason for a final thought, a deep breath or a last breath and bringing yourself into that moment to sync up the mind and body. Yoga is tremendous at doing that.

Goldberg: Performance is self-fulfilling. You always get what you expect because what you think in your mind goes into your body. It changes your body physiology, your muscle tension, increases your respiration and makes it shallower, and changes the blood-flow, and that's going to affect performance. If I'm focusing on the wrong things or thinking about the wrong things, I'm going to get physically tight and lose my endurance. That's going to affect my performance by killing my endurance, tightening up my muscles and wrecking my mechanics.

Hanson: I get what everyone's talking about, but my point is that it's all one thing. Where is your brain? It's in your body. That's why *Heads-Up Baseball* was so well received, because it's a baseball book. It's not that we set aside 15 minutes for the mental game, and then the rest of practice is the physical game. That makes no sense. It's strictly a semantic device.

Weintraub: That's big. If you want to create an ideal state, think good thoughts and have good body language. Well, it's easy to have good body language when you think good thoughts, and vice versa. There's so much to learn about the brain and the heart. It's amazing and there's so much more to go. I would love to see if in a thousand years there's a significant understanding of this connection and also of the brain in general. The mind-body connection is huge. Sometimes people try to take shortcuts to win the mental side of the game, but it doesn't work.

Jaeger: Huge. Yoga. Doing things like meditation, things that get you in tune to your body. You know we're in our heads a lot in our society, thinking a lot. We have 10,000-15,000 thoughts a day, and it might be more than that. So, mind-body connection is actually a cool idea. It sounds funny, but it's important to get in our body. I don't just mean if you're doing bicep curls, get into your biceps. I mean, get in tune with your body: feel your legs, feel the earth, feel your body as this one beautiful mechanism, this one beautiful piece instead of just getting heady and being above the shoulders and thinking of our body more from our head space. Think of your body more from a holistic place.

Gilbert: There isn't a mind-body connection because the mistake we make in our culture is thinking they are two words, mind and body. There's one word, mind-body, because anything that happens in our mind affects our body and anything that happens in our body affects our mind. They are totally connected. They're not separate.

Back in the 50's, no ball player ever lifted weights. They thought you'd be muscle-bound and you would never be able to hit or throw the ball. Now we realize that's totally ridiculous. We're at the stage now of developing the body. The next stage will put a whole lot of time into developing the mind, because that's where the power is.

Success

Rickertsen: Subjective.

Bell: Process.

Brubaker: Leaves clues.

Maher: Progress towards goals.

Hanson: To be individually defined.

Dixon: Inevitable if you have a relationship with practice.

Dedman: Success is found in the process, not in the result.

Margolies: It's what you make out of it. It's what you want in life.

Tully: John Wooden had it. Success is knowing that you have done everything you possibly could do to prepare.

Afremow: I'll quote Muhammad Ali: 'Success is not achieved by winning all the time. Real success comes when we rise after we fall.'

Gordon: Is meant to be shared. We have success not for just ourselves. The success we create is meant to be shared with others. A true success is about helping others be successful.

Toole: Derek Jeter and the Yankees. I was a Yankees fan growing up. In the late 90s, they won the World Series.

Dehmer: Defined in many ways, but Coach John Wooden said it the best. 'It's just a matter of you going out there and trying to compete your best when your best is needed.'

Janssen: Success is something you've got to define, what it means to you. A lot of times it is wins and losses. They're not only focused on success, but they're also focused on significance and having a huge impact, not just on a player's life for a few years, but on a person's life for their lifetime.

Goldberg: Success is a by-product of doing the right things. Success is something that will meet you at the end of the journey without you looking for it. I think of success as a paradox. The more you try to be successful, the further away it goes. The less you focus on the outcome and success, the more success you'll have.

Springer: We all want it, but we don't always get it. Be OK with it as long as I gave my best effort. Success is how you feel. 90% of a Quality At Bat is how you feel when you walk up to the plate. Do I know that I can hit or I am hoping to hit? Just because you don't get the result doesn't mean it wasn't a success.

Weintraub: Knowing you did your best. Peace of mind is this amazing thing. A lot of times an athlete will come back when I review this concept and say it's doing your best. I say yes, you're right, but it's the peace of mind that comes from knowing you did your best. If you have peace of mind, then you're not worried about the outcome, so it's much easier to focus on the task at hand. Peace of mind is a big deal in performance and even a bigger deal when you look at self-esteem and quality of life.

Gilbert: S-U-C-C-E-S-S-I-S-N-O-W-H-E-R-E. Write all those letters together and some people will read it as 'Success is nowhere', and some people will read it as 'Success is now here.' Success has a lot to do with perception. People have to have a vision of what they want, like Martin Luther King's vision. He knew what he wanted. When he was in school to become a minister, he took a couple of speech courses and he got C's in them. Imagine if he thought, 'Well, I'll never be a successful orator, because these professors gave me C's.' Imagine Martin Luther King getting a C in a speech class, but he did.

Cain: Success is not something that you pursue. I spent a lot of years of my life trying to be successful, whether it was financial success or working with championship teams or whatever it was. Success is not something you pursue. It's like a butterfly: you can never quite catch it. It always gets away from you. Success is something that you attract, and something that you become by becoming a successful person, someone who reads, who works to become more, who's never satisfied with where they're at, who is always looking not to get more but to become more. If you want more success, you have to become more successful. That happens by expanding your knowledge and expanding the actions you take on a daily basis.

Jaeger: A byproduct of having a great process and not focusing on success, just focusing on doing what you need to do. Whatever you call it, success or whatever the byproduct is, great. It is what it is, but that word can be very dangerous. Success is being great at your process, really knowing what your process is, and really committing to it. That may not lead to success in wins or losses, but it gives you a much better chance. The word success is tricky for me. I really try to stay away from that and focus on really being great at your process. By the way, success is great. It's nice to look back at the end of the season and say, 'I was very successful at staying with my process and it led to me being as good as I can be and the team being as good as it can be.'

Failure

Hanson: Essential.

Maher: Adjustments.

Afremow: Failure is temporary.

Rickertsen: Temporary, but necessary.

Dixon: Part of the game, deal with it.

Bell: A necessary ingredient for success.

Dehmer: It's the first attempt in learning.

Jaeger: Preoccupation with the past or the future, and to me it can be a teaching point, but it's something that can really be a trap too.

Gordon: Is a gift if you are willing to learn and grow from it. Every failure has made me who I am and made me stronger.

Margolies: I was going to be sarcastic and say it's what other people think, but failure is also up to you. We decide to be failures in life, and a lot of that is how we've been trained. That really is unfortunate.

Brubaker: Necessary. If you want to get that success, you have to go through a lot of failure. There's no such thing as an overnight success. An overnight success is made through thousands and thousands of nights of failure.

Gilbert: There's no failure, just feedback. Once Thomas Edison was asked how he dealt with the 14,000 times he failed in trying to develop the light bulb. He said, 'I didn't fail 14,000 times. I learned 14,000 ways how not to develop the light bulb.'

Cain: Necessary part of success and the neighbor to success on the highway to excellence. Failure is positive feedback. If you want more success, you have to fail more. If you're in sales, the best way to make more money in sales, the best way to get more yes's, is to get a lot more no's. Those who fail will fail their way to success if they keep going.

Dedman: Failure is necessary, no question about that. We're always spending all of this time trying to avoid failure, instead of trying to be relentless in the process. The thing that I've found in my career is that I've had to have failure to learn. I was learning at other times also, but the greatest leaps I've made in self-improvement, which have led me to be better across the board in my life, have stemmed from those failures.

Springer: Failure is something we are going to do. You've got to learn how to fail yet still be confident. Not only in baseball, but in life. Don't beat yourself up. I give you permission not to be perfect. I give you permission not to get three hits. I need you to compete with confidence with an attainable goal to hit the ball hard. I struck out six times in one day in a doubleheader. I played another 4 years. I didn't get released.

Weintraub: You have to put quote marks on that word. It's a stepping stone to success. Michael Jordan in the Nike commercial said, 'Twenty-six times I've been trusted by my teammates to take the last second shot to either tie or win the game and I missed. Because of that I succeeded.' He didn't say in spite of that, he said because of that. Just like Thomas Edison didn't fail ten thousand times to make the light bulb—ten thousand times it didn't work. That's why he found the one that did.

Tully: Failure is not permanent unless you let it be. You can either be a loser or a learner. Two weeks before the big win over the Soviet Union, the United States lost to the Soviet Union 10-3 at Madison Square Garden on national television. It was a devastating loss for everybody except Herb Brooks, who happened to be in there. We interviewed him after the game and asked what he thought of the game. We expected him to say it was really humbling and humiliating. Instead, he said, 'We learned some things.' Wow. If you can stand back as an athlete or a coach in the face of the most massive defeat and say we learned some things, then you never lose. You're a learner, not a loser.

Goldberg: Stepping stone to success. It's the most important thing an athlete can learn to do. How you handle your setbacks and your failures will make the difference between becoming a champion or stalling out and quitting. Failure is critical and it's feedback. I like to use the cliché that it's the 'breakfast of champions'. Failure tells you what you did that didn't work and what you need to do differently next time. If you want to be successful in your life on and off the field, you've got to learn how to manage your failures.

Omaha

Dixon: Memories.

Maher: Great baseball experience.

Bell: Rosenblatt. Vanderbilt.

Rickertsen: College World Series.

Tully: It's where they all want to be. It's what it's all about.

Dehmer: Tradition in my family. We go every year. Fun.

Janssen: For a lot of people, it's that vision, that dream, that carrot, that pinnacle that most people are striving for.

Afremow: Omaha is the ultimate outcome goal, as well as a great state of mind. Always have an Omaha mentality in everything you do.

Cain: A sign in the Cal State Fullerton dugout: Opportunistic. Makeup. Attitude. Hustle. Always put team first. The center of America. The word that, anytime I hear it, puts chills down my spine.

Toole: I went to Omaha and every College World Series game growing up. I would always request to work the championship just to see the dogpiles. When I hear Omaha, I think of dogpiles!

Gordon: The team that has the greatest chemistry, the greatest ability to focus, the greatest talent, effort and desire to win will be the one that walks away with the championship.

Brubaker: It's where you end up after you trust the process and build that championship culture. You can't focus on that destination. You have to focus on the journey. Ultimately, as you focus on the journey and all of the controllables and right things, it will lead you to Omaha as a college baseball player.

Dedman: Omaha is obviously a pinnacle for Division One baseball. For us in Division Two, it's Cary, North Carolina. You have to have goals, but that's part of the result. You want to put that at the top of the Christmas tree, but you've got to start from the ground up.

Springer: Omaha is what you are playing for. You don't play the game on paper. You play the game on the field. There are going to be upsets, and some of the teams that have the best talent aren't going to go there. Get 35 guys pulling the same way every pitch, every breath to win the game.

Gilbert: Who is the only Major League Baseball player who played in the Little League World Series? Well, I won't give it away. If you know the answer, email it to me at *sendmeastory@aol.com* and I'll send you a free copy of one of my books.

Margolies: I was thinking of Peyton Manning. One of my alma maters has been in Omaha, because I went to the University of Virginia. For any sport, at any level, when you look at what the championship is, maybe it's the goal for everybody. If you ask a player in the NFL, are they going to the Super Bowl, the first thing is, 'Yes, of course we are!' I would expect that, if you're a college baseball player, your goal is to help get your team to Omaha.

Jaeger: Omaha goes back to the word success. To me it's a destination. It's the future. It is a special place to be. The idea of conjuring up this special place that we're going to end up at puts the cart before the horse. Instead of saying the word Omaha, I would come back to, 'What's your process today, and can you be great at it?'

Goldberg: Performing under pressure. Think of party time. The bigger the game, the more you want to have fun and relax. The bigger the game, the more things stay the same. The biggest mistake athletes make is to get to the big setting and try too hard because 'Now it counts.' The bigger the game, the more you want to relax, enjoy it, and have fun, because your muscle memory is there and you want to relax and let it come out.

Weintraub: Reminds me of a coach I was talking to recently who had a great regular season. Their team came up a little short in the post season, and they didn't use the word failure, but you could tell in their body language and their tone of voice that in this coach's mind, it was a failure as a season. That's crazy.

Omaha is very useful for motivating. Think about how great it's going to feel. Get up at six in the morning to go lift. It's a fantastic place. They need to do something about the winds and the field so it's not a different game when college baseball gets there. It is not the end all be all. It is an amazing thing to qualify and participate in the World Series. Certainly, we want to use whatever works and enhances motivation to have good behavior.

Hanson: That makes me think of a poem that I used teaching sports psychology years and years ago. It's about these people riding on a train, and he says that all the metal will become scrap, all the people are going to die, but you ask a guy where he's going and he says, 'Omaha.'

The Limited by Carl Sandburg

I am riding on a Limited Express,
    one of the crack trains of the nation.
Hurtling across the prairie into blue haze and dark air
    go fifteen all-steel coaches holding a thousand people.

(All the coaches shall be scrap and rust and all the men and women laughing in the diners and sleepers shall pass to ashes.)

I ask a man in the smoker where he is going and he answers: "Omaha."

The point is that he is looking through a perspective that is very small, as opposed to what is really going on here. If you pull back from the guy on the train as if on Google Earth, you can see the whole train, then you see the whole state, the whole country, the whole world, then the stars. It's all a matter of perspective. In baseball, Omaha, of course, means the College World Series, but as people focus on it, they're seeing something that isn't there. It's much more about the journey, but even that trivializes it. So when I hear 'Omaha', I think of that poem more than I think of the College World Series, because people don't really quite get what's going on. I don't mean it in a negative way, that's where they're at. There are lots of things I'm into right now, and I may think later that I was missing it. So, it brings up the cosmic joke of being human and what you're paying attention to. That's what I really like, the play of it all and understanding deeper and deeper what's really going on, although that isn't necessarily always the best way to win.

I interviewed Pete Rose on the mental aspect of hitting, and what impressed me was that he kept it really simple. He's a hit king and I'm not, because I may think about something in a little more complicated way, but I enjoy that. That's me, and I know who I am. I know that in order to succeed, you need to simplify and pick something and go with it, but I love having it bigger context and understanding the bigger context of, let's say, Omaha.

THE CLOSER

Recommended Reading

What are the top books that a baseball player or coach must read?

Cain: If you want to start with one of mine I would say *The Mental Conditioning Manual.* That's going to be the foundation, the whole program. I would say get into *Champions Tell All,* a book where I've interviewed ten champion athletes. From a baseball player standpoint, I have included Matt Carpenter who is now a Major League Baseball All-Star, Casey Weathers who was a first round draft pick and Olympic medalist, Ben Orloff who was a college All-American, now an assistant coach at UC Irvine and who played in the College World Series, Justin Toole who played nine positions in nine innings in a minor league game, Josh Ludy who went from bench player to the Big 12 player of the year, Bryan Kervin from TCU who used the mental game, as he says, to save his life when he was batting with some illness. I didn't write *Champions Tell All.* They wrote it. I interviewed them, got their words, captured it, and put it down on paper. It's them telling their story about how the mental game has made a difference in their career and in their life. For the athletes listening, it's always better to understand the system: *The Mental Conditioning Manual,* and then understand how other athletes like yourself have applied it through *Champions Tell All.* Obviously *The Daily Dominator* is your one page a day read to make sure that you are building the blocks and the muscles of mental toughness.

I would recommend *Heads-Up Baseball* by Ken Ravizza and Tom Hanson, which is hands down the best book I've ever read.

Janssen: I've always loved Ken Ravizza and the great stuff that he's done. He's been a tremendous mentor for me and he's a guy who has had such great experience and success in the baseball world. *Heads-Up Baseball* by him and Tom Hanson is absolutely critical reading. If you are serious about the game, that's a book you've got to read.

A book that I really loved is Joe Torre's *Ground Rules for Winners*. It's a little bit older now, but Joe Torre is one of those guys who really understood today's generation of players and had a great sensitivity in his management.

I'm going to put in *The Team Captain's Leadership Manual*. It's fortunately our best-selling book. As a player, if you want to get to that championship level, you have to help other people be their best and help them through their worst points too. Hopefully some of the tips in *The Team Captain's Leadership Manual* will help players to be not just great players but great leaders.

Dixon: *The Power of Now* is a really good book by Eckhart Tolle. *Relentless* is a fantastic book. *The Slight Edge* by Jeff Olson talks about the little things done over a period of time that make success. The two most important books I've read lately, which are in congruence with each other, are *The War of Art* and *Turning Pro* by Steven Pressfield. There are so many great books and valuable resources at our disposal. We just need to use them.

Springer: The Bible would be number one. I read a lot of Christian books. I'm a Christian and I have a lot of faith. Audio CD's are so under-valued and under-used, it's amazing. We give ourselves too much credit to remember what we're taught. If you like what we're talking about right here, get my CD and listen to it. If somebody makes you good and you don't have something with that guy talking for 15 or 20 minutes, you're an idiot.

Jaeger: I know Brian Cain has a great book and Ken Ravizza has a great book. *The Mental Game of Baseball* is a great resource. I would push them more toward stuff that I have studied, *The Power Of Now* by Eckhart Tolle or the *Tao Te Ching* by Stephen Mitchell, 81 poems about the art of living. *The Way Of Zen* by Alan Watts is a lot heavier, it's pretty deep. It gives you a little introduction to Zen and some background. Those are the main books I would put out there.

Obviously I like our own book. My mom was a writer and she really made me write in a way that was simplified. There's a whole section on mental practice with breathing, visualization, and imagery, and there's a chapter on meditation. That would also be a really good book for someone starting out. There's a whole chapter on game management and life management as well.

Hanson: *The Inner Game of Tennis* is really, really good. I would suggest *The Road Less Traveled, Greatest Salesman in the World, Get the Life You Want* by Richard Bandler, *Way of The Peaceful Warrior, Love is Letting Go of Fear, Ask and It Is Given.* My good stuff mostly comes from outside of baseball, because it is humans doing an activity, it isn't baseball. But now, with *Heads-Up Baseball 2.0*, we're interviewing high-end players and coaches and pulling it together. It has a lot of really, really good stuff from baseball. I would say that baseball is one place to look for how to play better baseball, but if you want the real edge, you look outside of baseball.

Brubaker: Your go-to bible should be *Toilets, Bricks, Fish Hooks and PRIDE* by Brian Cain. That's a great read whether you're an advanced mental game athlete, or this is your first step into becoming a master in the mental game.

The second book I recommend is something that would prepare you for life after baseball. Eventually the cover wears off of that ball, and eventually you can't swing the bat anymore. Everybody should read *Think and Grow Rich* by Napoleon Hill. This will help you develop your mindset while you're playing the game, but it will serve you well after your baseball career is over. For shameless self-promotion, if you want to pick up a copy of one of my books, you can do that too, but I would defer to those two first.

Dedman: *The Mental Keys to Hitting* by Dorfman is a must for hitters, but there are a lot of athletes who can get great stuff out of that. Books that don't relate necessarily to athletics can be very useful. *Good to Great* is one of them, because it explains the physiological nature, myelin and nerve endings and stuff like that, explaining how skill is actually acquired. That's an important thing for both athletes and coaches to understand. If you understand that, you can practice smarter. *Good to Great*, *The Mental Keys to Hitting*, and any other book by Dorfman, certainly by Cain. *So What, Next Pitch!* is a great one, plus he's got some great ones on leadership as well. Obviously Ravizza's *Heads-Up Baseball* is a terrific book.

Maher: *Mindset* by Carol Dweck is on how to set your mind on growth, development and improvement rather than getting fixed in some rut. Another would be *The Way of Baseball: Finding Stillness at 95 mph* by Shawn Green, a former major league player. It deals with being in the moment, dealing with the process, letting things go. The third book is *The Noticer* by Andy Andrews, about being able to slow yourself down by noticing, being able to deserve things and not make judgments about them. Those are three that I know for a fact have been seen as worthwhile by major league players.

Gordon: There is no doubt that *Energy Bus* and *Training Camp* are essential for athletes. Baseball players will get a ton from *Training Camp*. In terms of other books, *The Inner Game of Tennis* would be a great book for any athlete and especially baseball players, because it's all about the process and the moment. Jim Fannin has a great book on the zone, which has a great process.

Weintraub: I am working on *Leadership Training for Baseball*, so when that gets out we'll put that on the list. Certainly Harvey's books are at the top of my list. The *Mental Game of Baseball* and *Coaching the Mental Game* are challenging to read. They are like a textbook. You're going to go slow. Don't be in a hurry when reading those books.

Mental Keys to Hitting and *Mental ABC's of Pitching* are easy reads. There's no reason for every pitcher not to have *The Mental ABC's of Pitching*. It's such great stuff and such an easy read.

When I was a pitching coach, we actually would photocopy a chapter and read it that day out on the field as a part of practice. People reading this who are Harvey fans already know about those books, but might not know about his other three. He has a trilogy that's an autobiography, so you can check into that if you're interested.

Other books: *Mind Gym* is awesome. Ken Ravizza's book *Heads-Up Baseball* is great. Tony Robbins' work is fantastic. I would put *Man's Search for Meaning* as a must-read, but I know a lot of people won't read it. That's OK. Maybe they can just read the CliffNotes, but it wouldn't have the same impact as reading the whole book.

One thing that is interesting to me is Harvey's background as a teacher. He taught literature and there is so much information in books, so go out there and read fiction, read nonfiction, read baseball history, read biographies, read a lot and get to where you actually like to read because there is so much information available to us. When we spend a little too much time on Facebook and Twitter, we miss a lot of opportunities to learn from books.

Rickertsen: The book that got me into sports psychology was *Mind Gym* by Gary Mack. When I was in college, I picked it up off the shelf, flipped through it, bought it, read it, and absolutely loved it. The reason I liked it so much was that it's not written in a textbook form, it's written in 2-3 page chapters. There are great examples from lots of different sports, not just baseball, and different examples of athletes and their stories. That book got me excited about sports psychology. That was the first one I ever read, so I always like to recommend that to people.

Two of my favorites, although they're getting a little bit older now, are *Heads-Up Baseball* by Ken Ravizza and *The Mental Game of Baseball* by Dorfman. They still have great information in them and are very easy to read.

Gilbert: Number one is *How I Raised Myself From Failure To Success In Selling* by Frank Bettger. Read the first chapter over and over and over again. My most recent book is *Think Better Win More*. I wrote a book called *Thank God You're Lazy*. I find that most athletes just don't read books, but it's a good idea to read it. They listen to CDs and watch DVDs. Anything and everything that Brian Cain has done is fabulous stuff.

I would definitely not read a sport psychology textbook. It's not going to help you too much. My area isn't sport psychology. It's applied sport psychology. I'm just interested in the application. I'm not interested in theory. I'm interested in practice, not in the lab. I'm interested in what works in the real life, in putting the theory into practice.

Based on my experience, what has really helped a lot of athletes over time is calling my hotline because it's every single day. The number is (973) 743-4690, and I don't just have athletes call my hotline, I probably have more salespeople than athletes. Every day I'm thinking, 'What can I say today that will help you do better, help you sell more, help you get higher grades, help you win more, help you improve?' I'm not saying that every day you're going to say, 'Wow, that really helped!'

Every once in a while there will be a story like this: There are three frogs sitting on a log and one frog decided to jump off the log. How many frogs are left on the log? Most people say two. There are three frogs, one jumped off. Three minus one is two. It's a riddle. The answer is three, because the frog decided. It doesn't mean it did jump. There's a big difference between decision and action.

How many times in my life did I take my books home from high school and decide to study on Friday or over the weekend? I never did study. There's a big difference between decision and action. Knowledge minus action equals nothing. K - A = 0. If you don't use these things, you gain nothing. It's all about putting the stuff into practice. When you put things into practice, some things will work and some things won't.

Probably the best-selling book of all time in sport psychology is *The Inner Game Of Tennis* by Tim Gallwey. There's *The Inner Game Of Golf, The Inner Game Of Work, The Inner Game Of Music, The Inner Game Of Skiing*, but all of his books are based on one formula: P=P–I: **P**erformance equals **P**otential minus **I**nterference. The goal of a sport psychology consultant is to take the big interference and make it little interference. Basically, you want to play without thinking. Carl Yastrzemski said, 'I think about baseball as soon as I wake up in the morning. I think about baseball all day. I dream about baseball all night. The only time I don't think about baseball is when I'm playing it.'

Tully: I've been coaching for 20 years and the best resource I've ever seen to help coaches and student athletes gain confidence and learn about their mental game is *Think Better, Win More: How Sports Psychology Can Make You a Champion*, available on Amazon. If you're a coach, I'll make it available for everyone on your team.

Second is *The Inner Game of Tennis*, one of the finest books about the mental game ever done.

Third is *My Life In Baseball: The True Record* by Ty Cobb. I read that book when I was about 10 years old. Talk about influences on your life! From an early age that taught me a lot of about the mental game and the relentless psychological warfare that Cobb waged out there on the field. That stuck with me all these years. Those three books are really good resources for any player or coach.

Toole: My favorite book growing up was *Mind Gym* by Gary Mack. It was the first sports mental game book that I got my hands on, so that's always in my favorites. Obviously Brian Cain has written a lot of books, Harvey Dorfman, *Heads-Up Baseball*, all of these different books are awesome.

Toughness by Jay Bilas is a great book. *Relentless: From Good to Great to Unstoppable* by Tim Grover, Michael Jordan's trainer, has a different way of looking at stuff. Those are ones that I've really become a fan of lately.

Margolies: I like Ravizza's book *Heads-Up Baseball*. I've found *Head Games* by Walter Herbison to be useful. It's a book in a binder, but it's got some really nice little things to help work on skills. I've read *Mental Ball*. There are some exercises in it that are really good, and there's some stuff by Dorfman.

One book I recommend for a lot of athletes that has nothing to do with baseball or the individual sport they're in, unless they're a football player, is *Win Forever* by Pete Carroll, the coach of the Seahawks. He talks about competition, how we compete every day with ourselves, with and against our teammates, and it all goes to making us better. When you look at how we compete every single day and if you include working on your mental skills in that, you can get better at competing every day. You can compete in that pressure cooker every day, rather than it just coming around on game day, you become a better athlete. The problem I have with books, including my own, (that doesn't mean I don't want people to go buy it, because I do), is that it's really hard to translate ideas from a book to yourself. Self-help books are a billion dollar industry. You can get a self-help book for everything from being a good person to mental training, whatever you want to do. It's hard to make that step unless you have guidance, and that's why there are people like me, because there's a step that people miss by just reading, rather than by having a few conversations with somebody to get that missing step.

Dehmer: Any of Brian Cain's books are excellent. He's one of the main contributors to our team's success early on in adopting the mental game and helping me take it to another level. He has a lot of good information.

My book *The 1-Pitch Warrior* is a great coach or player book, but *The 101 Tools*, my second book, is great for coaches. There are 101 chapters on all kinds of stuff from practice planning to mental game strategies to measuring the process that they can really learn from. I would be surprised if they didn't pick up two or three new things that they would be real excited about to implement in their next season.

Mindset is a really, really excellent one. Another one is *David and Goliath* by Malcolm Gladwell, one of my favorite writers. He doesn't talk about baseball-specific stuff, but a lot about being the underdog and overcoming that, and the underdog isn't maybe what we think it is. It's a really, really good book that every coach should read.

Bell: *The Hinge: The Importance of Mental Toughness* is a good book. It took me 20 years to write that book. *Heads-Up Baseball* obviously. I love Dorfman's book, *The ABCs of Pitching*. Those are the good ones, the staples. The mental game is very simple. We make it more complicated than it is.

Afremow: One of the best things anyone can do for themselves is to become an avid reader and a lifelong learner. Read as much as you can. 'Always a student' is a good philosophy to embrace, whether in baseball or life in general. Rather than listing specific books, I would recommend to read everything you can get your hands on in terms of the mental game. There are so many good books out there.

Second, read biographies of great athletes and coaches, because you learn how they overcame adversity, that success didn't happen overnight, and that it's a process. I would definitely recommend biographies.

Third, read novels. Stories that have nothing to do with baseball will help get your mind off baseball during the grind of a long season. Just as watching a movie can be a good way for regeneration, reading novels can as well. Don't be intimidated by books. A lot of athletes will tell me they hate reading or they look at it as a grim duty in the classroom, but if you really get involved in reading and find some good books, which you will, it can add a lot to your life.

Question Review

What are the top books that a baseball player or coach must read?

Cain

The Mental Conditioning Manual

Champions Tell All

The Daily Dominator

Heads-Up Baseball by Ken Ravizza and Tom Hanson

Janssen

Heads-Up Baseball by Ken Ravizza and Tom Hanson

Joe Torre's Ground Rules for Winners

The Team Captain's Leadership Manual

Dixon

The Power of Now by Eckhart Tolle

Relentless

The Slight Edge by Jeff Olson

The War of Art and *Turning Pro* by Steven Pressfield

Springer

The Bible

Christian books

Audio CD's

Jaeger

The Power Of Now by Eckhart Tolle

Tao Te Ching by Steven Mitchell

The Way Of Zen by Allen Watts

Hanson

The Inner Game of Tennis

The Road Less Traveled

Get the Life You Want by Richard Bandler

Way of The Peaceful Warrior

Love is Letting Go of Fear

Ask and It Is Given

Heads-Up Baseball 2.0

Brubaker

Toilets, Bricks, Fish Hooks And PRIDE by Brian Cain

Think and Grow Rich by Napoleon Hill

Dedman

The Mental Keys to Hitting by Harvey Dorfman

Good to Great

So What, Next Pitch! by Brian Cain

Heads-Up Baseball

Maher

Mindset by Carol Dweck

The Way of Baseball: Finding Stillness at 95 mph by Shawn Green

The Noticer by Andy Andrews

Gordon

Energy Bus

Training Camp

The Inner Game of Tennis

Weintraub

The Mental Game of Baseball by Harvey Dorfman

Coaching the Mental Game

Mental Keys to Hitting

Mental ABC's of Pitching

Mind Gym

Heads-Up Baseball

Man's Search for Meaning

Rickertsen

Mind Gym by Gary Mack

Heads-Up Baseball by Ken Ravizza and Tom Hanson

The Mental Game of Baseball by Harvey Dorfman

<u>Gilbert</u>

How I Raised Myself From Failure To Success In Selling by Frank Bettger

Think Better, Win More

Thank God You're Lazy

The Inner Game Of Tennis by Tim Gallwey

<u>Tully</u>

Think Better, Win More: How Sports Psychology Can Make You a Champion

The Inner Game of Tennis

My Life In Baseball: The True Record by Ty Cobb

<u>Toole</u>

Mind Gym by Gary Mack

Heads-Up Baseball

Toughness by Jay Bilas

Relentless: From Good to Great to Unstoppable by Tim Grover

<u>Margolies</u>

Heads-Up Baseball by Ken Ravizza and Tom Hanson

Head Games by Walter Herbeson

Mental Ball

Win Forever by Pete Carroll

<u>Dehmer</u>

1 Pitch Warrior

Mindset

David and Goliath by Malcolm Gladwell

Bell

The Hinge: The Importance of Mental Toughness

Heads-Up Baseball

The ABCs of Pitching

Afremow

Everything you can get your hands on in terms of the mental game

Biographies of great athletes and coaches

Novels that have nothing to do with baseball

The Future of the Mental Game

As more and more people become educated on the importance of the mental game while technology continues to evolve, where do you see the future of mental training?

Dixon: You'll find that successful programs at any level are using the mental game. The problem that people are discovering with the mental game is that they're taking it too far. They feel they have to be in this perfect situation to be successful, which is not possible. The mental game is absolutely important, but when it's said and done, when the umpire says 'Play ball!,' you compete and you do whatever it takes to win. The mental practice and all that stuff is used during practice.

I'd like to see the mental game in five to ten years geared more towards yes, a breath is important, and perception and control and controllables, and routine and all of that stuff, but living with honor and practice with passion and being the best is the only option. They are all the same thing, just different verbiage. I see the culture of the mental game changing a little bit, where it's going to create success in the athletic arena, but it's also going to create the foundation for everything that you do, to be the best at it.

Janssen: You're definitely going to see a lot more online training and video training materials. You'll have a lot more real-time evaluations. That's something that we're doing. We're moving towards 'gameification' and a point system with our Leadership Academy, so you'll see a lot of that as well. It's exciting what technology allows you to do. I'm doing a lot of Skype consulting with people long distance. Obviously it's great to be there in person, I love to do that whenever possible, but when I've got seven different schools and a crazy travel schedule, Skype is a great way to connect with people, even though we may be 2,000 miles apart.

Cain: With social media, the Internet and technology, everything is happening faster. A lot of people aren't searching because they are OK in their comfort zone. Trent Dilfer, quarterback for the Tampa Bay Buccaneers once said, 'Growth happens on the edge of discomfort.' Ken Ravizza says, 'You have to get comfortable being uncomfortable.' People need to stretch and grow. Unfortunately, there's a big disconnect in NCAA athletics between what goes on in the administration and what the athletes' needs really are.

Every athletic department in the country will have five to ten strength and conditioning coaches, but no sports psychologist on campus. You'll start to see a lot of athletic departments hire full-time sports psychology and peak performance coaches in their departments. It's very, very needed. If we're going to talk about excellence and providing the absolute best opportunity for our athletes, then let's really do it.

Hanson: I have a way of measuring things. If you go into the business world, they say if you want to improve something, measure it. Well, everyone says the mental game is really important, but very few people are measuring it. There are people who do it, but my mental game profile, the Play Big Profile, measures the guy's mental game. What's underneath the surface? What's going on in the guy's inner umpire and his lower brain, his reptilian brain? I can measure it. I can take a guy and tell you accurately what this guy's makeup is like, and I have never met him. It could be a female, I wouldn't know, but I could tell you about the person, that player's makeup and whether I would draft/recruit them or not.

It's like it's too far in ahead of its time, or there's something that has people not jumping up and down to see this. If you want to measure some guy's mechanics, here's the video breakdown. What I can do is break down a guy's mental game the way video breaks down a guy's mechanics. That ought to be really interesting to people, because they all say the mental game is 80-90% of success. OK, let's measure. What have you got? But they don't really want to do that. There's a fear, because it's all about safety or survival, and I get that. The same with the energy stuff and the tapping. It freaks people out. I understand that. The whole point of *Play Big*, which is a fictional story, was to introduce people to tapping without their having a problem. My yips people will tap. They'd stand on their head and drink flat Dr. Pepper if I said that's what they should do because they're hurting so badly. But when you're not hurting, you want to stay mainstream and status quo. But people need to get this to be great, to look to things that are beyond the normal.

I use tapping and other energy psychology techniques, and I understand why someone would not do that, but I'm constantly looking to the cutting edge. What's better, what's better, what's better, how do we do that better? What's really going on here? That's what excites me. All these mental game guys send their people to me with the yips. Why? If it's a big league issue, don't you want to learn how to work with big league issues? People will get more into that, and that's what I see. It will become more integrated, so there is no 'mental game' and 'physical game'. It's baseball, and this view will become much more normal.

I've got a program called *Effortless Power Hitting*, a revolution in how to coach. It's a massive upgrade in the basics on how to coach a player with mechanics. People who get it get into it, but most people aren't so interested. They just want to know how to keep their hands inside the ball. I present a great way to teach it, but they'll be much more open to dealing with reality. Reality, as I see it, is how people actually learn and what's actually going on.

Jaeger: If you were to ask me this 10 or 15 years ago, I don't know if I would have been so optimistic, but it's like a powder keg right now. Ken Ravizza started it. I don't mean he was the first sports psychologist, but especially in the baseball world he really gave the thing a big push. Brian Cain is out on the road touching so many people. I think the world of him.

It's part of the world now. I feel like this has become part of the culture. Twenty years ago, if you were on tour in golf with a sport psychologist, they think, 'Well, what's wrong with you?' Nowadays you get the feeling, if you don't have a sports psychologist on tour, they'll wonder what's wrong. That weird dynamic seems to have shifted to where it's almost expected, and if you're not doing it, it's like you're just not part of the norm.

I'm encouraged. I feel like it's moving in such a great direction. Maybe a big word is acceptance. I feel that it is now accepted as a field of training and development. Thank goodness that the stigma is basically gone. People are looking at it for enhancement and development. Yes, there are things that need correction, too, but I am very encouraged by it.

Maher: There are a lot of opportunities for qualified mental skills consultants to make an impact at the collegiate and professional levels, as long as they stick with the basics of providing good service. Technology is good, but technology shouldn't be the driver. The use of video is great, digital is great, and I'm supportive of that, but it has to be seen as the means to an end and not an end in itself. As we move in that direction, we have to watch out for people hawking products and claiming quick fixes.

Weintraub: Five or 10 years is not very long for the evolution of mental training. The work that they're doing at IMG is impressive. I'm friends with those guys and love what they're doing: from heart math, studying the rhythm of the heartbeat to vision training and bio feedback stuff out there.

Ultimately, the best mental skills coaches that I know don't use gimmicks. They talk to people, they connect with them, they understand where they're at, help them increase the awareness of where I am and where I want to go, and then develop logical strategies for how to get from A to B. I don't think it should be changing significantly. I hope it becomes more part of the standard culture. The fact that sports psychology is so outside the expectations of training causes a lot of people to miss information that is right there available to them. The stereotypes against the word psychology mean that it's just not standard like weight training is.

50 years ago, there was a stigma against weight training but that was clearly enhanced in peoples' minds and now everyone does it. I thought sports psychology was going to do the same thing, but it hasn't yet. There are some interesting reasons for that, but it is getting more and more accepted and mainstream. There are a lot of great coaches out there helping that happen.

Gordon: I see it continuing to build and grow in the field. I believe more and more people are realizing importance of it. More and more teams are going to get it, and they have started to really focus on it.

On the mental side, we're going to have more and more focus on technology, just as nutrition and fitness have improved tremendously. We'll start having more mental toughness sessions. We can see what Michael Gervais has done with the Seattle Seahawks. There are a lot of great people on the mental side. It's going to be a big part of everyone's process going forward. You have to make it a part of your team and of your culture.

We can't lose sight of the human factor, the part where the magic happens. You want to leave room for magic. You don't want to be so in your head that you overthink, you want to be in that moment. You can train yourself to be in the moment, to allow the magic to happen, where the zone comes in, where this silence leads to this big bang in your mind and in your play. That's the part that I don't think we can capture, because it's uncapturable. I believe that's where God lives to be honest. Miracles happen that we can't explain. You always want to make room for the supernatural. When the supernatural happens, you realize there's a lot more to this game and to our mind than just our senses.

Afremow: It will be a lot of fun to find out. There's going to be some really good brain training technology that will help with focus and concentration. At the end of the day, the human connection and traditional psych services, talking with another player as part of a self-discovery process, will always trump technological advancements. The coach will always be important, and obviously the sports psychologist will always be important in terms of helping the player with increased self-awareness and learning mental skills and strategies.

Brubaker: We are at a really interesting intersection with the advent of technology. There are mental training apps that are going to be commonplace. More and more video work is done on iPads, such as reviewing game film. However, there is a point of diminishing returns with that. An iPad and an app can't help you close your eyes, visualize and breathe deep in absolute quiet and focus on quieting your mind from digital distraction. We need to be careful with it, but it's a beautiful thing.

Tully: Epigenetics immediately comes to mind. Epigenetics is about how the experiences of one generation can influence many generations to come. My family came from Ireland, victims of the Potato Famine in the mid-1800s. My father grew up in the Depression. That made an impression not only on the way he looked at the world, but there's some thought that it actually affects your genes and changes your genes in some way.

I'm looking for more connections between the physical and the mental, enzymes or certain brain synapses that make us different, people who have a bit more of this chemical or a bit less of that chemical. There's a tension between that in science, what's innate and what's learned, nature or nurture. I expect more of that kind of research to come forward. Since we have more tools now, the information is going to come fast and furious. Anybody who can assimilate all that information and put it into a book is going to have a really good life.

Margolies: I make MP3's for athletes with relaxation and imagery training on them. I can do those now really simply on my computer or on my iPhone. When I started out, we were using reel-to-reel tapes. There are things that we can do with videotape. You watch videotape of yourself hitting, then I want you to do it in a different way than you've done it in the past. You're not looking just at technique. As you're looking at it, you're using your imagination to encode that in your brain. By isolating good swings, let's get rid of the bad swings. Let's just look at some of the good swings. With video editing, we can do things like that.

I work with a company in Dallas called Mental Training, Inc. which has The Mental App. It's a pretty cool app for your iPhone or Android. It helps you track goals. It's got video, so you can learn the techniques and track your goals. Your coach can watch your goals, so it's got some really good things.

There are things like Lumosity and brain training. I work with a company in Arizona that has a golf program that works on brain training as opposed to sports psychology, although they mix it back and forth. It has to do with a lot of attention kinds of exercises like using a grid to help your memory and your searching skills. A lot will have to do with video.

For years, I've been teaching people how to journal. You can keep a journal now on your phone, and it will remind you when it's time to journal so you can create that habit. I use an app myself called Mood Meter, produced by Yale University. It has to do with emotional intelligence, becoming self-aware of what your moods are. It will ping you when it's time to assess your mood, and you can look at yourself over time. If you don't like the way you're feeling, if you've been sad or not been relaxed, and you see that right in front of you over the course of a couple weeks, you can start to change that. As we change our thoughts, we change our emotions. We can go from somebody who's not very happy with life and what they're doing right now to somebody who really is.

Dedman: Twitter has been an enormous, accessible opportunity for young players and coaches alike. A lot of people spend a lot of time giving their thoughts and sharing their thoughts on there. Most people certainly don't have an inordinate amount of time or money to go to speakers in person, to buy books, DVDs, CDs, etc, so the Internet has become a great resource, if you're choosing the right people to follow, to get quick bursts of information. It's great to dive in. We go to the American Baseball Coaches Association Convention each year as a staff, and it's outstanding to hear from so many great speakers and it's a great week. It's like going to a Tony Robbins event. It's this giant wave of information and energy. It's a great experience that can propel you forward. I think that's important. The mental game is as much about pursuing relentlessness and aggressiveness and confidence in your darkest hour as it is when you are excited about it and ready to start. The internet, because of its consistency and how it's always there and Twitter continues to feed you small bits, you can get a greater wealth of knowledge through that. It's just so consistent and ubiquitous that everybody can continue to read different tweets from different people, if you're following the right people, and get a lot of good information.

Dehmer: I see it evolving into almost every Division 1 program having their own mental game coach. A lot of athletic programs are starting to have their own, but it's going to be a situation where it's more prevalent, like a strength and conditioning coach was maybe 10 or 15 years ago. I see this being very much the same, where there weren't a lot of teams who were doing speed and agility work, and now if you're not doing that, people would laugh at you. It's become a mainstay. That's the direction that the mental game, actually having the ability to coach it and teach it on a consistent basis, is really going. The teams that have already started are creating a competitive advantage and edge for themselves, and that leaves everybody else catching up.

Toole: It has taken off. Quality At Bats. Steve Springer has things he can add on your phone or that you can get on YouTube. Riding to the field, you can throw in a 5 or 10-minute CD to key yourself into things. Guys are big on making videos of past successful performances, as easy as saving something to your phone. With the way technology is, sports psychology and the mind game is going to take off in terms of how easy it is to get hold of. Not only is that going to be beneficial for the field, but for the players, because it's so easy for them to do that.

Final Thoughts

Do you have any further advice for baseball players out there striving to improve their performance and get to the next level?

Gordon: Enjoy the game, have fun, and every day give your best. Give your best and let God do the rest. If you do that day in and day out, you're going to be just fine.

Cain: The key thing to understand is that if you want more, you've got to become more. Part of becoming more is reading this, not just once, but continually. Trade in your sports talk radio for educational, life-changing material like we're providing here, and some day they'll be talking about you on the sports talk radio.

Don't be a fan. I get the question all the time, 'Well, who do you want to win?' I can't answer that. I don't know. I'm not a fan. I'm not wanting teams to win. I want athletes and coaches to go out there and perform at their best, and if they do, everything else will take care of itself. I'm thinking about who's going to follow their routine better? Who's going to play one pitch at a time? Who's going to compete more?

What can we learn today that's going to help us get better for the next game and the next year? I don't consider myself a fan. If I don't have people, teams or athletes that are playing, I don't watch. I'm more into working on myself and becoming more myself so I can help those athletes when I do get the chance to work with them. The last thing I can say to the athletes is, if you want to be great, you've got to work on your mental game as much as your physical game, and reading this is a great way to do that.

Dixon: Understand that there is no finish line. To be the best is a constant, every day grind and it doesn't look pretty at the top. It's painful and it's lonely and it's filled with failure and it's not this glorified moment. To be the best, you've got to understand that you're going to get dirty, you're going to fail, you could potentially be lonely, but you've got to love it. Augie Garrido, when we were inducted into the Cal State Fullerton Hall of Fame, gave a great speech. One sentence that came out of his mouth I'll remember for the rest of my life. He said, 'You've got to love the hate.' So many people want to avoid the hate, the fear and the pain, but that's what creates greatness. When you see fear, you've got to run towards it. Don't run away from it. Enjoy the grind, enjoy the process, take the lids off expectations, and have a heck of a time doing it.

Goldberg: Do you want to play well? Do you want to hit well? Focus on seeing and reacting, rather than thinking. What gets hitters into trouble is they go up to the plate and they're thinking, 'What's he going to throw me? I've got to get a hit. I've got to advance the runners. I haven't hit in six games.' That's focusing on thinking. Do you want to do well? You have to focus on seeing the ball and reacting, nothing else. You've got to train yourself, when thoughts pop in your head, to not focus on them, just let them go. You can't stop them, but you have an ability to let them go and keep your focus on what's important.

Hanson: Check out *Play Big Baseball* if anything has piqued your interest. At *PlayBigBaseball.com*, sign up for something that'll be free and get into the conversation. It's a process, an ongoing evolution, not something you just get. The mental game is not a box you check. It's a constant evolution, even as basic as 'one pitch at a time'. I could say 'one pitch at a time', and they respond, 'Yes, yes, I do that.' No, you don't. I interviewed Homer Bailey, who has two no-hitters, and he expressed how he feels that he's not very good at it. If you've thrown two big league no-hitters, and then you tell me you're really good at playing one pitch at a time, I'll believe you, but beyond that, it's much more that you don't know what you don't know.

Janssen: Keep seeking out opportunities and coaching and ways to get better. I had the opportunity to hear Bill Walsh speak when I was working with Stanford's Leadership Academy. Bill Walsh had so much success with the San Francisco 49ers. He was the architect of the West Coast offense. Here's a guy who, even at the last part of his career, still had an insatiable desire to get better, to learn more, to figure out ways to motivate people. If Bill Walsh, one of the best coaches out there, is still seeking out learning opportunities, all the rest of us mere mortals can try to do the same and follow after him. Definitely continue to keep learning every single day. You can learn something and get better. It goes back to working the process. If you take advantage of every single day, trying to get better physically and mentally, with video and all this stuff that's out there now for athletes, you can't help but grow as a player and as a person.

Springer: There are a lot of good baseball people. I feel I'm one of them, but I'm not the only one. You keep learning and build your own philosophy. I didn't invent this. I learned it from a lot of good people, coaches and teammates. Fortunately, God gave me the ability to speak it. You keep learning, keep working and keep talking baseball. You bring in what you like and get rid of what you don't. Now, you have your philosophy!

Maher: Always check in with yourself why you're doing what you're doing. Recognize that everybody's not going to be able to play professional baseball in the major leagues. Ask yourself why you are doing what you're doing. Where does this fit into your life? How are you growing and developing and learning from what you're doing? That will be helpful not only on the field, but in your future life and career, wherever that takes you.

Weintraub: I always like to close each of my elite athlete audios the same way. It is a crisp, convenient and inspirational library of lessons, each under five minutes, available on iTunes, Amazon and places you would buy songs. Each one ends the same way. The message to the players is that you're capable of making outstanding achievements, including an ideal focus one pitch at a time, staying positive through adversity, and approaching your potential as an athlete. These aren't easy goals and they won't be achieved overnight, but remember to have fun, because you get to play ball with your friends. Take it one step at a time because that's all anyone can do in this challenging test called life and you'll be well on your way.

Rickertsen: My advice would be to know that wherever you are, you can always get better. I would argue that one of the most effective ways to get better is by exploring the mental game. A lot of athletes either don't realize how impactful their mental game is on their performance or they don't know how to fix it. My best advice is to find somebody. You can contact me if you want, I'm happy to answer questions if you're just curious. Read anything you can get your hands on. Talk to your teammates, your coaches, or other people that have had success or are learning about the mental game for themselves. It can be a very powerful piece to performance. It's not getting the emphasis that it needs yet in sports, but it can improve performance leaps and bounds. Look into it a lot of different ways. Look on the Internet. Talk to somebody who teaches it or teammates. Really start to dig into it, and in most cases you'll start to see a significant improvement in performance or at least the consistency of your performance.

Bell: Every single one of us should get ready for the hinge moment. That's the real importance of being mentally tough, to perform your best when it matters the most. That's all we've got to keep in mind. You don't know when it's coming, but it's coming. It doesn't mean you try harder, it means relax more and trust more. That's all we've got to do is trust.

Afremow: All players should think gold and never settle for silver or bronze. Always strive to be the absolute best you can be. That is our ultimate victory, so go for the gold.

Brubaker: Two things: make your bed, and I mean that literally, take pride in paying attention to detail. How you do anything is how you do everything. Get out of the rack and make your bed, and you have already made progress, you have already manufactured one win for yourself, and you haven't even left your bedroom. It's developing attention to detail outside of your sport. It is understood that you need great attention to detail inside your sport, but you can hone those skills and become a more disciplined person off the field. It will only benefit you on the field.

For the younger players, play other sports. We have become a society of specialization, but when we do that, we are not quite as athletic. A lot of college coaches are looking for two or three-sport athletes today, and the benefit of that isn't only physical. It's being exposed to different coaching and communication styles. Everybody motivates a little differently. Learning how to adapt and adjust to different philosophies won't just serve you well as a college athlete, it will also serve you well as a college student and when you're dealing with that difficult boss when you get out of college.

Gilbert: Yogi Berra, whom I see all the time because he used to live in Montclair, said, "A full mind is an empty bat. You can't think and hit at the same time." Brian Cain's concentration grids are key stuff.

For coaches, I'd like to stress the importance of telling stories. The other day we were talking about how the world is changing and this person said, 'The most important communication tools are the computer, the iPad and the iPhone.' I said, 'No. The most important communication tool is a story.' That's what it's all about. Stories communicate. So, when I see my students after I haven't seen them in years, I say, 'What did you get out of my course?

What do you remember the most?' They always say, 'The stories.' That's what sticks to our brains. So I'd like to end with a story.

I live in Bloomfield, New Jersey. Right next door is a town called Glen Ridge. I know this is a true story because the wrestling coach at that time in Glen Ridge was one of my graduate students, Angelo Cuervo. There was a kid in town, Tom Mapother. He had a single mom and he didn't have much money. The reason Angelo knew him so well is because he used to drive him home after practice. Tom was a wrestler. He wasn't a good student. He had a learning disability, and he wasn't a good wrestler. In the ninth grade, he didn't even win a match. In the tenth grade, he might have won a few. In the eleventh grade he won a few more. Angelo said, 'You know, Tom, if you stick it out your senior year, you're going to have a winning record.'

Every summer he used to get into a fight with his mother because he wanted to go out for the high school football team, but he was a small kid, 120 – 130 pounds. Before his senior year, he said, 'Mom, this is my last chance. My last chance my whole life to play football. Please sign the release. Please let me play.' She finally relented and let him play. Just as she predicted, halfway through the season he got hurt. He hurt his leg. He didn't hurt his leg so badly that he needed an operation, but he hurt his leg badly enough that the school doctor said, 'You're not going to be able to wrestle this year.' The kid was heartbroken because this is the only thing people knew of him. Angelo told him he could have been the manager of the team, but that would have been too painful for Tom to be around the sport and not be able to wrestle.

He went out for the senior play, and, who knows how, he got the lead role in the play *Guys and Dolls*. The girl who had the female lead made sure a New York theatrical agent was at the opening of *Guys and Dolls* at Glen Ridge High School. The agent was there and he saw nothing in the girl, no potential, no possibility, no hope, but he saw a spark in the kid, Tom. He spoke to the kid and said, 'You should take acting lessons. I want to keep in touch with you.' Eventually, he signed the kid and he became the kid's agent. Four years later, this kid is dancing in his underwear on the big screen in a movie called *Risky Business*. His name was Tom Cruise.

What I'd like to end with is that anybody could count the number of seeds in an apple. Just cut the apple open, you could count the number of seeds. Nobody could count the number of apples in a seed. Nobody could tell you what potential is. Don't let anybody tell you about your potential. Don't let anybody steal your potential and don't let anybody steal your dreams.

Tully: Be mindful in practice. Work on what you're working on while you're working on it. If you tell yourself that you're going to be working on your secondary lead, then darn it, work on your secondary lead. Work on the line drive that's hit right to you. Work on your crossover step. Work on setting your feet to throw. Once you identify that one thing, do it. Ask somebody who you respect, your skipper or coach, what do I need to add to my game? Wade Boggs is a tremendous example of that. Everybody knew he could hit but no one thought he could field, so he took thousands of ground balls and became an adequate third baseman. Some people say he became a better than adequate third baseman. That's real genius there. It sounds so obvious, but people don't do it. Identify what you need to do, and make sure you do it.

Margolies: The most important thing to remember is that if they can be calm, confident, motivated, focused, and if they can play the game in a carefree manner, they're going to be a lot more successful, because that's when you're in the zone. If we practice, the skills that are associated with being calm, confident, motivated, focused and carefree, they're going to be able to slip into the zone at will.

Dedman: The most important thing is to be relentless. That's the single most important skill as a player or as a coach. It just means that you can continue to get up off the mat when you get knocked down. When you feel great, you keep going. When you don't feel so great, you find a way to fake it 'til you make it or fake it 'til you find it. Continue to learn, progress, read books, listen to audio, tapes, listen to podcasts and other useful bits of information and make it part of your life. If you're just listening to it, it's not very useful, it's not long-term, but if you can find a way to make it a part of the way that you think by surrounding yourself with it, then it can become who you are and that's when it's powerful.

Dehmer: If there's anything I can do for them in any way, shape, or form, whether they're players or coaches, reach out to me and I would love to help. This is one of my passions—creating programs of excellence and helping guys strive to be their best. I'd encourage them to reach out and hopefully I could help them in some way.

Toole: Just go out there and believe that you can do it. If you have a good mindset, good work ethic and a good attitude, anything is possible. When I was in high school, kids told me that the reason I played on the varsity team was because my Dad was the coach. They told me I wasn't very good, wasn't very fast, wasn't very big. I didn't get a lot of scholarships out of college, but that didn't stop me from chasing my dreams. I was lucky enough to have parents who supported my dreams. Ever since I was little, I wanted to be a major league baseball player, and my parents never once told me that was a dumb idea. I was fortunate enough to have people who allowed me to chase my dream. My biggest advice would be that if somebody has a dream, whether you want to be a teacher, a fireman, a lawyer or the president, if you have a dream and you want to do it, work hard and good things can happen to you. You never know what's going to happen. Don't let anyone tell you that you can't do something. It's crazy what the mind will do when you put it to work and think positive. If you've got a dream, go ahead and chase it.

EXTRA INNINGS

Bonus Interview

Featuring:

Ken Ravizza

Legendary Performance Trainer and Author of *Heads-Up Baseball*

Heads-Up Baseball is one of the greatest baseball psychology books ever written and has been referenced by so many of the sport psychologists and performance coaches throughout the Mental Game VIP program. Thank you for all of the great work that you have done and continue to do in the game of baseball... but rumors are building that Heads-Up Baseball 2.0 is in the works! What can the baseball community expect to learn when that is released?

Ravizza: Basically, I've been working on that the last two years with Tom Hanson and it's been fascinating looking at the changes that have taken place from when we did the first book. I think the first book was, I wouldn't necessarily agree with the greatest book of all time in baseball, but it was a solid book and it took me 25 years of working with athletes before I wrote the first book. I know today a lot of people work two weeks and they're writing a book, but that was very helpful to learn from all those coaches and athletes and get that information and put it out there.

I don't think there really was a lot of new stuff in *Heads-Up Baseball*, but it was a pulling together of things where it provided a structure and a framework for coaches. I think coaches have been doing the mental game throughout their coaching career, but what we did in *Heads-Up Baseball* was provide a structure and a framework where this related to that and they can see that. So many coaches said, "I'm already doing it," and I even, when I do clinics, really hammer them with, "You're already doing this stuff, you know?" It's not like this mental game is something new and revolutionary. Good coaches coach the mental game.

Heads-Up Baseball 2 was after 20 years from writing the first book really looking at what's changed. What has changed is the environment that athletes are brought up in. We were talking about this in spring training. Many of our US players have never had a summer job. Many kids in high school today don't have a summer job. Someone comes and cuts the lawn. They don't do it. They don't have these jobs where you learn a lot about responsibility and sometimes going to work when you don't want to go to work. It's a different young person that we're dealing with today. Being a university professor for the last 41 years, I really see how the students have changed and it is dramatic. The whole social media aspect that the young kids are dealing with is that they want everything quick. They want the instant gratification. They want the quick fix and one of the difficulties with sport is, and it's not just baseball, but sport is analog in a digital world, meaning there's no way around it. You have to pay your dues and you have to do the work. You have to go through the blood, sweat, and tears. There's absolutely nothing magical that's going to help you dominate over anyone. It's going to be a struggle, it's going to be a battle and that takes hard work, so when we say hard work, if you've never had a job, you don't know what hard work is. Now, the athletes that have had to work, they have an advantage, no question.

The thing *Heads-Up Baseball 2* is really looking at is what are the pitfalls in the mental game. When you get an athlete, that I would say, is 'too internal', they're focused too much on routines, too much on the at-bat and they're not competing. Where they get what we call 'too internal' is a mistake. Another one is they do their routines, but there's no meaning in the routine and that becomes an issue. Also with the athlete today, I'm learning from the college teams, we have to talk about how you compete. In this age of specialization and showcasing, it's more about showcasing your skills than it is competing and being on a team. Being on a team is critical, because when you're on a team, you're not just a one-man band taking care of you. You're supporting your teammates and that, ironically, helps you get your head out of your rear end and support somebody else.

Young kids today don't play Wiffle ball and they don't do sandlot. So at the college level we have to teach kids how to compete, because they know how to showcase but 'How do I compete when the pressure is on?' That's a whole other thing besides just showcasing my skills.

The final part in *Heads-Up Baseball 2,* besides the competing and being on a team, would be the issue of a really old school thought and that is knowing yourself, knowing yourself as a ball player, knowing what your strengths are, knowing what your weaknesses are, knowing how to use your experience and learn from it. That's basically where *Heads-Up Baseball 2* is going.

As a former sport psychology professor at Cal State Fullerton, do you have any tips for students?

Ravizza: Enjoy what you're doing and realize it isn't going to be easy. Learn to compensate, adjust and keep moving forward. I think that's very important. I think learning how to spend time by yourself alone, without the cell phone, without the computer, without all the stuff, but just being able to sit and be with yourself and start looking at your own personal experience in the world that you're in.

How have the best players you have coached learned to slow the game down in 'pressure' situations?

Ravizza: It's a skill that you have to work with and it's not like you learn it one time and you have it. For those of you reading that follow the World Cup, you saw that Brazil team that had some of the best soccer players in the world on it. When Germany scored the second goal on them, you could see the fear and panic look in their eyes. One thing I've learned over my years of doing this is that confidence is fragile. I think we build up this false bravado that 'I'm the man, I'm going to dominate, I'm the guy,' which is a joke and it's so superficial that it's ridiculous to me. What the athlete has to learn is how to compensate and adjust, how to learn to be uncomfortable, how to learn to bounce back from adversity, and how to learn from their failures and not be so damn preoccupied with having to feel just right to perform well, but instead learn to have good crappy days.

If you were a coach, how would you create pressure situations in practice?

Ravizza: I think the way that you would create them in practice is explain to them what you're trying to do and really be clear what that is, so they understand. During BP, instead of taking 15 pitches, cut down the number of pitches and increase the quality of the pitches. This is where situational hitting is good. You've got to practice being on-deck, you've got to practice slowly getting in there, you've got to practice working it, and during BP practice stepping out. For the coaches that are reading, you try to make practice more game like, meaning like when you're doing a bullpen, do bullpens in pairs, where one guy works it, the other guy sits. He makes about 15-17 pitches, then he sits and the other guy gets up. Then he goes 17 and the other guy sits, because that's what you do in the game. Now, are there bullpens where you want to work quick, are there bullpens where you want to take your 50-60 pitches? Yes, but you've also got to practice game like situations. With teams that I work with at the college level, we practice making errors. We practice what we're going to do after we make an error and that's stuff that I've learned from coaches like Dave Snow and Mike Weathers.

One thing I've got to be real clear on in all of this is that I've just had the privilege of being around great coaches, such as Augie Garrido, Marcel Lachemann, Joe Maddon, and Mike Scioscia. You just learn from these people and that's just so important.

What aspect of sports psychology do you find the most difficult to teach?

Ravizza: I get excited by all of it. I mean the more challenges, the better. I still get excited about the challenges that come your way. I think the thing I run into the most is that the athletes can be very hard on themselves and the need to forgive themselves and move forward. I think that's the hard thing, especially for the perfectionist athlete, who just gets so hard on himself. Sometimes, they've got to learn to just step back and laugh a little bit.

Million Dollar Question

What do you know now that you wish you knew then?

Ravizza: Great question. I think I learned it real early in my teaching career as a university professor. When I first started, I was trying to be like everybody else and I was overwhelmed, because I was inadequate and I wasn't good enough. About my sixth month into teaching, I finally came to a conclusion after not enjoying trying to be like everyone else. I was listening to a song by Neil Young, where he was talking about you've got to be yourself, not like everyone else. That really resonated with me. It was at that time that I stopped trying to be like everyone else and started to do what I do and that was the first thing that jumped out at me. There's so many levels to that which are so important.

The second thing that's been very important is that as teachers and coaches we give so much to other people that it becomes important that you've got to do some of those things for yourself and take care of yourself as you're doing the work with others. That's very, very important. I can't emphasize that enough and that's something that I constantly have to deal with. At my desk at home, I have a little sign that says, 'Take care of me.' Sometimes I'm so busy taking care of everyone else. The caring is important, but you've also got to take care of yourself.

Hot Seat

Positive Energy

Ravizza: Use what you've got. Sometimes it's not positive. Sometimes it's have a good shitty day.

Confidence

Ravizza: Fragile.

Championship Culture

Ravizza: Who knows? Clueless. I have no idea what champions do. I've seen it done so many different ways. There's no one way to do it.

Routines

Ravizza: Consistency. Something to go to when the garbage hits the fan and the garbage will hit the fan.

Process

Ravizza: Keep the process greater than the outcome. It's all about outcomes, but you've got to stay on the process. It's real clear to me that people bring me in to work with them for one reason and that is to win. Let's be real clear about that, but to win, you've got to focus on the process and do what you do. You can't do more. I finished my ninth Olympic Games with Russia. Recipe for failure in the Olympics is go to the Olympics and try to do the best you've ever done. It's not going to work. You've got to go to the Olympics, or the biggest competition, and you've go to do what you do. You don't have to bring it up a level, because if you've got to bring it up a level, man, you were shortchanging yourself before. You got cracks in your armor and you'r going to be found out.

Controllables

Ravizza: Got to make sure you focus on them, because there's very little you have control of. You've only got control of yourself, your attitude, your effort and your focus. Other than that, you'll get swallowed up in things if you don't focus on the controllables.

Mind-Body Connection

Ravizza: Mind, body, spirit, emotion. It's what being is about and they're all related. You've got to have the spirit as well, and by spirit I mean the purpose and the passion for what you're doing. It becomes critical, no question.

Success

Ravizza: Success is controlling the controllables and doing everything you can. I had one World Cup athlete I worked with and he responded to me after his final game in Brazil. He said, "Ken, I did everything I could, I played to the best of my ability." That's fantastic, man. That's fantastic.

Failure

Ravizza: Failure is positive feedback, information, stuff for you to learn from.

Omaha

Ravizza: Do what you do.

If you have had a positive experience with the *Mental Game VIP* Program and would like to share a testimonial to be featured in future editions, please e-mail Testimonials@MentalGameVIP.com

FOR MORE FROM MATT MORSE, VISIT MATT-MORSE.COM!

Made in the USA
Lexington, KY
27 November 2019